# Nuances of Sexual Consent

Sexual consent represents the willingness to engage in sexual behaviour with another person. This book presents a collection of research studies that sought to uncover intricacies related to how people experience, communicate, or perceive such willingness. Is consent sexy? To what extent are descriptions of nonconsensual sex discomforting? Do past instances of nonconsensual sex affect how people experience consent in subsequent relationships? Can you be willing to have sex but not want to? When two people go home together after a date, does that mean they are consenting to have sex? What roles do gender or sexual orientation play regarding sexual consent? Does consent matter for interactions with sex robots? These questions and more are the focus of the studies described within. The many nuances underlying a person's willingness to engage in sexual behaviour emphasise that the process of sexual consent must be ongoing and requires mutual respect between those involved.

*Nuances of Sexual Consent* is a significant new contribution to sexuality studies and will be a great resource for researchers, instructors, and advanced students of Psychology, Sociology, Cultural Studies, Gender Studies, and Philosophy. The chapters in this book were originally published as a special issue of the journal *Psychology & Sexuality*.

**Malachi Willis** is Research Associate in the MRC/CSO Social and Public Health Sciences Unit at the University of Glasgow, UK. He primarily researches the nuances of sexual consent, which he conceptualises as a person's willingness to engage in a particular sexual behaviour with a particular person within a particular context.

# Nuances of Sexual Consent

*Edited by*
**Malachi Willis**

LONDON AND NEW YORK

First published 2022
by Routledge
4 Park Square, Milton Park, Abingdon, Oxon, OX14 4RN

and by Routledge
605 Third Avenue, New York, NY 10158

*Routledge is an imprint of the Taylor & Francis Group, an informa business*

Chapters 1–5, 7 and 8 © 2022 Taylor & Francis
Chapter 6 © 2020 Charlotta Holmström, Lars Plantin and Eva Elmerstig. Originally published as Open Access.

With the exception of Chapter 6, no part of this book may be reprinted or reproduced or utilised in any form or by any electronic, mechanical, or other means, now known or hereafter invented, including photocopying and recording, or in any information storage or retrieval system, without permission in writing from the publishers. For details on the rights for Chapter 6, please see the chapter's Open Access footnote.

*Trademark notice*: Product or corporate names may be trademarks or registered trademarks, and are used only for identification and explanation without intent to infringe.

*British Library Cataloguing-in-Publication Data*
A catalogue record for this book is available from the British Library

ISBN13: 978-1-032-23186-0 (hbk)
ISBN13: 978-1-032-23187-7 (pbk)
ISBN13: 978-1-003-27618-0 (ebk)

DOI: 10.4324/9781003276180

Typeset in Myriad Pro
by codeMantra

**Publisher's Note**
The publisher accepts responsibility for any inconsistencies that may have arisen during the conversion of this book from journal articles to book chapters, namely the inclusion of journal terminology.

**Disclaimer**
Every effort has been made to contact copyright holders for their permission to reprint material in this book. The publishers would be grateful to hear from any copyright holder who is not here acknowledged and will undertake to rectify any errors or omissions in future editions of this book.

# Contents

|   |   |   |
|---|---|---|
| *Citation Information* | | vi |
| *Notes on Contributors* | | viii |
| 1 | Introduction<br>*Malachi Willis* | 1 |
| 2 | Is consent sexy? Comparing evaluations of written erotica based on verbal sexual consent<br>*Jennifer L. Piemonte, Staci Gusakova, Marissa Nichols and Terri D. Conley* | 5 |
| 3 | Using vignette methodology to study comfort with consensual and nonconsensual depictions of pornography content<br>*Kate Dawson, Chris Noone, Saoirse Nic Gabhainn and Padraig MacNeela* | 28 |
| 4 | Sexual consent and sexual agency of women in healthy relationships following a history of sexual trauma<br>*Kristen P. Mark and Laura M. Vowels* | 50 |
| 5 | South African women's constructions of sexual consent<br>*Kayla Beare and Floretta Boonzaier* | 64 |
| 6 | Complexities of sexual consent: Young people's reasoning in a Swedish context<br>*Charlotta Holmström, Lars Plantin and Eva Elmerstig* | 77 |
| 7 | People perceive transitioning from a social to a private setting as an indicator of sexual consent<br>*Kristen N. Jozkowski and Malachi Willis* | 93 |
| 8 | Reprogramming consent: implications of sexual relationships with artificially intelligent partners<br>*Ellen M. Kaufman* | 107 |
| | *Index* | 119 |

# Citation Information

The chapters in this book were originally published in the journal *Psychology & Sexuality*, volume 11, issue 4 (2020). When citing this material, please use the original page numbering for each article, as follows:

## Chapter 1
*Introduction to the special issue on sexual consent*
Malachi Willis
*Psychology & Sexuality*, volume 11, issue 4 (2020) pp. 266–269

## Chapter 2
*Is consent sexy? Comparing evaluations of written erotica based on verbal sexual consent*
Jennifer L. Piemonte, Staci Gusakova, Marissa Nichols and Terri D. Conley
*Psychology & Sexuality*, volume 11, issue 4 (2020) pp. 270–292

## Chapter 3
*Using vignette methodology to study comfort with consensual and nonconsensual depictions of pornography content*
Kate Dawson, Chris Noone, Saoirse Nic Gabhainn and Padraig MacNeela
*Psychology & Sexuality*, volume 11, issue 4 (2020) pp. 293–314

## Chapter 4
*Sexual consent and sexual agency of women in healthy relationships following a history of sexual trauma*
Kristen P. Mark and Laura M. Vowels
*Psychology & Sexuality*, volume 11, issue 4 (2020) pp. 315–328

## Chapter 5
*South African women's constructions of sexual consent*
Kayla Beare and Floretta Boonzaier
*Psychology & Sexuality*, volume 11, issue 4 (2020) pp. 329–341

## Chapter 6
*Complexities of sexual consent: young people's reasoning in a Swedish context*
Charlotta Holmström, Lars Plantin and Eva Elmerstig
*Psychology & Sexuality*, volume 11, issue 4 (2020) pp. 342–357

## Chapter 7
*People perceive transitioning from a social to a private setting as an indicator of sexual consent*
Kristen N. Jozkowski and Malachi Willis
*Psychology & Sexuality*, volume 11, issue 4 (2020) pp. 358–371

## Chapter 8
*Reprogramming consent: implications of sexual relationships with artificially intelligent partners*
Ellen M. Kaufman
*Psychology & Sexuality*, volume 11, issue 4 (2020) pp. 372–383

For any permission-related enquiries please visit:
http://www.tandfonline.com/page/help/permissions

# Notes on Contributors

**Kayla Beare** is a master's student at University College London, UK, who studies Women's Health and specialises in women's understandings of sexual consent and how broader social contexts inform these understandings. She is an Advancing Womxn scholar and has worked with the Disrupting Gender Based Violence group.

**Floretta Boonzaier** is Professor of Psychology at the University of Cape Town, South Africa; Co-Director of the Hub for Decolonial Feminist Psychologies in Africa; and Co-Chair of the Global Africa Group of the Worldwide Universities Network. She teaches in feminist, critical, social, and decolonial psychologies, with special interests in intersectional subjectivities, youth subjectivities, gendered and sexual identifications, participatory methodologies, and sexual and gender-based violence.

**Terri D. Conley** is Professor of Psychology at the University of Michigan, USA. She studies gender differences in sexuality, monogamy, and nescience.

**Kate Dawson** is a post-doctoral researcher with the Active Consent Programme at the School of Psychology, NUIG. Kate's research interests include pornography, sexual consent and aggressive behaviour, sex education, and adolescent health.

**Eva Elmerstig** is Associate Professor and Senior Lecturer in health and society, and the field of sexology at Malmö University, Sweden. Her research is focused on sexual functions, sexual dysfunctions, gender norms/ideals connected to sexual situations, and sexual health and diseases.

**Staci Gusakova** is a candidate in the joint Psychology and Women's Studies Ph.D. program at the University of Michigan, USA.

**Charlotta Holmström** is Associate Professor in the Department of Social Work and Director for the Centre for Sexology and Sexuality Studies at Malmö University, Sweden. Her research area is prostitution policies, sexual and reproductive health and rights, and sexuality norms among youth.

**Kristen N. Jozkowski** is William L. Yarber Endowed Professor in Sexual Health in the Department of Applied Health Science at the School of Public Health at Indiana University, Bloomington, USA. Her research focuses on sexual violence prevention and sexual consent and refusal communication.

**Ellen M. Kaufman** is a doctoral student in Informatics at Indiana University, Bloomington, USA, and a Graduate Research Assistant at Kinsey Institute. She received her M.A. in Communication, Culture, and Technology from Georgetown University, USA, where her research focused on the ethics of emerging 'sex robot' technology and artificial intelligence. Her work continues to explore the intersection of technological innovation and digital intimacy.

**Padraig MacNeela** is Senior Lecturer at the School of Psychology, NUIG, Ireland. Padraig leads the Active Consent Programme and research team. Padraig's research interests include sexual health, youth research, community engagement, and risky behaviour.

**Kristen P. Mark** is Associate Professor in Health Promotion and Director of the Sexual Health Promotion Lab at the University of Kentucky, Lexington, USA. Her research is in the area of sexual health and romantic relationships.

**Saoirse Nic Gabhainn** is Professor in Health Promotion and Project Leader in the Health Promotion Research Centre and the World Health Organisation Collaborative Centre for Health Promotion Research.

**Marissa Nichols** is a student in the Master of Social Work Program at the University of Michigan, USA.

**Chris Noone** is Lecturer at the School of Psychology, NUIG, Ireland. Chris is a graduate of NUI Galway, Ireland, and Leiden University, the Netherlands. Chris has been involved in research in health, cognitive, and LGBT+ psychology.

**Jennifer L. Piemonte** is a candidate in the joint Psychology and Women's Studies Ph.D. program at the University of Michigan, USA.

**Lars Plantin** is Professor of Social Work in the Department of Social Work at Malmö University, Sweden. His main area of expertise is sexuality, youth, and family research. He has published books and articles on HIV, sexual and reproductive health, parenting, and everyday family life.

**Laura M. Vowels** is Doctoral Student in Psychology at the University of Southampton, UK, and a couples therapist in private practice in the UK. Her research is in the area of close relationships and sexual functioning.

**Malachi Willis** is Research Associate in the MRC/CSO Social and Public Health Sciences Unit at the University of Glasgow, UK. He primarily researches the nuances of sexual consent, which he conceptualises as a person's willingness to engage in a particular sexual behaviour with a particular person within a particular context.

# Introduction
Malachi Willis

Sexual consent is a timely topic across the globe. People – media, laws, society – are actively thinking about sexual consent and what it means. The past decade has witnessed an exponential increase in empirical articles on sexual consent (Willis et al., 2019). *Psychology and Sexuality* aimed to continue this momentum with a special issue of peer-reviewed research on sexual consent. Addressing the continued need for more complex conceptualisations of consent and more varied samples in this area of research (Muehlenhard et al., 2016), the seven papers that compose this special issue consider novel nuances of sexual consent and demonstrate diversity in several ways.

First, much of the past academic literature on sexual consent focused on individual consent behaviours and paid little attention to the contexts in which they occur (Muehlenhard et al., 2016). Now, one of the trends in recent consent research is an emphasis on how sexual consent varies by context (Beres, 2014; Jozkowski et al., 2018; Willis & Jozkowski, 2019). The researchers represented in this special issue used diverse methodologies to ask complex questions about sexual consent and to provide nuanced insights. Specific approaches included experimental vignettes, focus groups, content analysis, and semi-structured interviews.

Second, with few exceptions, studies on sexual consent have relied on samples primarily comprising White heterosexual cisgender college students in North America (Muehlenhard et al., 2016; Willis et al., 2019). Continuing *Psychology and Sexuality*'s tradition of publishing international research, the studies included in this special issue spanned Africa, Europe, and North America. And only two of the studies exclusively relied on data from college students. In addition to providing diverse samples regarding geographic region and age, the teams that conducted the present research on sexual consent were themselves diverse in career stage (i.e. student, postdoctoral, early career, and established) and discipline (i.e. psychology, sexology, public health, social work, women's studies, and informatics).

This special issue advances our understanding of sexual consent – each study in its own way. Some authors conceptualised consent as an internal experience of willingness, others as an external communication of agreement, and still others as perceptions of an interaction. Even though definitions of sexual consent varied across studies, all authors aimed to elucidate key aspects of consent in unique contexts.

## Present collection of sexual consent research

Piemonte et al. (2020, this issue) examined whether people perceive explicit verbal consent communication to be sexy. Using written erotica, these researchers manipulated the way fictional characters communicated their willingness to engage in sexual behaviours verbally or nonverbally. Across two studies, Piemonte et al. (2020) found that adults in the United States generally rated the erotica as similarly sexy disregarding the type of consent communication – indicating the potential for consent education tactics to be situated in a sex-positive approach that emphasises the sexiness of open sexual communication. Because these vignettes followed heterosexual scripts, it was not surprising that lesbian and gay participants rated them as less sexy than did bisexual and heterosexual participants.

Dawson et al. (2020, this issue) also considered sexual consent within the context of written erotica. These researchers investigated people's comfort with consensual and nonconsensual pornographic content. Using structural equation modelling and vignettes they had developed in a three-round Delphi study, Dawson et al. (2020) found that young adults studying at an Irish university were relatively less tolerant of written accounts of nonconsensual sexual encounters if they had more positive attitudes and perceived norms toward establishing sexual consent. While the initial set of written erotica included sexual interactions between two female or two male characters, the final set used for analysis only depicted heterosexual encounters.

Mark and Vowels (2020, this issue) more directly assessed the relationship between consent and non-consent by interviewing women who had been sexually victimised but were in a healthy sexual relationship at the time of the study. In a sample of adult women primarily from the United States (but also Canada, Australia, England, and New Zealand), Mark and Vowels found that sexual consent post-sexual trauma was ever-evolving and could be explicit or implicit. Participants in this study also discussed the complexities associated with feeling empowered to voice their sexual wants and needs. While more than a third of this sample identified as bisexual, lesbian, pansexual, queer, or questioning, almost all participants were partnered with men at the time of the study and primarily referenced sexual consent in the context of heterosexual relationships.

Beare and Boonzaier (2020, this issue) focused on sexual consent from women's perspectives as well and provided some insight regarding sexuality. These researchers facilitated focus group discussions with female university students in South Africa. Participants discussed sexual consent as willingness that is distinct from desire. And in a sample in which more than a quarter of participants identified as gay, queer, or bisexual, sexual orientation was discussed as being relevant to consent: identifying as a sexual minority can empower women to more readily refuse unwanted sexual advances from men than identifying as heterosexual.

Holmström et al. (2020, this issue) sought to understand the complexities of sexual consent in Sweden – a country that recently introduced new sexual assault legislation that prioritises the need for evidence from the defence that a person communicated their willingness to engage in sexual activity. Specifically, they conducted focus groups with young people who varied regarding their post-secondary educational pathways. Their participants discussed understanding the many nuances regarding sexual consent but voiced that challenging sexual scripts is difficult. Using vignettes to facilitate conversations, Holmström et al. manipulated the gender of the fictional characters to prompt discussions of consent in same-sex relationships; however, participants tended to reference their own heterosexual interactions. One theme that young people in this study emphasised was that transitioning from a public to a private setting is an indicator of sexual consent.

Jozkowski and Willis (2020, this issue) focused on this specific transition in their study. These researchers developed a staggered vignette protocol that presented a consensual heterosexual sexual encounter over the course of 11 segments. After each segment, participants reported whether they thought the characters were willing to engage in various sexual behaviours. Jozkowski and Willis found that the consent cue most strongly associated with increases in consent perceptions was the transition from a social to a private setting. A nuance of this effect was that male participants were particularly likely to think that the female character was willing to engage in sexual behaviour if she was the one to invite the male character home in the vignette.

Finally, Kaufman (2020, this issue) shed light on the vast intellectual frontier that may lie before contemporary sexual consent researchers in her application of consent to digisexuality, which involves technology-enhanced sexual interactions. Using content analysis, this study examined data from online forum discussions wherein users described their interactions with 'Harmony,' an artificially intelligent smartphone application that supports sex robot technology. Kaufman found that 'Harmony' users approached sexual interactions – including consent negotiations – as if they were a game. This gamification might promote flawed internal ethics regarding how people perceive others' willingness to engage in sexual activity; the extent that these beliefs extend to sexual interactions with other humans remains unknown.

## Directions for future sexual consent research

Even after this collection of articles, there remains a need for more complex conceptualisations of consent and more varied samples. Going forward, researchers should continue being creative in their study designs to assess how sexual consent varies across contexts. For example, experience sampling methodology might be employed to investigate how consent varies within a person from one sexual encounter to the next. And while the samples included in this special issue began to address the lack of diversity regarding geographic region and age inherent to previous sexual consent research, there are several other individual differences for researchers to investigate going forward: race/ethnicity, social class, ability, spirituality, and so on. We also encourage research on sexual consent regarding modern trends in sexuality, such as online dating, sexting, hooking up, or consensual nonmonogamy.

Of particular relevance to *Psychology and Sexuality*, the existing academic literature on sexual consent continues to be sorely limited on matters of sexual orientation and gender identity. Even though a few studies in this special issue provided data regarding consent and sexuality, these insights were consistently secondary to the primarily heterosexual and cisgender framework underlying the research questions and study designs. Going forward, scholars should more critically consider how to incorporate sexual or gender diversity in their research.

## Concluding remarks

I am excited for the future of sexual consent research and am eager to keep pushing the field forward with you. If you are examining sexual consent within the context of sexualities or plan to, please consider submitting your work to *Psychology & Sexuality*. I thoroughly enjoyed guest editing this special issue on sexual consent, and I am overwhelmingly grateful to everyone who made it possible.

- To Drs. Daragh McDermott and Todd Morrison, thank you for leading *Psychology and Sexuality* as co-editors and for entrusting me to deliver a rigorous and engaging special issue.
- To my amazing anonymous reviewers, thank you for dedicating your time and energy to providing comprehensive and helpful feedback to the authors.
- To all of the authors who submitted their work to be considered for this special issue, thank you and your research teams for moving the literature on sexual consent forward and for letting me be involved in the process of disseminating your findings.
- To Dr. Kristen Jozkowski, thank you for the last several years of mentorship and for the many years of collaborating on sexual consent research to come.
- To the readers of this special issue, enjoy!

## Disclosure statement

No potential conflict of interest was reported by the author.

## ORCID

Malachi Willis http://orcid.org/0000-0002-3173-3990

## References

Beare, K., & Boonzaier, F. (2020). South african women's constructions of sexual consent. *Psychology & Sexuality*. https://doi.org/10.1080/19419899.2020.1769158

Beres, M. A. (2014). Rethinking the concept of consent for anti-sexual violence activism and education. *Feminism & Psychology, 24*(3), 373–389. https://doi.org/10.1177/0959353514539652

Dawson, K., Noone, C., Nic Gabhainn, S., & MacNeela, P. (2020). Using vignette methodology to study comfort with consensual and nonconsensual depictions of pornography content. *Psychology & Sexuality*. https://doi.org/10.1080/19419899.2020.1769159

Holmström, C., Plantin, L., & Elmerstig, E. (2020). Complexities of sexual consent: Young people's reasoning in a swedish context. *Psychology & Sexuality*. https://doi.org/10.1080/19419899.2020.1769163

Jozkowski, K. N., Manning, J., & Hunt, M. (2018). Sexual consent in and out of the bedroom: Disjunctive views of heterosexual college students. *Women's Studies in Communication, 41*(2), 117–139. https://doi.org/10.1080/07491409.2018.1470121

Jozkowski, K. N., & Willis, M. (2020). People perceive transitioning from a social to a private setting as an indicator of sexual consent. *Psychology & Sexuality*. https://doi.org/10.1080/19419899.2020.1769162

Kaufman, E. M. (2020). Reprogramming consent: implications of sexual relationships with artificially intelligent partners. *Psychology & Sexuality*. https://doi.org/10.1080/19419899.2020.1769160

Mark, K. P., & Vowels, L. M. (2020). Sexual consent and sexual agency of women in healthy relationships following a history of sexual trauma. *Psychology & Sexuality*. https://doi.org/10.1080/19419899.2020.1769157

Muehlenhard, C. L., Humphreys, T. P., Jozkowski, K. N., & Peterson, Z. D. (2016). The complexities of sexual consent among college students: A conceptual and empirical review. *Journal of Sex Research, 53*(4–5), 457–487. https://doi.org/10.1080/00224499.2016.1146651

Piemonte, J. L., Gusakova, S., Nichols, M., & Conley, T. D. (2020). Is consent sexy? comparing evaluations of written erotica based on verbal sexual consent. *Psychology & Sexuality*. https://doi.org/10.1080/19419899.2020.1769161

Willis, M., Blunt-Vinti, H. D., & Jozkowski, K. N. (2019). Assessing and addressing the need for more diverse samples regarding age and race/ethnicity in sexual consent research. *Personality and Individual Differences, 149*, 37–45. https://doi.org/10.1016/j.paid.2019.05.029

Willis, M., & Jozkowski, K. N. (2019). Sexual precedent's effect on sexual consent communication. *Archives of Sexual Behavior, 48*(6), 1723–1734. https://doi.org/10.1007/s10508-018-1348-7

# Is consent sexy? Comparing evaluations of written erotica based on verbal sexual consent

Jennifer L. Piemonte, Staci Gusakova, Marissa Nichols and Terri D. Conley

**ABSTRACT**
Whether "consent is sexy' is a topic that has been broadly debated, with some contending that asking for consent 'ruins the mood' and is, therefore, distinctly not sexy. In the current research, we investigated whether consent is sexy by comparing evaluations of written erotica based on whether the characters expressed explicit verbal consent. In Study 1, we compared brief excerpts of erotic fiction in which verbal sexual consent was either present or absent and determined that U.S. adults judged the stories similarly and, if anything, considered the excerpts with verbal consent sexier. In Study 2, we generated erotic stories that followed familiar, heterosexual scripts and compared evaluations of erotica with consent expressed explicitly and verbally to erotica with consent expressed implicitly through no resistance. Participants considered both versions equally as sexy, indicating that public concerns about consent ruining sexual dynamics are potentially unwarranted. We discuss the potential utility of sexual media in normalising sexual consent as an erotic aspect of sexual scripts.

## Introduction

Many United States (U.S.) Americans have encountered the phrases 'affirmative consent' or 'enthusiastic consent,' which both refer to a new model of sexual consent following a paradigm shift from 'no means no' to 'yes means yes' (Beres, 2018; Dougherty, 2015). This model of sexual consent has recently risen in part thanks to the nationwide surge to address sexual assault on college campuses; the idea is that explicit communication will prevent misunderstandings of implicit cues and thus reduce sexual assault (Jozkowski et al., 2017; Jozkowski & Humphreys, 2014). Although scholarship indicates that implicit communication invites neither misunderstandings nor sexual assault (Beres, 2010; Hickman & Muehlenhard, 1999), pressure has increased around verbally affirming one's desire to engage in partnered sexual activity. However, this practice has been traditionally rare (Lindgren et al., 2009; T. P. Humphreys, 2004) and has received backlash at its implementation (Humphreys & Herold, 2003; Jozkowski, 2015a). People claim aversion to 'yes means yes' because it ruins the mood of sexual scenarios (Young, 2014). Yet feminist and other activist or campus groups have pushed back, using slogans such as 'party with consent' and 'consent is sexy' to promote positive associations with sexual consent (Jozkowski, 2015b; Madden et al., 2018). Initial evidence has suggested that these campaigns are received positively on campus, but research has only examined reactions to the visuals (i.e. posters) or otherwise assessed people's awareness and understanding of the campaign issue (Hovick & Silver, 2019; Thomas et al., 2016).

The present research built on previous literature on how people perceive sexual consent. People generally report thinking that verbal affirmative consent is awkward, ruins the mood, and is overall unsexy (Beres, 2010; Blunt-Vinti et al., 2019; Curtis & Burnett, 2017; Foubert et al., 2006; T. P. Humphreys, 2004; Lindgren et al., 2009). After all, the slogan 'consent is sexy' was developed to address this shared cultural belief (consentissexy.net). But to the best of our knowledge, no peer-reviewed research has empirically tested the validity of that claim. Do people find consent sexy? Or does the presence of verbal consent reduce the eroticism of a sexual scenario?

In the present research, we tested these questions in an online experiment by asking participants to evaluate sexually explicit media. Media are primary vehicles for sexual scripts, or the cultural guidelines for sexual situations and what people can expect from them (Gagnon & Simon, 2005). Erotic media is especially associated with people's sexual behavioural intentions (Collins, et al., 2011; Hust et al., 2014). Therefore, we used passages of erotic fiction to examine whether incorporating consent dialogue affects their appeal. Across two studies, we compared how sexy U.S. American adults found excerpts of written erotica based on the presence or absence of affirmative verbal consent.

## *Sexual scripts*

The current research was informed by sexual scripts theory, which describes how sex and sexuality can be organised by sets of cognitive schemata including norms, roles, and meanings associated with a given sexual concept or scenario (Simon & Gagnon, 1986, 2003). Sexual scripts guide expectations for sexual interactions and inform individuals' cognitions and affect. People learn sexual scripts through social processes and internalise largely heterosexual norms, cultural scenarios, and gender roles (Kim et al., 2007; Sakaluk et al., 2014). According to the theory, individuals adapt and internalise the scripts and subsequently apply or enact them in their own lives (Frith & Kitzinger, 2001). Indeed, many scholars evidence the prominent role of sexual scripts in informing both people's sexual knowledge and behaviour (Greene & Faulkner, 2005; Grello et al., 2006; Littleton et al., 2009; Maticka-Tyndale & Herold, 1997).

As primary sources of sexual socialisation, sexual scripts in media are therefore key sites of communicating a given culture's sexual norms, values, and activities (Metts & Spitzberg, 1996). Essential components of dominant (e.g. heterosexual) sexual scripts include traditional gender roles, or gender-stereotyped sexuality (Eaton et al., 2016; Wiederman, 2005). Men are expected to pursue sex with women and persist tenaciously despite rebuffs, whereas women are expected to gatekeep their sexuality and be more interested in romantic relationships than physical sexuality (Jozkowski et al., 2017; Willis, Hunt et al., 2019). Consent is thus a gendered process whereby men seek it and women provide it (Bay-Cheng & Eliseo-Arras, 2008; Hust et al., 2017; Muehlenhard & Rodgers, 1998; Shumlich & Fisher, 2018).

## *Consent scripts*

Behaviours to indicate consent and refusal can be largely categorised as 1) either verbal or nonverbal and 2) either explicit (language or behaviours that are clearly sexual) or implicit (language or behaviours indicate interest in sexual activity; Hickman & Muehlenhard, 1999; Willis, Canan et al., 2019). 'No response' is also a commonly reported consent cue, described as passively allowing sexual activity to progress (Hickman & Muehlenhard, 1999).

People report far more experience with 'no response' cues and implicit, as opposed to explicit, consent behaviours in their own lives (Beres, 2010; Beres et al., 2004; Humphreys & Herold, 2007; Muehlenhard et al., 2016). Given our cultural context, this is expected: prototypical sexual encounters are depicted as unfolding wordlessly, seamlessly, and spontaneously (Beres, 2007; Dune & Shuttleworth, 2009; Haffner, 1995/1996). The idea of romance and passion as requiring subtlety and mystery is not commonly seen as compatible with explicit verbal sexual communication (Blunt-Vinti et al., 2019).

Beliefs about the required implicitness of sexuality are compounded by women and men's sexual roles. If a man verbally communicates during sex, he risks feeling or being perceived as unsure, partner-focused, or otherwise ill-equipped to lead the sexual encounter, all of which would contradict his prescribed role, inviting negative affect (Foubert et al., 2006; Humphreys, 2004). Meanwhile, women are also supposed to be silent – but about their sexual interest or desire. This poses a bind for women: they are expected to simultaneously gatekeep their sexuality, or risk being stigmatised and perceived as promiscuous, at the same time as asserting explicit affirmative consent to partake in sexual activity (Jozkowski et al., 2017; Kitzinger & Frith, 1999). To navigate these conflicting demands, women have indirectly expressed sexual consent and desire, usually via implicit or 'no response' cues (Righi et al., 2019; Shumlich & Fisher, 2018).

In sum, sexual consent scripts, as they have traditionally existed, emphasise nonverbal communication, implied sexual consent, and traditional gender roles that hold that men pursue sexual conquests while women should avoid promiscuity by not engaging in sex too readily (Curtis & Burnett, 2017; Fantasia, 2011). These beliefs clearly conflict with contemporary pushes for affirmative consent standards, as has been previously covered by sexual consent researchers (e.g. Beres, 2010; Jozkowski, 2015b). We suggest that the aversion people have to the idea of explicit verbal consent may be in part due to the tension affirmative consent practices have with the dominant set of cultural sexual scripts. However, sexual scripts are both a vehicle for sexual socialisation as well as fluid and malleable, like other cultural norms (Berkowitz, 2005; Metts & Spitzberg, 1996). Therefore, it is possible that dominant sexual scripts can begin incorporating explicit verbal consent as a standard component. If the practice can become normalised, perhaps affirmative consent would be considered erotic or arousing, as opposed to awkward and uncomfortable.

## *Sexual media*

Sexual scripts are frequently conveyed through media, particularly sexually explicit media, including pornographic videos and written erotic stories (Seabrook et al., 2017; Stevens & Smith, 2016; Ward, 2003). Just as people learn dating and relationship scripts from popular media, they learn sexual scripts from erotic media (Jozkowski et al., 2019; Zurbriggen & Morgan, 2006). Sexual media can affect an individual's perception of what is normative or acceptable sexual behaviour and, moreover, affect subsequent behaviours related to sexual activity (Brown & L'Engle, 2009; Kohut & Fisher, 2013; Van Oosten et al., 2017). Some young people report actually seeking out erotic and sexual materials (e.g. visual pornography) to supplement education or resources they receive from official providers (such as school-based sex education; Hare et al., 2015; Wood et al., 2002; Zillmann, 2000).

However, sexually explicit media do not frequently include models of explicit or verbal consent. In an analysis of the consent behaviours present in 50 of the best-selling pornographic films of 2015, implicit and nonverbal consent cues were portrayed much more frequently than explicit or verbal consent behaviours (Willis, Canan et al., 2019). Furthermore, in a study of adolescents who had seen pornography in the United Kingdom, only 13% of females and 23% of males reported that online pornography had informed them about giving consent (Martellozzo et al., 2016). The ubiquity of implicit communication methods could imply that verbal dialogue is inappropriate during sexual encounters. Indeed, across multiple studies, interviewees demonstrated aversive reactions to verbal sexual consent, a communication process that they suggested risks rejection, embarrassment, and decreased arousal (Curtis & Burnett, 2017; Foubert et al., 2006).

Verbal communication has a greater presence in written erotica than in visual sexual media (Warren, 2019). Dialogue is a primary component of a story, and narrative writing relies on conversations between characters to convey the motivations and emotions of the characters and the tone of the setting, whereas films can use visual cues and more subtle portrayals of nonverbal communication. It stands to follow that written sexual media may be a more comfortable or appropriate context for verbal or explicit consent behaviours than visual sexual media, where explicit dialogue about consent may feel out of place. We therefore used erotic fiction as the type of sexually explicit media in which to investigate how people perceive consent.

Erotic fiction is differentiated from romantic novels by the degree of explicit sexual content (such as the language used, details of sexual activity, and emphasis on sex between characters as opposed to relationships between characters) and ultimately by whether 'the text is designed primarily to arouse' (Warren, 2019, p. 2). However, peer-reviewed research has only investigated people's perceptions of sexual consent outside of explicitly erotic or arousing stimuli. For example, Lim and Roloff (1999) asked participants to read a version of a vignette about 'Sue' and 'Tom,' two undergraduates who go on a date and subsequently have sexual intercourse. Participants reported how consensually they perceived the situation to be, which varied the interpersonal dynamics between the characters (such as indicating coercion, an unequal power balance, or impairment from alcohol; Lim & Roloff, 1999).

Humphreys (2007) also investigated perceptions of consent in written vignettes depicting a sexual scenario, this time about 'Lisa' and 'Kevin' watching a movie together. Though not a dry, clinical passage, the vignette also cannot be considered sexually explicit material based on the criteria outlined by Warren (2019). The most explicit sexual detail is that Kevin 'brushed his hand slowly against her breast' and the couple is described to have 'missed the rest of the movie having sex' (Humphreys, 2007, p. 310). Both of these research studies use written sexual scenarios to investigate perceptions of consent, but both focused primarily on people's recognition or understanding of consent given the supplied sexual scenario. Contrastingly, for the current study we were interested in people's evaluations of the supplied sexual scenario, given the presence or absence of explicit verbal consent.

### *Current research*

In the present research, we sought to assess whether people perceive sexual scenarios containing explicit verbal consent as more or less sexy than scenarios containing implicit consent. Our primary aim was to examine both the campaign slogan ('consent is sexy') and the backlash to the campaign which claims that explicit consent is decidedly *not* sexy. To do so, we explored how people perceive written sexual media based on the presence or absence of clearly expressed sexual consent.

We used written sexual erotica for several reasons. First, written erotica poses many advantages over visual sexual stimuli for an initial research study. In general, erotica is considered to harbour more equal or egalitarian sexual power dynamics, making it more universally appealing to both women and men (Hyde & Delamater, 2017). This may be in part because there is more gender and sexual diversity in production and consumption of written erotica than of pornographic videos and films (Warren, 2019). Second, we wanted the women and men in our studies to find the sexually explicit material equally as appealing, so it was important to avoid pornographic films or videos because they are received much more positively by men than women (Carvalho et al., 2018; Chadwick et al., 2018; Janssen et al., 2003) and are watched more often by men than women (Hald & Štulhofer, 2015; Peter & Valkenburg, 2016).

Finally, research indicates that written erotica, just like other forms of sexual media, is a promising vehicle for sexual socialisation and location for encountering sexual scripts (Seabrook et al., 2017; Ward, 2003). People indeed internalise sexual interactions and sequences of behaviours as they are depicted in mainstream porn and erotica (Jozkowski et al., 2019; Lindgren et al., 2009). Furthermore, erotica can also promote sexual communication, and we suggest sexual consent, too. In a study by Kimberly et al. (2018), erotic literature introduced individuals to different sexual behaviours as well as increased their comfort and ability to discuss such sexual behaviours with a partner. The erotic literature aided individuals in facilitating dialogue around sexual activity. If explicit verbal sexual consent was encountered in an already titillating context, perhaps it would be less awkward, or at least disrupt the flow of the encounter less than people currently expect (Fantasia, 2011).

Using sexually explicit material meant that participants would encounter explicit verbal consent in an already arousing scenario, which we posited may provide insight regarding how people would feel and respond to affirmative consent in their own sex lives, as opposed to how they perceive consent in non-sexually charged scenarios (e.g. neutrally written sexual stories or vignettes). In the present research, we assessed the effects of verbal consent on perceived sexiness of the scenario by comparing ratings of erotica excerpts that contained explicit verbal consent to excerpts that omitted it.

Across two studies we examined evaluations of written erotica with and without explicit verbal consent. People demonstrate negative reactions or pessimism when asked directly about their attitudes towards sexual consent (e.g. Jozkowski et al., 2017). We investigated whether this concern is warranted. If verbal consent dialogue can be incorporated into a familiar sexual script, for example, perhaps the practice will not disrupt eroticism as some anticipate. Thus, we predicted that participants would evaluate the erotica excerpts favourably despite the presence of explicit consent.

Given the predominance of heteronormative sexual scripts among erotic media (Kim et al., 2007; Séguin et al., 2018), we focused on perceptions of consent among heterosexual encounters – those involving one woman and one man. People are more familiar with consent scripts that follow traditional gender roles (i.e. the man instigates, and the woman responds; Sakaluk et al., 2014) and research has even demonstrated that sexual minorities draw on heteronormative sexual scripts (Courtice & Shaughnessy, 2018). Therefore, it is reasonable for participants of varying sexual orientations to encounter and evaluate erotica depicting heterosexual encounters.

## Study 1

In this study, we examined how appealing people perceive sexual scenarios based on the inclusion or exclusion of explicit verbal consent. We employed an online survey in which respondents read a brief excerpt of erotic fiction depicting a heterosexual encounter. Half of the participants read original text excerpts, wherein the characters engaged in consensual sexual activity that followed an expected heterosexual script, meaning consent was implicit and nonverbal. The other half of the participants read the experimental versions of the excerpts, in which the researchers added explicit verbal consent. Participants indicated their appraisals of the excerpts, including how sexy they found them and how much they wanted to read more of the story.

## Method

### Participants

Undergraduate research assistants recruited participants by posting the survey link on Craigslist volunteer forums between January and March of 2018. The survey was advertised as a short research study on perceptions of short online stories. Four hundred and twenty-one individuals completed the dependent measure. However, we excluded three participants who were not from the U.S. and 16 participants whose responses indicated that they were not taking the survey seriously (i.e. responding facetiously in the open-ended fields for demographic questions, completing the survey by clicking straight down the columns in the questionnaire, missing the negatively worded item, or finishing the survey in under two minutes). The final sample included 402 individuals between the ages 18–87 ($M = 42.9$, $SD = 14.5$). The majority of participants were White (83.1%) and over half were male (63.4%). See Table 1 for full demographics.

Importantly, these participants were largely older than traditional undergraduate students: only 10.4% of the sample were younger than 25. Although we did not ask participants if they were currently college students, 46.6% of the sample indicated that they have already completed a degree in higher education. As previously mentioned, the current sample provides a novel contribution to the literature because college students and other young people are frequently the subjects of study when it comes to sexual consent (Willis, Blunt-Vinti et al., 2019).

Table 1. Demographics.

| Variable | Pilot Study | Study 1 | Study 2 |
| --- | --- | --- | --- |
| Participants N | 233 | 402 | 449 |
| Age M (SD) | 23.8 (9.6) | 42.9 (14.5) | 35.0 (10.7) |
| Gender N (%) | | | |
| Women | 175 (75.1) | 141 (35.1) | 192 (42.8) |
| Men | 40 (17.2) | 255 (63.4) | 250 (55.7) |
| Other | 3 (1.3) | 1 (0.2) | 3 (0.7) |
| No response | 15 (6.4) | 5 (1.2) | 4 (.9) |
| Race/Ethnicity N (%) | | | |
| African American/Black | 10 (4.3) | 10 (2.5) | 35 (7.9) |
| Asian/Asian American | 16 (6.9) | 10 (2.5) | 25 (5.6) |
| European American/White | 163 (70) | 331 (83.1) | 347 (78.5) |
| Hispanic/Latino/Latina/Latinx | 13 (5.6) | 8 (2) | 22 (4.9) |
| Native/Indigenous | 1 (0.4) | 6 (1.5) | 2 (.4) |
| Multi-Racial/Other | 12 (5.1) | 32 (8) | 12 (2.7) |
| Highest schooling completed N (%) | | | |
| Less than high school | 1 (0.4) | 9 (2.3) | 3 (.7) |
| High school diploma/GED | 145 (62.2) | 199 (50.5) | 138 (31) |
| College degree | 61 (26.2) | 138 (45) | 261 (58.7) |
| Master's degree | 10 (4.3) | 34 (8.6) | 33 (7.4) |
| Doctoral or Professional degree | 1 (0.4) | 14 (3.5) | 10 (2.2) |
| Current college students | – | – | 64 (14.4) |
| Sexual orientation | | | |
| Heterosexual | – | – | 383 (86.1) |
| Lesbian or Gay | – | – | 20 (4.5) |
| Bisexual | – | – | 35 (7.9) |
| Other | – | – | 7 (1.6) |
| Marital Status | | | |
| Single, never married | – | – | 242 (54.4) |
| Married | – | – | 164 (36.9) |
| Separated | – | – | 3 (.7) |
| Divorced | – | – | 24 (5.4) |
| Widowed | – | – | 3 (.7) |
| Other | – | – | 9 (2) |

(not all percentages will total 100 due to missing data from participant omission)

## Procedure

The initial page of the survey contained the informed consent and age requirement (18 years or older). By clicking 'next,' individuals indicated their agreement to participate and confirmed their age. Participants were then advised that they would be reading a story that describes sexual experiences or scenarios and should expect sexually explicit content and language. After advancing to the next screen, Qualtrics Research Suite randomly assigned participants to one of eight conditions (four erotica passages that contained verbal consent between the female and male characters and four that did not). All participants then completed the same dependent measure asking their evaluations of the story that they read. The final page of the survey contained demographic questions and an open-ended question where participants could provide feedback or report issues. The university's institutional review board for research for human subjects approved all methods. All data were anonymous, and we conducted all analyses with IBM SPSS Statistics 25.

## Materials

### Erotica excerpts

Three trained undergraduate research assistants reviewed over 100 erotic fiction stories, available for free consumption online at literotica.com, fanfiction.net, remittancegirl.com, archiveofourown.org, nifty.org, and erotic-stories.mobi. They aggregated excerpts of stories that (1) depicted a scenario between one woman and one man, (2) did not depict sadomasochistic or other fetishistic activities, and (3) could be easily modified to depict two versions: one with verbal consent and one where the sexual activity 'just happened.' Because we wanted to begin by testing how the addition of affirmative verbal consent into typical sexual scenarios would affect people's appraisals of them, we aimed for the 'control' excerpts to reflect traditional heterosexual scripts (commonly depicted in mainstream sexual media like erotic fiction, pornographic videos, and romance novels).

The research assistants aggregated 25 excerpts that were then assessed among a larger team of ten undergraduate research assistants, who anonymously rated the excerpts on arousability. The top five excerpts were presented to the authors for quality assurance. Four final excerpts were chosen based on their comparable content (i.e. a sexually charged situation between a woman and man who are depicted with internal feelings of consent; Willis, Blunt-Vinti et al., 2019) and their varying story contexts (i.e. a lustful encounter, familiar friends, an apprehensive couple, and romantic lovers). In this way, we hoped to explore how people view sexual consent while accounting for potential differences in preferences for sexual scenarios (such as a preference for graphic depictions of sex acts versus verbose representations of erotic feelings, or preferences for familiar versus unfamiliar partners).

Working with the authors, the three trained undergraduate research assistants modified the four excerpts so that each had two versions: one where the sexual activity unravelled without affirmative dialogue (we termed these stories the 'just happens' condition, referring to the dominant sexual script in both sexual media and reported behaviour; Jozkowski, and Peterson, 2013) and one where the male character obtained verbal consent from the female character (we termed these versions the 'verbal consent' condition). We aimed for consistency in how consent was obtained (i.e. the man obtaining it from the woman) between the four verbal consent stories to minimise effects from different depictions of gender roles. We chose the man obtaining consent from the woman because that is in line with prevalent understandings of how sexual consent occurs. Please see Appendix A for all erotica excerpts used in Study 1.

## Measures

### Erotica assessment

For this research we developed items intended to assess perceived sexiness and appeal of a given piece of media. The authors and trained undergraduate research assistants collectively wrote statements to which participants could respond on a six-point Likert scales with endpoints ranging from 1 = *Strongly Disagree* to 6 = *Strongly Agree*. We intended that the items measure the participants' attitudes towards the erotica, rather than their inner affective state. Thus, the items were written to elicit the participants' appraisals of the excerpt and we narrowed our list to the seven items upon which all members of the research team agreed: 'I was engaged in this story,' 'I found this story appealing,' 'This story was exciting,' 'I found this story sexy,' 'If given the opportunity, I would like to read more of this story,' 'This story was realistic,' and 'I found this story boring.' We wrote the final item in the opposite direction than the other items – that is, negatively worded – to reduce participant acquiescence.

Undergraduate research assistants posted a pilot version of this study, including the erotica excerpts and items we developed, to their social media accounts and solicited volunteer participants. A sample of 233 anonymous individuals completed the survey (see Table 1 for demographics). A correlational analysis revealed that all seven items were significantly correlated, $ps <.001$ (see Table 2 for inter-item correlations). Furthermore, there was no risk of high partial correlation as all correlations were large and significant, as opposed to only one inter-correlation (Hair et al., 2010, p. 102).

To demonstrate the statistical interrelation between items, we conducted an exploratory factor analysis with varimax rotation and a loading cut-off of .6 (reduced thresholds are suggested when testing fewer variables than the recommended dozens for an Eigenvalue greater than 1; Hair et al., 2010; Fields, 2005). The seven items constituted two factors and accounted for 70.1% of the variance. The first factor comprised all the items except for 'This story was realistic,' which comprised

**Table 2.** Inter-item correlations for Study 1 and Study 2 dependent measure items.

| Item | 1 | 2 | 3 | 4 | 5 | 6 |
|---|---|---|---|---|---|---|
| 1. I was engaged in this story. | – | .832*** | .776*** | −.657*** | .701*** | .704*** |
| 2. I found this story appealing. | .794*** | – | .840*** | −.642*** | .764*** | .736*** |
| 3. This story was exciting. | .787*** | .857*** | – | −.669*** | .806*** | .765*** |
| 4. I found this story boring. | −.687** | −.683*** | −.748*** | – | −.647*** | −.615*** |
| 5. I found this story sexy. | .741*** | .801*** | .799*** | −.663*** | – | .764*** |
| 6. If given the opportunity, I would want to read more of this story. | .647*** | .765*** | .737*** | −.575*** | .719*** | – |
| 7. I found this story awkward.[†] | −.543*** | −.608*** | −.608*** | −.606*** | −.656*** | −.539*** |

*Study 1 correlations are located above the diagonal line; Study 2 correlations are below.
** $p < .05$
***Correlation is significant at $p < .001$
[†]This item was not included in Study 1.

the second. We dropped the second factor's item from the current research because our aim was to assess how sexy people find a piece of erotic media that also contains explicit verbal consent, and we would not necessarily expect something sexy or erotic to also be realistic – especially when its media associated with fantasy.

The final set of six items included: 'I was engaged in this story,' 'I found this story appealing,' 'This story was exciting,' 'I found this story sexy,' 'If given the opportunity, I would like to read more of this story,' and 'I found this story boring' and demonstrated strong internal coherence (Cronbach's alpha = .926).

## Demographics

The final page of the questionnaire asked participants to indicate their age, race/ethnicity, gender, and highest level of education completed.

## Analysis

The aim of this study was to compare how sexy U.S. adults find excerpts of written erotica based on the presence or absence of affirmative verbal consent. Because we have not determined the external validity of the dependent measure items, we approached the present research's primary analyses without the assumption that all items assess the same exact construct. To test each specific item, we conducted one-way multivariate analyses of variance (MANOVAs) to examine the six items across the independent variables at once, to account for the multiple means being tested and reduce risk of type 1 error that accumulates with increased analyses (Hair et al., 2010).

We first assessed for differences in participant appraisals of the erotica excerpts across the four story types, finding that Story 3 received significantly less positive ratings than Stories 1, 2, and 4. Given that we were not interested in participant appraisals between the stories, but rather across them in comparing evaluations of passages that contain versus omit verbal consent, we decided to control for story version in our mean comparisons between 'verbal consent' and 'just happens.' We did so by creating a dummy variable for story version (1–4 for each of the four stories) and including that variable as a covariate in the MANOVA assessing the dependent measure items across experimental conditions.

We also tested whether women and men differed in their perceptions of the erotica but found no evidence of a gender difference. We again used a MANOVA to reduce risk of type 1 error while testing for mean differences in the six outcome items.

Our primary analyses consisted of a multivariate analysis of covariance (MANCOVA) comparing means on the dependent measure items between the 'verbal consent' condition to the 'it just happens' condition, while controlling for which of the four stories were read by participants by including that variable as a covariate. We created a dummy variable to indicate condition with 0 = 'verbal consent' and 1 = 'it just happens.'

# Results

## Exploratory analyses

### Story differences

We conducted a one-way multivariate analysis of variance (MANOVA) of the six outcome items, comparing participant ratings across the four story versions. The stories differed significantly, Wilks' $\lambda = .83$, $F(18, 1112.06) = 4.26$, $p < .001$. Pairwise comparisons between the four erotica stories revealed that participants found one of the four stories (the one featuring an apprehensive couple) significantly less preferable compared with the other three stories on five of the six dependent measure items, $ps < .05$. Importantly, the apprehensive couple story differed from the other three most significantly on the item *I found this story sexy*, with an overall mean (that is, across both consent conditions) of 2.65 compared with overall means of 3.69, 3.53, and 3.75.

### Group differences

We conducted a one-way MANOVA testing for gender differences in scores on the six outcome items. Results indicated that women and men rated the passages similarly, Wilks' $\lambda = .985$, $F(6, 389) = .96$, $p = .45$, $\eta^2 = .02$.

## Primary analyses

Overall, participants provided approximately average evaluations of the erotica passages: the means of the dependent measure items ranged between 3.29 to 3.71 (see Table 3), which surrounds the midpoint (3.5) of a six-point scale.

The MANCOVA model indicated no overall difference in participant assessment of the erotica based on the presence or absence of explicit verbal consent, Wilks' $\lambda = .975$, $F(6, 394) = 1.71$, $p = .118$, $\eta^2 = .03$. The descriptive and test statistics for individual items are presented in Table 3.

Three of the individual items demonstrated significant differences between conditions: 'I found this story appealing,' 'I found this story sexy,' and 'If given the opportunity, I would want to read more of this story.' We note that all effect sizes are very small, with $\eta^2 s < .02$. However, our goal in this study was to determine whether verbal consent reduced the sexiness of the passage. We found, if anything, the opposite was true, albeit by this small margin. For all three items, participants rated the erotica excerpts with verbal consent more favourably than the excerpts lacking it. That is, participants considered the excerpts with verbal consent more appealing and sexier; they also indicated greater interest in reading more of the erotic story.

# Study 2

In Study 1, people did not differ in their appraisals of erotic fiction based on the inclusion versus exclusion of affirmative consent. As such, we did not find evidence to suggest that how sexy people perceive a sexual scenario is dampened by the presence of explicit verbal consent.

Table 3. Descriptive and test statistics for Study 1 dependent variables.

|  | 'Just happens' condition (SD) N = 204 | 'Verbal consent' condition (SD) N = 198 | df | F | p | $\eta^2$ |
| --- | --- | --- | --- | --- | --- | --- |
| I was engaged in this story. | 3.55 (1.50) | 3.82 (1.37) | 1 | 3.64 | .06 | .009 |
| I found this story appealing. | 3.40 (1.44) | 3.74 (1.40) | 1 | 5.58 | .02* | .014 |
| This story was exciting. | 3.23 (1.46) | 3.52 (1.49) | 1 | 2.71 | .06 | .009 |
| I found this story boring. | 3.31 (1.54) | 3.26 (1.47) | 1 | .093 | .76 | .000 |
| I found this story sexy. | 3.23 (1.56) | 3.58 (1.52) | 1 | 5.27 | .02* | .013 |
| If given the opportunity, I would want to read more of this story. | 3.37 (1.58) | 3.71 (1.59) | 1 | 4.57 | .03* | .011 |

1 (low) – 6 (high)* $p < .05$

Participants preferred one of the four stories (the one featuring an apprehensive couple) significantly less than the others. In re-assessing the excerpts from the apprehensive couple story, we realised that both the 'just happens' and 'verbal consent' versions of this story failed to include explicit sexual activity. Rather, the characters seem to be preparing for a sexual encounter, whereas the excerpts from the other three stories include explicitly sexual language and depict kissing as the minimum sexual activity. Therefore, we aimed to reproduce our findings from Study 1 with a more consistent and controlled experimental manipulation and in additional examples of erotic fiction. In Study 2, we again assessed whether the inclusion of affirmative consent detracts from the erotic appeal of a sexual scenario by comparing the perceived sexiness of erotic fiction with and without explicit verbal consent.

## Method

### Participants

The participants for Study 2 were recruited on Amazon Mechanical Turk. The survey was advertised as a short research study on perceptions of short sexual scenarios and respondents were paid 1.00 USD for completing the study. Inclusion criteria were being 18 years of age or older and being a resident of the U.S. Data were collected during May 2019.

We conducted a power analysis and determined that we needed a minimum of approximately 200 participants in each of the two conditions (or approximately 50 participants per each of the eight cells). Based on our previously described pilot test of 233 individuals, we expected about 20% of participants to fail the attention check. Therefore, we recruited more than 400 participants to account for the 20% of participants we expected to fail the attention check. Four hundred and ninety-seven individuals completed the dependent measure. We excluded all participants who failed the study attention check, which asked, 'In the story portion that you read, did someone consent to sex using words?' Answer options included 'Yes,' 'No,' and 'I'm unsure.' Participants failed the attention check by either responding 'I'm unsure' ($n = 33$), responding 'No' even though they were assigned to 'verbal consent' conditions ($n = 7$), or responding 'Yes' despite reading 'just happens' versions ($n = 8$).

The final sample comprised 449 U.S. adults between ages 18–75 ($M = 35.0$, $SD = 10.7$). Most participants were White (78.5%) and heterosexual (86.1%). Just under half of the sample were women (42.8%), and just over half indicated they had never been married (54.4%). As in Study 1, the current sample was primarily non-college students (85.6%) which contributes a new population of study to the current literature on sexual consent (Willis, Blunt-Vinti et al., 2019). Once again, only 10% of the participants were under age 25. For full demographics, please see Table 1.

### Procedure

The procedure was identical to Study 1 with two exceptions. First, the initial page of the survey also contained information on participant payment. Second, we included an attention check after the dependent measures but before the demographics.

### Materials

#### Erotica excerpts

Given the variance between the different erotica stories in Study 1, we emphasised consistency across the erotic fiction we used as study materials. Specifically, we ensured the four chosen excerpts in Study 2 were of similar lengths and included comparable levels of sexual activity between the characters. After selecting new erotica excerpts, we pilot tested them for ratings of preference and arousability among adult volunteers in the U.S. (specifically, a large university town and community).

The authors reviewed and aggregated excerpts of erotic fiction stories using the same websites identified in Study 1. For these stimuli, we were careful to keep excerpt length, storytelling point of view, and level of sexual explicitness consistent across all four chosen stories. In all of the 'just happens' versions, narrative descriptions indicate that the sexual activity is consensual via cues of 'no response.' For example, the text indicated an implied consent with passive nonverbal cues such as 'her legs parted.' Meanwhile, excerpts in the 'verbal consent' condition incorporated explicit verbal consent cues as defined by Jozkowski et al. (2019). We specifically ensured that these portions of dialogue were explicit, not implicit (i.e. sexual desire or behaviour was not implied or alluded to, but rather directly expressed) and that affirmative consent was provided verbally by the female characters (to avoid misperceptions of nonverbal or implied consent). For example,

> "How far do you want to take things?" Michael asked, trailing his hands down her stomach. "I've wanted to have sex with you for a long time," she admitted, propping herself up on her elbows, a smile playing around the corners of her mouth.

Once again, we followed the traditional heterosexual script of male initiators of sexual activity and obtainers of consent and female gatekeepers of sexual activity and consent providers.

Additional material design included ensuring that consent was obtained at the same chronological location of each story, since it is important that consent come prior to the specific sexual activity, especially intercourse (Hall, 1998). This reduced the risk of participants evaluating the erotica based on their preference for where consent comes sequentially in the sexual script. Finally, we eliminated any narrative text that described a character's internal monologue to reduce variance in erotica assessment introduced by individual differences in how participants may interpret alignment between the characters' internal feelings of consent and their sexual consent behaviours (Willis et al., 2019).

The four final erotic fiction excerpts (see Appendix B) all depicted a sexually charged situation between one woman and one man that culminated in vaginal-penile intercourse. The writing style and story contexts varied less than in Study 1 given that the excerpts primarily described sexual feelings and activities and included less detail about character dynamics or familiarity. In this way, the current study is a more controlled test of the effect that affirmative, verbal consent has on how people perceive sexual scenarios.

## Measures

### Erotica assessment
Participants responded to the same six items that were in Study 1. To interrogate the claim that direct communication about sexual consent is awkward, we added one item to our dependent measures: *I thought this story was awkward*. Participants again indicated their agreement using six-point Likert scales with endpoints ranging from 1 = *Strongly Disagree* to 6 = *Strongly Agree*. Please see Table 2 for inter-item correlations.

### Demographics
We included additional demographic questions regarding whether participants were currently college students, their current marital status, and their sexual orientation.

## Analysis

In Study 2, we again used MANOVAs to examine the seven items at once. We assessed differences in participant appraisals of the erotica excerpts across the four story types, but nothing of significance emerged. Thus, we determined that we did not need to control for which of the four stories the participants read in our primary analyses.

We also explored group differences with multivariate analyses to test whether people of different genders and sexual orientations perceived the erotica differently. We employed MANOVAs in these cases to be able to identify whether any individual items were noteworthy in driving any overall group differences while controlling for increase of type 1 error.

Women and men differed in their responses to the item 'If given the opportunity, I would want to read more of this story' such that women more strongly agreed than men ($p = .05$). However, we decided not to control for gender in our primary analyses for several reasons. First, the gender difference on this item is expected because research indicates that women are more familiar with written sexually explicit media, while men report more experience with visual forms (Peter & Valkenburg, 2016; Warren, 2019). Second, including gender as a covariate in our analyses did not change the significance nor effect sizes of our results. Finally, the difference between women and men on 'I would want to read more of this story' is preliminary and fell on the cusp of significance. Because the purpose of the current study was to investigate perceived sexiness (and women and men did not differ on the item 'I found this story sexy'), we did not include gender as a covariate in assessing participants' evaluations of the erotica across consent condition.

We also found an overall significant difference between sexual orientation categories. However, the groups were highly unequal in number with 383 heterosexual participants, 20 same-sex oriented participants, 35 bisexual participants, and 7 participants who indicated 'None of the above/Prefer not to answer.' Therefore, it was not appropriate to run pairwise comparisons to home in on the specific orientation categories that significantly differed. Given that no analyses of interest to the current research yielded different results based on the removal of sexual minority participants, we elected to keep all participants (who passed the attention check) in the study. Because we were not controlling for story version, gender, nor sexual orientation, we compared means on the seven dependent measure items between the 'just happens' and 'verbal consent' conditions by conducting a MANOVA. In this way, we avoided increasing type 1 error, and also presented the simplest statistical model. We again created a dummy variable to indicate condition with 0 = 'verbal consent' and 1 = 'it just happens.'

## Results

### *Exploratory analyses*

### *Story differences*
Using a MANOVA to compare participant ratings across the four story versions on the seven dependent measure items, we found no significant differences, Wilks' $\lambda = .95$, $F(21, 1261.12) = 1.10$, $p = .34$, $\eta^2 = .02$.

### *Group differences*
Using a MANOVA testing for gender differences in scores on the seven outcome items. Results indicated a marginally significant difference overall, Wilks' $\lambda = .96$, $F(8, 433) = 2.033$, $p = .04$, $\eta^2 = .04$. Examining the individual items, however, reveals that only 'If given the opportunity, I would want to read more of this story' yielded a significant difference between women ($M = 3.94$, $SD = 1.53$) and men ($M = 3.57$, $SD = 1.59$). For all other items, mean scores between women and men differed by less than .03 of a scale point (see Table 4). Addressing this slight disparity by including gender as a covariate in our primary analyses did not change the results, so we elected not to control for this gender difference.

The MANOVA comparing the outcome item means between sexual orientation groups indicated an overall significant difference, Wilks' $\lambda = .92$, $F(21, 1249.64) = 1.78$, $p = .02$, $\eta^2 = .03$. Heterosexual and bisexual participants rated the erotica excerpts more favourably on the individual items than did lesbian and gay participants (see Table 4). Removing lesbian and gay participants from our analyses

**Table 4.** Study 2 descriptive statistics by gender and sexual orientation.

|  | Women M (SD) | Men M (SD) | Heterosexual (SD) | Lesbian/Gay M (SD) | Bisexual M (SD) | Other M (SD) |
|---|---|---|---|---|---|---|
| N | 192 | 250 | 383 | 20 | 35 | 7 |
| I was engaged in this story. | 4.51 (1.2) | 4.51 (1.2) | 4.6 (1.2) | 4.0 (1.1) | 4.4 (1.5) | 3.7 (1.4) |
| I found this story appealing. | 4.30 (1.3) | 4.22 (1.4) | 4.3 (1.3) | 3.9 (1.9) | 4.1 (1.6) | 4.0 (1.2) |
| This story was exciting. | 4.29 (1.4) | 4.18 (1.4) | 4.3 (1.4) | 3.9 (1.9) | 4.1 (1.6) | 3.4 (1.5) |
| I found this story boring. | 2.46 (1.4) | 2.57 (1.5) | 2.5 (1.4) | 3.6 (2.0) | 2.8 (1.6) | 3.1 (1.2) |
| I found this story sexy. | 4.46 (1.4) | 4.36 (1.4) | 4.5 (1.4) | 4.0 (1.5) | 4.2 (1.5) | 4.3 (1.1) |
| I thought this story was awkward. | 2.54 (1.5) | 2.81 (1.6) | 2.7 (1.6) | 3.4 (1.9) | 2.7 (1.6) | 3.0 (1.3) |
| I would want to read more of this story. | 3.94 (1.5) | 3.57 (1.6) | 3.8 (1.6) | 3.1 (1.7) | 3.9 (1.6) | 3.0 (1.2) |

did not change this research's findings, nor did removing participants who indicated 'Other' for their sexual orientation, so we included them in this sample.

## Primary analyses

In this study, participants gave these passages of erotica more favourable overall ratings than the passages in Study 1. Every single item's average was on the side of the six-point scales that indicates a more positive appraisal; in other words, the boring and awkward items yield means below 3.5 while the rest of the item means range from 3.7 to 4.5, see Table 5.

The MANOVA comparing participant ratings of the 'verbal consent' erotica excerpts to the 'it just happens' excerpts on the dependent measure items indicated no overall difference in participant assessment of the erotica based on the presence or absence of explicit, verbal consent, Wilks' $\lambda = .975$, $F(7, 441) = 1.59$, $p = .135$, $\eta^2 = .03$. Participants evaluated the erotica passages similarly across experimental condition. None of the individual items yielded a significant difference across conditions, $ps > .05$. Descriptive and test statistics for individual items are presented in Table 5.

## Discussion

The purpose of this research was to examine the effects of explicit verbal consent on the appeal of a sexual scenario. We conducted two studies comparing how sexy participants found a given excerpt of erotica, based on whether the characters expressed explicit verbal consent.

Participants evaluated the passages of erotica depicting traditional 'sex just happens' scripts and the passages of erotica incorporating explicit verbal consent equally as sexy and appealing. Findings from Study 1 suggested U.S. adults judged the stories similarly and, if anything, considered the excerpts with verbal consent to be sexier. In Study 2, participants considered both versions equally as sexy. Overall, people's appraisals of how sexy they found the erotica did not differ based on the presence or absence of affirmative verbal consent. Despite claims that such direct negotiations of

**Table 5.** Descriptive and test statistics for Study 2 dependent variables.

|  | 'Just happens' condition M (SD) N = 222 | 'Verbal consent' condition M (SD) N = 227 | df | F | p | $\eta^2$ |
|---|---|---|---|---|---|---|
| I was engaged in this story. | 4.62 (1.21) | 4.42 (1.23) | 1 | 3.13 | .078 | .007 |
| I found this story appealing. | 4.27 (1.39) | 4.24 (1.28) | 1 | 0.07 | .797 | .000 |
| This story was exciting. | 4.34 (1.44) | 4.13 (1.34) | 1 | 2.57 | .110 | .006 |
| I found this story boring. | 2.45 (1.53) | 2.64 (1.45) | 1 | 1.89 | .170 | .004 |
| I found this story sexy. | 4.48 (1.48) | 4.33 (1.33) | 1 | 1.31 | .254 | .003 |
| I thought this story was awkward. | 2.61 (1.59) | 2.81 (1.58) |  | 1.76 | .186 | .004 |
| I would want to read more of this story. | 3.78 (1.61) | 3.70 (1.57) | 1 | 0.35 | .554 | .001 |

1 (low) – 6 (high).

consent are inorganic, disruptive, and unsexy, we found evidence that the inclusion of verbal consent in erotica is not associated with lowered appeal.

The consent dialogue used in the current research materials was direct, explicit, and verbal. These qualities are conventionally presumed incompatible with romance and passion, which are more closely associated with subtlety or spontaneity (Beres, 2007; Blunt-Vinti et al., 2019). Why did participants rate the excerpts with verbal consent just as – if not more – sexy than the excerpts without it? We suggest that because the consent dialogue was (1) written into a traditional sexual script (i.e. one in which the man seeks, and the woman provides, consent; Hust et al., 2017) and (2) encountered in an already sexually charged scenario, participants did not find it disruptive nor out of place. To the first point, the script's familiarity may have buffered against the unexpected consent dialogue, allowing participants to still find the excerpt sexy.

To the second point, engaging with explicit consent in an erotic context – rather than an educational, professional, or clinical one – may allow people to feel more positively towards consent and make more pleasurable associations with it. The primary contexts in which people are familiar with explicit verbal consent are not in bedrooms and boudoirs, but in the contexts of sexual assault prevention, clinical or professional training, and activism or advocacy spaces (Beres, 2018; Foubert et al., 2006; Hovick & Silver, 2019; Humphreys & Herold, 2003; Madden et al., 2018). These environments are intentionally unerotic and encountering explicit verbal consent outside of those spaces may invoke in people similar feelings and conceptual associations that they experience while in those spaces. Yet in the current research, people rated reading material with explicit verbal consent as arousing and sexy. Perhaps encountering explicit verbal consent within the context of sexually explicit media reduced unerotic associations and promoted arousing feelings. That affirmative verbal consent did not detract from the excerpts' appeal indicates that sexual communication need not be implicit or nonverbal in sexual media to maintain sexiness.

### *Contributions to literature*

This research provides a novel contribution to the literature on sexual consent, which has focused on assessing people's attitudes towards, beliefs about, and behaviours related to consent (Borges et al., 2008; Hall, 1998; Hickman & Muehlenhard, 1999; Humphreys & Herold, 2007; Hust et al., 2017; Jozkowski & Peterson, 2013; Jozkowski et al., 2014; Shumlich & Fisher, 2019). Many of these researchers have investigated the parameters of what constitutes consent, specifically exploring whether contextual changes affect expression and recognition of consent cues. Findings from the current studies suggested that incorporating consent into already arousing or erotic situations may promote favourable associations and experiences with those situations.

This research also contributes to the growing literature documenting the social processes by which we learn scripts through media, even – or especially – including sexually explicit media (Jozkowski et al., 2019; Seabrook et al., 2017; Stevens & Smith, 2016; Ward, 2003; Zurbriggen & Morgan, 2006). Participants rated the erotica excerpts favourably overall, indicating they were not opposed to the traditional scripts invoked in the gendered consent dynamic portrayed in the stories. Thus, various sexual scripts do seem to indicate shared knowledge in terms of expected norms for sexual interactions or encounters.

Scripting offers a mechanism to normalising or desensitising people to an unfamiliar process. Scripts are offered in a variety of contexts to assist people through interactions, including ordering food at a restaurant, successfully completing a job interview, recruiting participants for research, and many more. In the present research, sexual scripts offer a path to normalising or routinising verbal consent. Perhaps as people are exposed to the new script component (i.e. explicit verbal consent), their experiences with, and perceptions of, verbal consent will not be awkward or threatening.

## Translation and application

Normalising affirmative verbal consent in sexual media may have major effects on shifting sexual scripts culturally. Many young people turn to erotica for purposes of curiosity and active learning that often stem from a lack of formal comprehensive sexual education (Hare et al., 2015; Wood et al., 2002). They turn to these media because they are more sex positive and exploratory compared with sexual health curricula, which are often limited and restrictive (Stanger-Hall & Hall, 2011; Willis, Jozkowski et al., 2019). Additionally, numerous organisations dedicated to promoting affirmative consent and more positive sexual encounters include in their curricula educational programmes, social marketing, and activism (Jozkowski, 2015b; Madden et al., 2018). We suggest that all would do well to consider that people – especially young people – yearn for better resources and information around sexual communication. Including sexual consent under the umbrella of sexual communication could be a useful branding strategy in promoting sexual consent as an erotic process.

Currently, consent risks being primarily understood as a barrier to overcome to achieve a sexual encounter or as a strategy to reduce the risk of sexual assault. Neither of these purposes is compatible with conceptualising consent as sexy or leading to pleasure. Perhaps people could learn about verbal consent as a sexual script component in ways that emphasise or highlight sexual communication as a key factor for sexual pleasure and satisfaction. As demonstrated in the current research, when sexual consent is incorporated into a situation that is already arousing, sexually charged, and erotic, it seems that the allegedly unnatural or awkward dialogue of consent is less apparent than we might assume.

Finally, verbal consent scripts could contribute to people's self-efficacy, or their belief in their own ability to enact and negotiate consent in their own lives. Perhaps people believe that consent is not sexy because they find it difficult to imagine communicating their own consent in a way that seems erotic. The dialogue enacted in sexually explicit media could serve as a template of how to incorporate affirmative verbal consent in ways that contribute to arousal or do not disrupt the sequence of events. Obtaining or providing consent does not inherently ruin the mood and it can even be fun and sexy! Erotic media can contribute to the cultural push for enthusiastic consent by providing examples that fit in between 'no response' consent cues and a clinical, decidedly un-erotic exchange of consent.

## Limitations and future directions

The present research was an initial test of how sexy – or not – people find explicit verbal consent. We only compared people's perceptions of consent within the context of brief passages of erotica that depict a dominant heteronormative sexual script (in terms of the sequence of events and portrayal of gender roles). We strongly encourage conceptual reproductions using additional erotica and other sexually explicit materials, such as videos or images. Because men use visual pornography more than written erotica (Peter & Valkenburg, 2016), male participants may be more or less amenable to explicit sexual consent in a different media format. Perhaps men would report greater variance in perceived sexiness across consent conditions if the consent dialogue were incorporated, for example, into a pornographic video.

Examining one type of script as the basis for our erotica passages was helpful for reducing variance but prevented us from comparing effects of verbal consent on perceived sexiness across script dynamics. For example, the sexual scenario could be characterised by swapped gender roles and depict a woman seeking consent from a man. Same-sex encounters also have their own sets of norms and scripts. How do people perceive consent between partners of the same gender in sexual media? Future research promises to contribute to scholarship on consent scripts across a variety of sexual encounters.

For these studies, we developed original items, consisting of statements that assessed the sexiness or appeal of media. The present research was limited by the lack of external validity, given that we did not test the items we created against existing measures. However, they did demonstrate coherence in reliability analyses. Future research could systematically test the associations 'perceived sexiness' has with other evaluative measures and further develop this outcome, perhaps constructing a scale. Researchers could even incorporate measures of arousal (both self-report and physiological) and test the relationship between perceived sexiness and physical arousal.

Importantly, future work should also be designed to test comparisons across sexual orientation on this measure. The insufficient number of sexual minority participants to conduct group-based comparisons is another current limitation. Researchers should intentionally recruit participants and collect data to answer questions about how people of different sexual orientations relate to, or perceive, consent.

Finally, the present work only addressed perceptions of consent in fiction, and not in practice. Therefore, findings cannot be extrapolated to people's real behaviour. In the current studies, participants evaluated excerpts of erotica with consent dialogue that had been carefully written, edited, and pilot tested – all luxuries that individuals do not have when negotiating their own sexual encounters. However, it is possible that behavioural intentions and even consent behaviours could change after exposure to verbal consent scripts. Future work could also look at the relationships between consuming sexual media with verbal consent and individuals' personal sexual consent attitudes and behaviours. Perhaps with regular exposure to explicit consent as a critical component of a sexual encounter, people will be less likely to rely on nonverbal behaviours to communicate their intentions. Daily diary studies could be particularly useful for tracking media consumption and sexual activity. In sum, plenty of future directions exist for the critical work of promoting safer, more positive, and more pleasurable sex through the championing of explicit verbal consent.

## Disclosure statement

No potential conflict of interest was reported by the authors.

## Funding

This work was supported by the Horace H. Rackham School of Graduate Studies, University of Michigan [RRG REF-19481].

## ORCID

Jennifer L. Piemonte http://orcid.org/0000-0002-3043-8893

## References

Bay-Cheng, L. Y., & Eliseo-Arras, R. K. (2008). The making of unwanted sex: Gendered and neoliberal norms in college women's unwanted sexual experiences. *Journal of Sex Research*, *45*(4), 386–397. https://doi.org/10.1080/00224490802398381

Beres, M. A. (2007). 'Spontaneous' sexual consent: An analysis of sexual consent literature. *Feminism & Psychology, 17*(1), 93-108. https://doi.org/10.1177/0959353507072914

Beres, M. A. (2010). Sexual miscommunication? Untangling assumptions about sexual communication between casual sex partners. *Culture, Health & Sexuality, 12*(1), 1-14. https://doi.org/10.1080/13691050903075226

Beres, M. A. (2018). The proliferation of consent-focused rape prevention social marketing materials. In C. Dale & R. Overell (Eds.), *Orienting feminism* (pp. 181-196). Palgrave Macmillan. https://doi.org/10.1007/978-3-319-70660-3_10

Beres, M. A., Herold, E., & Maitland, S. B. (2004). Sexual consent behaviors in same-sex relationships. *Archives of Sexual Behavior, 33*(5), 475-486. https://doi.org/10.1023/B:ASEB.0000037428.41757.10

Berkowitz, A. (2005). An overview of the social norms approach. In L. P. Lederman & L. P. Stewart (Eds.), *Changing the culture of college drinking: A socially situated health communication campaign* (pp. 193-214). Hampton Press.

Blunt-Vinti, H., Jozkowski, K. N., & Hunt, M. (2019). Show or tell? Does verbal and/or nonverbal sexual communication matter for sexual satisfaction? *Journal of Sex & Marital Therapy, 45*(3), 206-217. https://doi.org/10.1080/0092623X.2018.1501446

Borges, A. M., Baynard, V. L., & Moynihan, M. M. (2008). Clarifying consent: Primary prevention of sexual assault on a college campus. *Journal of Prevention & Intervention in the Community, 36*(1-2), 75-88. https://doi.org/10.1080/10852350802022324

Brown, J. D., & L'Engle, K. L. (2009). X-rated: Sexual attitudes and behaviors associated with US early adolescents' exposure to sexually explicit media. *Communication Research, 36*(1), 129-151. https://doi.org/10.1177/0093650208326465

Carvalho, J., Czop, O., Rocha, M., Nobre, P., & Soares, S. (2018). Gender differences in the automatic attention to romantic vs sexually explicit stimuli. *Journal of Sexual Medicine, 15*(8), 1083-1092. https://doi.org/10.1016/j.jsxm.2018.06.008

Chadwick, S. B., Raisanen, J. C., Goldey, K. L., & Van Anders, S. (2018). Qualitative exploration of women's agentic engagement with sexual media. *Archives of Sexual Behavior, 47*(6), 1853-1858. https://doi.org/10.1007/s10508-018-1174-y

Collins, R. L., Martino, S. C., Elliott, M. N., & Miu, A. (2011). Relationships between adolescent sexual outcomes and exposure to sex in media: robustness to propensity-based analysis. *Developmental Psychology, 47*, 585-91.

Courtice, E. L., & Shaughnessy, K. (2018). The partner context of sexual minority women's and men's cybersex experiences: implications for the traditional sexual script. *Sex Roles, 78*, 272-285.

Curtis, J. N., & Burnett, S. (2017). Affirmative consent: What do college student leaders think about "yes means yes" as the standard for sexual behavior? *American Journal of Sexuality Education, 12*(3), 201-214. https://doi.org/10.1080/15546128.2017.1328322

Dougherty, T. (2015). Yes means yes: Consent as communication. *Philosophy & Public Affairs, 43*(3), 224-253. https://doi.org/10.1111/papa.12059

Dune, T. M., & Shuttleworth, R. P. (2009). 'It's just supposed to happen': The myth of sexual spontaneity and the sexually marginalized. *Sexuality and Disability, 27*(2), 97-108. https://doi.org/10.1007/s11195-009-9119-y

Eaton, A. A., Rose, S. M., Interligi, C., Fernandez, K., & McHugh, M. (2016). Gender and ethnicity in dating, hanging out, and hooking up: Sexual scripts among Hispanic and white young adults. *The Journal of Sex Research, 53*(7), 788-804. https://doi.org/10.1080/00224499.2015.1065954

Fantasia, H. C. (2011). Really not even a decision anymore: Late adolescent narratives of implied sexual consent. *Journal of Forensic Nursing, 7*(3), 120-129. https://doi.org/10.1111/j.1939-3938.2011.01108

Field, A. (2005). Discovering statistics using spss. In *Thousand oaks* (2nd ed.). CA:Sage Publications, Inc.

Foubert, J. D., Garner, D. N., & Thaxter, P. J. (2006). An exploration of fraternity culture; Implications for programs to address alcohol-related sexual assault. *College Student Journal, 40*(2), 361-373. Retrieved from https://psycnet.apa.org/record/2006-07935-015

Frith, H., & Kitzinger, C. (2001). Reformulating sexual script theory: developing a discursive psychology of sexual negotiation. *Theory & Psychology, 11*, 209-232.

Gagnon, J. H., & Simon, W. (2005). *Sexual conduct: The social sources of human sexuality* (2nd ed.). Routledge. (Original work published in 1973).

Greene, K., & Faulkner, S. L. (2005). Gender, belief in the sexual double standard, and sexual talk in heterosexual dating relationships. *Sex Roles, 35*(3-4), 239-251. https://doi.org/10.1007/s11199-005-5682-6

Grello, C. M., Welsh, D. P., & Harper, M. S. (2006). No strings attached: The nature of casual sex in college students. *Journal of Sex Research, 43*(3), 255-267. https://doi.org/10.1080/00224490609552324

Haffner, D. W. (1995/1996, December-January). The essence of 'consent' is communication. *SIECUS Report, 24*(2), 2-3. Retrieved from https://siecus.org/wp-content/uploads/2015/07/24-2.pdf

Hair, J. F., Black, W. C., Babin, B. J., & Anderson, R. E. (2010). *Multivariate data analysis pearson new international edition.* Pearson Education Limited.

Hald, G. M., & Štulhofer, A. (2015). What types of pornography do people use and do they cluster? Assessing types and categories of pornography consumption in a large-scale online sample. *The Journal of Sex Research, 53*(7), 849-859. https://doi.org/10.1080/00224499.2015.1065953

Hall, D. S. (1998). Consent for sexual behavior in a college student population. *Electronic Journal of Human Sexuality, 1*, 1–16. http://www.ejhs.org/volume1/consent1.htm

Hare, K. A., Gahagan, J., Jackson, L., & Steenbeek, A. (2015). Revisualising 'porn': How young adults' consumption of sexually explicit internet movies can inform approaches to Canadian sexual health promotion. *Culture, Health & Sexuality, 17*(3), 269–283. https://doi.org/10.1080/13691058.2014.919409

Hickman, S. E., & Muehlenhard, C. L. (1999). "By the semi-mystical appearance of a condom": How young women and men communicate sexual consent in heterosexual situations. *Journal of Sex Research, 36*(3), 258–272. https://doi.org/10.1080/00224499909551996

Hovick, S. R., & Silver, N. (2019). "Consent is sexy": A poster campaign using sex-positive images and messages to increase dyadic sexual communication. *Journal of American College Health, 8*(8), 817–824. https://doi.org/10.1080/07448481.2018.1515746

Humphreys, T. (2007). Perceptions of sexual consent: The impact of relationship history and gender. *Journal of Sex Research, 44*(4), 307–315. https://doi.org/10.1080/00224490701586706

Humphreys, T. P. (2004). Understanding sexual consent: An empirical investigation of the normative script for young heterosexual adults. In M. Cowling & P. Reynolds (Eds.), *Making sense of sexual consent* (pp. 209–225). Ashgate.

Humphreys, T. P., & Herold, E. (2003). Should universities and colleges mandate sexual behavior? Student perceptions of 'Antioch College's consent policy'. *Journal of Psychology & Human Sexuality, 15*(1), 35–51. https://doi.org/10.1300/J056v15n01_04

Humphreys, T. P., & Herold, E. (2007). Sexual consent in heterosexual dating relationships: Development of a new measure. *Sex Roles, 57*(3–4), 305–315. https://doi.org/10.1007/s11199-007-9264-7

Hust, S. J. T., Marett, E. G., Ren, C., Adams, P. M., Willoughby, J. F., Lei, M., Ran, W., & Norman, C. (2014). Establishing and adhering to sexual consent: The association between reading magazines and college students' sexual consent negotiation. *The Journal of Sex Research, 51*(3), 280–290. https://doi.org/10.1080/00224499.2012.727914

Hust, S. J. T., Rodgers, K. B., & Bayly, B. (2017). Scripting sexual consent: Internalized traditional sexual scripts and sexual consent expectancies among college students. *Family Relations, 66*(1), 197–210. https://doi.org/10.1111/fare.12230

Hyde, J., & Delamater, J. (2017). *Understanding human sexuality*. McGraw-Hill Education.

Janssen, E., Carpenter, D., & Graham, C. A. (2003). Selecting films for sex research: Gender differences in erotic film preference. *Archives of Sexual Behavior, 32*(3), 243–251. https://doi.org/10.1023/A:1023413617648

Jozkowski, K. N. (2015a). "Yes means yes"? Sexual consent policy and college students. *Change: The Magazine of Higher Learning, 47*(2), 16–23. https://doi.org/10.1080/00091383.2015.1004990

Jozkowski, K. N. (2015b). Barriers to affirmative consent policies and the need for affirmative sexuality. *University of Pennsylvania Law Review, 47*(4), 741–772. Retrieved from https://scholarlycommons.pacific.edu/uoplawreview/vol47/iss4/10

Jozkowski, K. N., & Humphreys, T. P. (2014). Sexual consent on college campuses: Implications for sexual assault prevention education. *Health Education Monograph Series, 31*(2), 30–36.

Jozkowski, K. N., Marcantonio, T. L., & Hunt, M. E. (2017). College students' sexual consent communication and perceptions of sexual double standards: A qualitative investigation. *Perspectives on Sexual and Reproductive Health, 49*(4), 237–244. https://doi.org/10.1363/psrh.12041

Jozkowski, K. N., Marcantonio, T. L., Rhoads, K. E., Canan, S., Hunt, M. E., & Willis, M. (2019). A content analysis of sexual consent and refusal communication in mainstream films. *The Journal of Sex Research, 56*(6), 654–665. https://doi.org/10.1080/00224499.2019.1595503

Jozkowski, K. N., & Peterson, Z. D. (2013). College students and sexual consent: Unique insights. *Journal of Sex Research, 50*(6), 517–523. https://doi.org/10.1080/00224499.2012.700739

Jozkowski, K. N., Sanders, S., Peterson, Z. D., Dennis, B., & Reece, M. (2014). Consenting to sexual activity: The development and psychometric assessment of dual measures of consent. *Archives of Sexual Behavior, 43*(3), 437–450. https://doi.org/10.1007/s10508-013-0225-7

Kim, J. L., Sorsoli, C. L., Collins, K., Zylbergold, B. A., Schooler, D., & Tolman, D. L. (2007). From sex to sexuality: Exposing the heterosexual script on primetime network television. *Journal of Sex Research, 44*(2), 145–157. https://doi.org/10.1080/00224490701263660

Kimberly, C., Williams, A. L., & Creel, S. (2018). Women's introduction to alternative sexual behaviors through erotica and its association with sexual and relationship satisfaction. *Sex Roles, 78*(1–2), 119–129. https://doi.org/10.1007/s11199-017-0771-x

Kitzinger, C., & Frith, H. (1999). Just say no? The use of conversation analysis in developing a feminist perspective on sexual refusal. *Discourse & Society, 10*(3), 293–316. https://doi.org/10.1177/0957926599010003002

Kohut, T., & Fisher, W. A. (2013). The impact of brief exposure to sexually explicit video clips on partnered female clitoral self-stimulation, orgasm, and sexual satisfaction. *The Canadian Journal of Human Sexuality, 22*(1), 40–50. https://doi.org/10.3138/cjhs.935

Lim, G. Y., & Roloff, M. E. (1999). Attributing sexual consent. *Journal of Applied Communication Research, 1*(1), 1–23. https://doi.org/10.1080/00909889909365521

Lindgren, K. P., Schacht, R. L., Pantalone, D. W., Blayney, J. A., & George, W. H. (2009). Sexual communication, sexual goals, and students' transition to college: Implications for sexual assault, decision-making, and risky behaviors. *Journal of College Student Development, 50*(5), 491–503. https://doi.org/10.1353/csd.0.0095

Littleton, H., Tabernik, H., Canales, E. J., & Backstrom, T. (2009). Risky situation or harmless fun? A qualitative examination of college women's bad hook-up and rape scripts. *Sex Roles, 60*(11-12), 739–804. https://doi.org/10.1007/s11199-009-9586-8

Madden, S., Janoske, M., Winkler, R. B., & Harpole, Z. (2018). Who loves consent? Social media and the culture jamming of Victoria's Secret. *Public Relations Inquiry, 7*(2), 171–186. https://doi.org/10.1177%2F2046147X18764216

Martellozzo, E., Monaghan, A., Adler, J., Leyva, R., Davidson, J., & Horvath, M. (2016). "... I wasn't sure it was normal to watch it ... " A quantitative and qualitative examination of the impact of online pornography on the values, attitudes, beliefs and behaviours of children and young people. Middlesex University. https://doi.org/10.6084/m9.figshare.3382393

Maticka-Tyndale, E., & Herold, E. S. (1997). The scripting of sexual behavior: Canadian university students on spring break in Florida. *Canadian Journal of Human Sexuality, 6*(4), 3137–3328. Retrieved from https://proxy.lib.umich.edu/login?url=https://search.proquest.com/docview/220808793?accountid=14667

Metts, S., & Spitzberg, B. H. (1996). Sexual communication in interpersonal contexts: A script-based approach. *Annals of the International Communication Association, 19*(1), 49–92. https://doi.org/10.1080/23808985.1996.11678928

Muehlenhard, C. L., Humphreys, T. P., Jozowski, K. N., & Peterson, Z. D. (2016). The complexities of sexual consent among college students: A conceptual and empirical review. *The Journal of Sex Research, 53*(4–5), 457–487. https://doi.org/10.1080/00224499.2016.1146651

Muehlenhard, C. L., & Rodgers, C. (1998). Token resistance to sex: New perspectives on an old stereotype. *Psychology of Women Quarterly, 22*(3), 443–463. https://doi.org/10.1111%2Fj.1471-6402.1998.tb00167.x

Peter, J., & Valkenburg, M. (2016). Adolescents and pornography: A review of 20 years of research. *The Journal of Sex Research, 53*(4–5), 509–531. https://doi.org/10.1080/00224499.2016.1143441

Righi, M. K., Bogen, K. W., Kuo, C., & Orchowski, L. M. (2019). A qualitative analysis of beliefs about sexual consent among high school students. *Journal of Interpersonal Violence*, 1–27. https://doi.org/10.1177%2F0886260519842855

Sakaluk, J. K., Todd, L. M., Milhausen, R., & Lachowsky, N. J., & Undergraduate Research Group in Sexuality. (2014). Dominant heterosexual sexual scripts in emerging adulthood: Conceptualization and measurement. *The Journal of Sex Research, 51*(5), 516–531.

Seabrook, R. C., Ward, L. M., Cortina, L. M., Giaccardi, S., & Lippman, J. R. (2017). Girl power or powerless girl? Television, sexual scripts, and sexual agency in sexually active young women. *Psychology of Women Quarterly, 41*(2), 240–253. https://doi.org/10.1177/0361684316677028

Séguin, L. J., Rodrigue, C., & Lavigne, J. (2018). Consuming ecstasy: Representations of male and female orgasm in mainstream pornography. *The Journal of Sex Research, 55*(3), 348–356. https://doi.org/10.1080/00224499.2017.1332152

Shumlich, E. J., & Fisher, W. (2019). An information-motivation-behavioral skills model of sexual consent. *Journal of Sexual Medicine, 16*(6), S11. https://doi.org/10.1016/j.jsxm.2019.03.481

Shumlich, E. J., & Fisher, W. A. (2018). Affirmative sexual consent? Direct and unambiguous consent is rarely included in discussions of recent sexual interactions. *Canadian Journal of Human Sexuality, 27*(3), 248–260. https://doi.org/10.3138/cjhs.2017-0040

Simon, W., & Gagnon, J. H. (1986). Sexual scripts: permanence and change. *Archives of Sexual Behavior, 15*, 97-120.

Simon, W., & Gagnon, J. H. (2003). Sexual scripts: origins, influences and changes. *Qualitative Sociology, 26*, 491-497.

Stanger-Hall, K. F., & Hall, D. W. (2011). Abstinence-only education and teen pregnancy rates: Why we need comprehensive sex education in the U.S. *PloS One, 6*(10), e24658. https://doi.org/10.1371/journal.pone.0024658

Stevens, A. J., & Smith, S. E. (2016). The impact of exposure to sexually oriented media on the endorsement of hookup culture: A panel study of first-year college students. *Mass Communication and Society, 19*(1), 74–101. https://doi.org/10.1080/15205436.2015.1070875

Thomas, K. A., Sorenson, S. B., & Joshi, M. (2016). "Consent is Good, Joyous, Sexy": A banner campaign to market consent to college students. *Journal of American College Health, 64*(8), 639–650. https://doi.org/10.1080/07448481.2016.1217869

Van Oosten, J. M. F., Peter, J., & Vandenbosch, L. (2017). Adolescents' sexual media use and willingness to engage in casual sex: Differential relations and underlying processes. *Human Communication Research, 43*(1), 127–147. https://doi.org/10.1111/hcre.12098

Ward, L. M. (2003). Understanding the role of entertainment media in sexual socialization of American youth: A review of empirical research on media influence on attitudes and behaviors. *Developmental Review, 23*(3), 347–388. https://doi.org/10.1016/S0273-2297(03)00013-3

Warren, A. L. (2019). Kiss and sell: Is there a market for erotica for 18- to 25-year-olds? *Interscript Journal, 2*, 1–19. http://ojs.lib.ucl.ac.uk/index.php/Int/article/view/2001/865

Wiederman, M. W. (2005). The gendered nature of sexual scripts. *The Family Journal, 13*(4), 496–502. https://doi.org/10.1177/1066480705278729

Willis, M., Blunt-Vinti, H. D., & Jozkowski, K. N. (2019). Associations between internal and external sexual consent in a diverse national sample of women. *Personality and Individual Differences, 149*, 37–45. https://doi.org/10.1016/j.paid.2019.05.029

Willis, M., Canan, S. N., Jozkowski, K. N., & Bridges, A. J. (2019). Sexual consent communication in best-selling pornography films: A content analysis. *The Journal of Sex Research, 57*(1), 52–63. https://doi.org/10.1080/00224499.2019.1655522

Willis, M., Hunt, M. E., Wodika, A., Rhodes, D. L., Goodman, J., & Jozkowski, K. N. (2019). Explicit verbal sexual consent communication: Effects of gender, relationship status, and type of sexual behavior. *International Journal of Sexual Health, 31*(1), 60–70. https://doi.org/10.1080/19317611.2019.1565793

Willis, M., & Jozkowski, K. N. (2019). Sexual precedent's effect on sexual consent communication. *Archives of Sexual Behavior, 48*(6), 1723–1734. https://doi.org/10.1007/s10508-018-1348-7

Willis, M., Jozkowski, K. N., & Read, J. (2019). Sexual consent in K–12 sex education: An analysis of current health education standards in the USA. *Sex Education, 19*(2), 226–236. https://doi.org/10.1080/14681811.2018.1510769

Wood, E., Senn, C. Y., Desmarais, S., Park, L., & Verberg, N. (2002). Sources of information about dating and their perceived influence on adolescents. *Journal of Adolescent Research, 17*(4), 401–417. https://doi.org/10.1177/07458402017004005

Young, C. (2014). *Campus rape: The problem with 'yes means yes'*. Time.com. https://time.com/3222176/campus-rape-the-problem-with-yes-means-yes/

Zillmann, D. (2000). Influence of unrestrained access to erotica on adolescents' and young adults' dispositions toward sexuality. *Journal of Adolescent Health, 27*(2), 41–44. https://doi.org/10.1016/s1054-139x(00)00137-3

Zurbriggen, E. L., & Morgan, E. M. (2006). Who wants to marry a millionaire? Reality dating television programs, attitudes toward sex, and sexual behaviors. *Sex Roles, 54*(1–2), 1–17. https://doi.org/10.1007/s11199-005-8865-2

## Appendices

## Appendix A. Erotica passages from Study 1

| 'Just happens' condition | 'Verbal consent' condition |
| --- | --- |
| **Story 1.**<br>*They shouldn't be doing this. Their hips snap to meet one another anyways. Her back is pressed against the door while he balances them and pulls her leg higher onto his waist, his shaft in engorged and do nothing to hide this fact when he pushes his hips against hers. She's still got far too many layers on but right now they don't have time to fully undress. He pushes her skirt down and panties aside enough to pull himself through, lining her up with his body.*<br>*There is little pause to catch their breath once he's inside her. They're moving in tandem again. He's not reserved in the slightest in these moments* | **Story 1.**<br>*They shouldn't be doing this. Their hips snap to meet one another anyways. Her back is pressed against the door while he does his best to balance them despite her leg creeping higher on his waist, her panties are wet and do nothing to hide this fact when he pushes his hips against her again. He's still got far too many layers on but right now they don't have time to fully undress. He pushes the fabric aside enough to pull himself through, lining her up with his body.*<br>*'Do you want this?' He asks quietly.*<br>*'Yes,' she responded without missing a beat, 'Do you?' she adds after a moment. 'Yes.'*<br>*They pause to catch their breath once he's inside her and it's a moment of intimacy they revel in as their eyes meet. The pause only lasts as long as it takes her body to adjust to him and then they're moving in tandem again. He's not reserved in the slightest in these moments and she revels in the sounds he pulls from him. This time they can't risk any sound so they settle for soft gasps.* |

*(Continued)*

(Continued).

| 'Just happens' condition | 'Verbal consent' condition |
|---|---|
| **Story 2.**<br>I put my hands on my hips, pushed my long, curly black hair over my shoulder and glared at him. He could so easily get my temper up.<br>I opened my mouth to give a smart-arse answer when he smiled and said: 'I want to be more than a friend. I want to fuck you.'<br>I slammed my mouth shut and was rendered speechless. He grabbed me by my arms, and pulled me to him. He kissed me so hard and passionately I would have melted right into him if he wasn't so forceful. Heat quickly spread from my lips to the rest of my body, centring on my sweet spot between my legs. Making me ache and pulse with need just from his kissing. He broke the hot kiss and put his face in my hair. Breathing my scent. I wondered if he could smell my feminine smell from my hot centre. I had never had sex before and I didn't want to tell him. He was taking steady deep breaths to control himself. I could feel his hard member on my belly. He felt so big and thick even through his bluish jeans.<br>'I want to take you right here. To lay you down on that lawn chair and fuck you so hard,' he said.<br>I jumped and trembled at his words. I was getting so nervous. 'No, I've never had sex before. I don't think I'm ready for that.' I was practically begging him to stop. | **Story 2.**<br>I put my hands on my hips, pushed my long, curly black hair over my shoulder and glared at him. He could so easily get my temper up.<br>I opened my mouth to give a smart-arse answer when he smiled and said: 'I want to be more than a friend. I have serious feelings for you.'<br>I slammed my mouth shut and was rendered speechless. He grabbed me by my arms, and pulled me to him. He kissed me so hard and passionately I thought I would melt right into him. His lips on mine felt so warm and he tasted so delicious! Heat quickly spread from my lips to the rest of my body, centring on my sweet spot between my legs. Making me ache and pulse with need just from his kissing. He broke the hot kiss and put his face in my hair. Breathing my scent. I wondered if he could smell my feminine smell from my hot centre. I needed him badly. I had never had sex before and I didn't know how to tell him. I wanted him and only him. He was taking steady deep breaths to control himself. I could feel his hard member on my belly. He felt so big and thick even through his bluish jeans.<br>'You don't know how bad I want to take you right here. To lay you down on that lawn chair and give both of us so much pleasure you will think you are flying to the stars,' he said.<br>I jumped and trembled at his words. I was getting so wet and hot just hearing him say it. 'Yes please make love to me. I want you so bad too!'<br>I was practically begging. |
| **Story 3.**<br>'Look, I know I said we didn't have to rush things. But I'm tired of waiting, Molly. I'm tired of it.'<br>He reached out and took her hands, pulling her close.<br>'No, I'm not ready,' Molly said.<br>'I don't want to wait anymore,' he replied. | **Story 3.**<br>'Look, we don't have to rush things. If you want to wait, I'll wait. I'll do whatever you want, Molly.'<br>'No,' she assured him, reaching out to take his hands and pull him close. 'No, I don't want to wait anymore.' |
| **Story 4.**<br>'My angel,' he replied, 'Take off your clothes.'<br>After they'd undressed ... He looked directly at her and said, 'You're going to sit on my face and suck me off to start with. So I can fuck you nice and slow the second time I come.'<br>Fuck. Her mouth watered. He was a fucking charmer alright. She wanted to just nail him to the bed right then and there, Jesus, he was too much, so she pounced on him and pulled him close, kissing him softly. | **Story 4.**<br>'My angel,' he replied, 'Take off your clothes.'<br>'What do you wanna do?' she asked him after they'd undressed ...<br>He looked directly at her and said, 'How about you sit on my face and suck me off to start with? So I can fuck you nice and slow the second time I come? You want that?'<br>Fuck. Her mouth watered as she said 'Yes, please. Please.' He was a fucking charmer alright. She wanted to just nail him to the bed right then and there, Jesus, he was too much, but she wanted to wait.<br>'Come here!' He begged, and she pounced on him and pulled him close, kissing him softly. |

## Appendix B. Erotica passages from Study 2

| 'Just happens' condition | 'Verbal consent' condition |
|---|---|
| **Story 1.**<br>*He leaned over her body and began kissing her neck. She could feel her slick thighs sliding together, trying to quell the throbbing.*<br>*His fingers slid down softly rubbing her nipples. He tweaked one as he bit her neck playfully. Her hands were on his shoulders, bracing herself, and a soft whimper escaped her lips.*<br>*He leaned close into her ear, letting his tongue glide along it. She closed her eyes as she felt his hands running down her stomach.*<br>*His fingers ghosted over her core, lightly touching her. As he slid one digit in between her pussy lips he uttered 'I'll bet you taste like honey.'*<br>*That was it, there was no turning back. Her legs parted and he cupped all of her delicate sex in his hand, feeling the heat radiating. His other hand fumbled with his jeans and scooped out his engorged dick and heavy balls.*<br>*He aimed the head of his shaft at her pulsing, dripping entrance and pushed inside. Their eyes locked and widened in unison at the incredible feeling.* | **Story 1.**<br>*He leaned over her body and began kissing her neck. She could feel her slick thighs sliding together, trying to quell the throbbing.*<br>*His fingers slid down softly rubbing her nipples. He tweaked one as he bit her neck playfully. Her hands were on his shoulders, bracing herself, and a soft whimper escaped her lips.*<br>*He leaned close into her ear, letting his tongue glide along it. She closed her eyes as she felt his hands running down her stomach. He whispered, 'Do you want me inside you?'*<br>*Her hips bucked and she gasped 'Fuck, yes.'*<br>*His fingers ghosted over her core, lightly touching her. As he slid one digit in between her pussy lips he uttered 'I'll bet you taste like honey.'*<br>*That was it, there was no turning back. Her legs parted and he cupped all of her delicate sex in his hand, feeling the heat radiating. His other hand fumbled with his jeans and scooped out his engorged dick and heavy balls.*<br>*He aimed the head of his shaft at her pulsing, dripping entrance and pushed inside. Their eyes locked and widened in unison at the incredible feeling.* |
| **Story 2.**<br>*They shouldn't be doing this. He moves towards her anyways. Their bodies snap to meet one another. Her back is pressed against the door while he balances them and pulls her leg higher up his waist. His shaft is stiff and engorged, and he does nothing to hide this fact when he pushes his hips against hers.*<br>*She's still got far too many layers of clothes on, but right now they don't have time to fully undress. He pushes her skirt up and panties aside enough to pull himself through, lining her up with his body.*<br>*The next thing they know he's inside her. They pause to catch their breath and it is a moment of intimacy they revel in as their eyes meet. The pause only lasts as long as it takes her body to adjust to him, and then they're moving in tandem again. He is not reserved in the slightest in these moments and she delights in hearing the sounds of pleasure that she pulls from him.* | **Story 2.**<br>*They shouldn't be doing this. He moves towards her anyways. 'I've got to have you, right here, right now,' he growled softly.*<br>*'What're you waiting for?' she asked, a devilish grin spreading across her face.*<br>*Their bodies snap to meet one another. Her back is pressed against the door while he balances them and pulls her leg higher up his waist.*<br>*His shaft is stiff and engorged, and he does nothing to hide this fact when he pushes his hips against hers. She's still got far too many layers of clothes on, but right now they don't have time to fully undress. He pushes her skirt up and panties aside enough to pull himself through, lining her up with his body.*<br>*'You want me to fuck you?' he asks quietly.*<br>*'Yes,' she responded without missing a beat.*<br>*The next thing they know he's inside her. They pause to catch their breath and it is a moment of intimacy they revel in as their eyes meet. The pause only lasts as long as it takes her body to adjust to him, and then they're moving in tandem again. He is not reserved in the slightest in these moments and she delights in the sounds of pleasure that she pulls from him.* |

*(Continued)*

(Continued).

| 'Just happens' condition | 'Verbal consent' condition |
|---|---|

**Story 3.**

He reached for the zipper on her dress as she met his lust-filled gaze. He eased it down, tantalisingly slowly. The silky material slipped over her skin and fell down to the floor.

She was leaned back against the bar, her back arched and her breasts on perfect display. His gaze drifted appreciatively over her naked body, head tilted to one side as if assessing where and how to touch her first, his desire evident by the bulge in his pants.

He cupped her ass and pulled her to him. Their chests were heaving with hot and heavy breath, their hips grinding, bucking for one another's warmth. There was a soft tinkling sound as his belt fell to the floor, and then his stiff shaft was released from the tight confines of his pants.

The heat generating from between her thighs beckoned the firm head of his cock. He pushed his way through her folds, all the way inside, and their moans filled the air. Her muscles clenched around him as he began to thrust lightly in his lusty hunger.

**Story 3.**

He reached for the zipper on her dress as she met his lust-filled gaze.

'I'm all yours,' she breathed, and he eased the zipper down, tantalisingly slowly. The silky material slipped over her skin and fell down to the floor.

She was leaned back against the bar, her back arched and her breasts on perfect display. His gaze drifted appreciatively over her naked body, head tilted to one side as if assessing where and how to touch her first, his desire evident by the bulge in his pants.

He cupped her ass and pulled her to him. Their chests were heaving with hot and heavy breath, their hips grinding, bucking for one another's warmth. There was a soft tinkling sound as his belt fell to the floor, and then his stiff shaft was released from the tight confines of his pants.

'Are you ready for this, baby?' he asked, glancing down at his throbbing manhood with a sly smile.

'Oooh, yes please!' she pleaded.

The heat generating from between her thighs beckoned the firm head of his cock. He pushed his way through her folds, all the way inside, and their moans filled the air. Her muscles clenched around him as he began to thrust lightly in his lusty hunger.

**Story 4.**

Michael could just see the waistband of her panties sticking out from the top of her skirt and it was the final straw. He reached forward and grabbed Samantha's thighs, pulling her on top of him on the chair.

Her lips melded with his and they kissed sensually before he parted her mouth and explored her tongue with his own. His hands clutched her waist before pulling up her shirt and releasing her breasts from her bra. Samantha felt his hair tickle her collarbone as he leaned forward, sucked one pointed nipple into his mouth, and played with the hardened tip with his tongue. He released her breast and leaned her back onto the table.

Then Michael reached under her skirt and rubbed against her amazingly soaked silk panties. She threw her head back with a cry as he caressed faster. He pulled her panties down to her ankles and touched the sweet, wet folds of her pussy with his hands. He opened her lips and rubbed gently at her delicate clit with his index finger. As he flicked and tapped in circles, Samantha's cries grew increasingly louder with an approaching climax.

Unable to take it, he slid his pants down his legs and finally unleashed his stiff cock to fresh air. Michael took it in his hand and pressed his precum-coated head into the budding lips where Samantha's legs met.

Her pussy expanded and tightened as he thrust, and the wildly hot and wet cave had his balls squeezing tighter and tighter. A heat began to build as he pounded rhythmically, bringing them both to the brink.

**Story 4.**

Michael could just see the waistband of her panties sticking out from the top of her skirt and it was the final straw. He reached forward and grabbed Samantha's thighs, pulling her on top of him on the chair.

Her lips melded with his and they kissed sensually before he parted her mouth and explored her tongue with his own. His hands clutched her waist before pulling up her shirt and releasing her breasts from her bra. Samantha felt his hair tickle her collarbone as he leaned forward, sucked one pointed nipple into his mouth, and played with the hardened tip with his tongue. He released her breast and leaned her back onto the table.

'How far do you want to take things?' Michael asked, trailing his hands down her stomach.

'I've wanted to have sex with you for a long time,' she admitted, propping herself up on her elbows, a smile playing around the corners of her mouth.

Michael reached under her skirt and rubbed against her amazingly soaked silk panties. She threw her head back with a cry as he caressed faster. He pulled her panties down to her ankles and touched the sweet, wet folds of her pussy with his hands. He opened her lips and rubbed gently at her delicate clit with his index finger. As he flicked and tapped in circles, Samantha's cries grew increasingly louder with an approaching climax.

Unable to take it, he slid his pants down his legs and finally unleashed his stiff cock to fresh air. Michael saw Samantha gazing at it and asked, 'Are you sure you want to do this?'

'Oh yes!' she pleaded, her voice hoarse with desire.

He took his cock in his hand and pressed his precum-coated head into the budding lips where Samantha's legs met. Her pussy expanded and tightened as he thrust, and the wildly hot and wet cave had his balls squeezing tighter and tighter. A heat began to build as he pounded rhythmically, bringing them both to the brink.

# Using vignette methodology to study comfort with consensual and nonconsensual depictions of pornography content

Kate Dawson, Chris Noone, Saoirse Nic Gabhainn and Padraig MacNeela

**ABSTRACT**
Spanking, whipping, and choking are examples of aggressive behaviours that can be performed in consensual sexual encounters. However, within the pornography research literature, such behaviours are often perceived as being nonconsensual, categorised as 'violent', and argued to predict sexual aggression. Viewing nonconsensual pornography may be associated with negative attitudes towards consent; however, viewing consensual pornography that features typically violent behaviour may not. In this study, we sought to more clearly distinguish between consensual and nonconsensual pornography depictions by using vignettes to examine individuals' consent attitudes in relation to these pornographic vignettes. We also sought to assess the hypothesis that more frequent pornography engagement will be associated with greater comfort with the nonconsensual vignettes. A series of pornography vignettes were developed by the researchers and categorised by a group of sexual consent experts as 'consensual' or 'nonconsensual' vignettes during a three-round Delphi study. The finalised vignettes were administered to a convenience sample of Irish university students ($n = 1121$). More frequent pornography engagement was not associated with greater comfort with the nonconsensual vignettes. Greater comfort with the nonconsensual pornography vignettes was negatively associated with attitudes towards establishing consent and the endorsement of sexual consent norms.

In the pornography literature, frequency of pornography engagement is the most commonly used method of assessing the link between pornography and sexual violence (Short et al., 2012). Much of literature in this area points towards a link between frequent pornography use and sexual coercion or aggression (Allen et al., 1995; Hald et al., 2010; Vega & Malamuth, 2007; Wright et al., 2015). A growing body of research indicates that engagement with pornography depicting nonconsensual activities is strongly correlated with committing acts of sexual aggression (Hald et al., 2010). However, research also shows that engagement with pornography depicting consensual depictions predicts sexual aggression. For example, one recent longitudinal study by Tomaszewska and Krahé (2018) found that frequent pornography engagement featuring consensual sex was associated with attitudes towards sexual coercion and was linked to future sexual violence perpetration.

One issue that may explain such confusion among findings relates to the items used to measure pornography content choices. There is considerable overlap in the definitions used to define violent and non-violent, as well as consensual and nonconsensual depictions of pornography. There is a need for more reliable measures to more clearly distinguish between different types of pornography that an individual chooses to engage with to obtain a clearer picture of the relationship between pornography content choices and sexual aggression.

## Defining consent in pornography

Meta-analyses have shown that engagement with violent pornography is a significant predictor of sexual aggression in cross-sectional and longitudinal studies (Hald et al., 2010; Wright et al., 2015). However, Wright et al. (2015) also found that, although pornography consumption was associated with actual acts of sexual aggression, the difference between viewing violent and non-violent pornography on acts of sexual aggression was non-significant. Therefore, despite the growing body of research, there is little clarity regarding which type of pornography is associated with violence. There are two key issues that could explain such inconsistencies in research findings.

First, the differences between 'violent' and 'nonconsensual' pornography have seldom been defined (Brown & L'Engle, 2009; Ybarra & Thompson, 2018; Ybarra, Mitchell, Hamburger, Diener-West, & Leaf, 2011; K. Dawson, Tafro et al., 2019). Research that has established links between aggressive behaviour and pornography has focused largely on broad categories such as 'violent/non-violent' pornography (Bauserman, 1996; Ybarra & Thompson, 2018). This is frequently described in terms of any sexual interaction which involves the use of force or coercion. For example, whipping, choking, and slapping are typically classified as violent behaviours within pornography research (Bridges et al., 2010). However, this means of categorisation may be problematic: 'whipping', for example, is often part of consensual sexual intimacies within bondage, dominance, sadism, and masochism (BDSM) sexual scripts. The context within which these behaviours occur is rarely elaborated upon; in other words, studies rarely distinguish consensual from nonconsensual acts. This is crucial to the valid assessment of pornography content choices and its outcomes.

The second issue is that, although some studies have provided definitions that distinguish between consensual and nonconsensual portrayals in pornography, individuals may not be able to reliably identify nonconsensual pornography content. In recent years researchers have begun to measure exposure to content that features nonconsensual or coercive sex (Davis et al., 2018; Landripet et al., 2019). For example, Davis et al. (2018) asked participants whether they saw pornography content that featured 'violence or aggression toward a woman or man that appears to be consensual (i.e., she/he appears to enjoy it or want it)' and 'Violence or aggression toward a woman or man that appears to be nonconsensual (i.e., she/he does not appear to enjoy it or want it)' (p. 314). These definitions help to provide greater clarity regarding pornography content engagement; however, they also rely on participants' subjective interpretation of consensual and nonconsensual content.

Consent scenarios are often interpreted differently by women and men (MacNeela et al., 2017), with young men more likely to believe that consent was present than their female peers. Previous research has shown that women and men differ in their interpretation of, preference for, and communication of consent, and that women are more distressed by nonconsensual depictions than men (Malamuth & Check, 1980; Malamuth, Heim, & Feshbach, 1980; Norris et al., 2004). Women and men also report different consent strategies. Women use passive consent strategies, perceive a greater need for sexual consent, are more likely to view consent as ongoing process, and desire that consent be clarified early during intimacy (Humphreys & Herold, 2007). In comparison, men are more likely to initiate sex, to view consent as a single event, and to assume that their partner has consented (Humphreys & Herold, 2007; Jozkowski, Sanders, Peterson, Dennis, & Reece, 2014). Such differences may help to explain why young women report seeing nonconsensual pornography more often than young men (Davis et al., 2018) – and might result in people reporting that they have not watched nonconsensual content, even though they have but have interpreted it as consensual.

In addition, social desirability may influence participants in answering truthfully about engaging with nonconsensual pornography; for example, responding to a statement like 'nonconsensual pornography use is unacceptable' may prompt a socially desirable response. But reading and responding to a scenario featuring nonconsensual content may be less likely to prompt such a response and thus provide a more authentic depiction of acceptability. Because of the potential ambiguity and possible misinterpretations that arise, there is a need for more objective assessment of nonconsensual pornography. The use of vignettes has been shown to have a number of specific advantages when conducting such sensitive research and may be particularly useful in the study of non-consensual pornography depictions. Such use may be indicative of individual consent-related attitudes.

## Sexual consent research

Individual consent attitudes, behavioural intentions, and beliefs are important regarding the commitment of acts of sexual aggression and may be a more reliable predictor of a person's likelihood to engage with nonconsensual pornography content (Tomaszewska & Krahé, 2018). Wright (2011) argued that pornography audience factors, like their existing sexual scripts, are important predictors regarding the replication of behaviours seen in pornography (Wright, 2013; Wright & Tokunaga, 2016). A person's attitudes towards establishing consent, their consent-related behavioural intentions, and beliefs about importance of consent are important variables that may be associated with whether an individual seeks consent in their relationships (Humphreys & Brousseau, 2010). These variables may also be important predictors of one's comfort with nonconsensual depictions in pornography (Foubert, 2000; Koopman et al., 2012).

Sexual consent is a multi-faceted construct that can be conceptualised as either an internal feeling of willingness, an external verbal or behavioural act, or a behaviour that is interpreted as willingness (Muehlenhard et al., 2016). Consent can be communicated by verbal or nonverbal means, using direct, indirect, or even passive signals (Hickman & Muehlenhard, 1999). Although verbal communication of consent may be the clearest form of communicating consent, research shows that individuals prefer to use indirect behavioural strategies during intimacy (Blunt-Vinti et al., 2019; Hickman & Muehlenhard, 1999; Humphreys, 2004; Jozkowski & Wiersma, 2015). Women and men use indirect cues to passively indicate their consent by not resisting their partner's advances (Humphreys & Brousseau, 2010). Indirect consent cues, such as token resistance and passive sexual behaviour, are commonplace in mainstream pornography (Willis et al., 2019). A preference for such representations may be reflective of an individual's approach to intimacy or beliefs about the acceptability of such behaviour.

Perceived sexual consent norms may be important predictor of pornography content choices. Indeed, the acceptability of pornography depictions is an important factor for content selection and continued engagement (Malamuth & Check, 1980; Parvez, 2006). Several studies support a positive relationship between beliefs about one's peer's sexual behaviour and ones' own sexual behaviour (Boone & Lefkowitz, 2004; Buunk, Van Deneijnden, & Siero, 2002; L'Engle & Jackson, 2008; Wallace, Miller, & Forehand, 2008). In this context, it has been argued that pornography use is associated with setting and reinforcing certain norms. For example, some studies show engagement with pornography was associated with holding certain perceptions regarding sexual behaviour and treatment of women (Koletic et al., 2019; Wright & Stulhofer, 2019). Although there is a dearth of research regarding pornography and sexual consent, we may hypothesise that individuals' engagement with nonconsensual depictions in pornography is reflective of having less positive attitudes towards consent. Alternatively, engaging with nonconsensual pornography may activate or reinforce positive attitudes towards nonconsensual behaviours (Wright, 2011).

## Theoretical foundation

A number of theories have been presented in the debate on the potential association between pornography and sexual violence. Some have argued that there is little to no effect on aggression because so few people engage with nonconsensual and violent pornography and that positive societal influences, which penalise acts of aggression, act to deter the application of sexually aggressive scripts (Diamond et al., 2011; Ferguson & Hartley, 2009; Fisher & Grenier, 1994). Others have suggested that pornography poses a risk to those who consume it (Dabreu & Krahé, 2014; Kingston et al., 2009) by contributing to a culture of sexual callousness, particularly regarding increased personal tolerance of violence against women (Zillmann & Bryant, 1982). This link is hypothesised to exist through the normalisation of sexual violence following frequent exposure to media that includes violence or degradation (Krafka et al., 1997). Some have argued that this leads to users needing to consume greater amounts of pornography and more extreme content to become aroused, thus increasing demand for aggressive and nonconsensual content (Dines, 2010; Paul, 2010; Sun, 2011). These hypotheses are based on script theory, whereby sexual scripts are acquired through watching pornography, which provides a framework from which individuals learn how to behave (Bandura, 1986; Gagnon & Simon, 1973; Wright, 2011). If this is the case, in this study, we should expect to see a relationship between higher rates of pornography consumption and greater perceived comfort associated with nonconsensual sexual vignettes.

Gender is also an important variable to explore in this context. A person's gender is argued to be associated with the strength of pornography effects (Wright, 2011). On average, men engage with pornography more often than women and are more accepting of it (Willoughby et al., 2014). Men have consistently been found to report significantly higher endorsements of rape myths compared with women (Hayes et al., 2016; Suarez & Gadalla, 2010) and are also more likely to be perpetrators of sexual violence (Muehlenhard, Peterson, Humphreys, & Jozkowski, 2017). A combination of these factors could mean that men are generally more comfortable with a wider variety of pornography and less sensitive to portrayals of sexual violence. We may therefore predict that males will more likely report greater comfort with the nonconsensual vignettes than females. Although we cannot examine the direction of the relationships between comfort with nonconsensual pornography vignettes and a person's attitudes towards sexual consent in the present study, the use of consensual and nonconsensual pornography scenarios allowed us to explore which of these factors are important in determining whether or not an individual may be likely to engage with pornography depicting nonconsensual content. Using a method that distinguishes between depictions of consensual and nonconsensual content will help to further understand which factors are related to nonconsensual pornography engagement and person's content choices.

## Present study

The present study aimed to test a new approach using vignettes to measure a person's comfort with consensual and nonconsensual pornography to further understand what factors are associated with watching nonconsensual pornography. Below, we provide our rationale for using vignette methodology and for assessing comfort with pornography.

Gould (1996) found evidence for the reduced impact of social desirability on participants' responses to vignette questions. It has been argued that the non-personal and hypothetical nature of a vignette is less threatening to the reader (Wilks, 2004), an issue that is likely to affect responses. This may be particularly the case when asking pornography viewers about their engagement with nonconsensual pornography. Gould (1996) argues that providing hypothetical situations, rather than relying on individuals to provide information about their own experiences, may allow participants greater freedom in their responses. Although the use of hypothetical scenarios does not determine whether an individual has engaged in a behaviour, it provides information about their attitudes, which have been shown to predict nonconsensual sexual behaviour (Gidycz et al., 2007; Tomaszewska & Krahé, 2018; Zinzow & Thompson, 2011). Using vignettes, researchers have the potential to gather data on sensitive topics from larger samples, with minimal risk of distress to participants (Wilks, 2004).

The use of a vignette-based methodology is exploratory in the sense of investigating whether written vignettes describing pornography vignettes have the potential to be used as a proxy for how video-based pornography might be interpreted. The validity of vignettes, with respect to being consensual or nonconsensual, can be maximised if the appropriate stakeholders (who have in-depth knowledge of sexual consent) are involved in the construction of the vignettes (Aguinis & Bradley, 2014). Therefore, the current study aimed to develop an alternative method to explore consensual and nonconsensual pornography engagement. There is a dearth of evidence linking existing sexual consent attitude measures to applied implications, like specific types of pornographic content. We aimed to use vignettes to investigate the relationship between attitudes towards sexual consent and decisions that pertain to real-world choices.

It has been suggested that individuals will be repulsed by pornography that does not reflect their own desires (Parvez, 2006). In this context, studies show that individuals are more likely to experience discomfort when reading nonconsensual pornography vignettes, in which the victim is not aroused by the assault (Malamuth & Check, 1980). More recent studies indicate those with high victim empathy, a key component in reducing rape myth acceptance and rape likelihood, report greater discomfort in response to nonconsensual representations (Foubert, 2000; Koopman et al., 2012). Reader discomfort therefore may imply an unwillingness to choose to engage with the pornography content described. In this study, we used the term 'comfort' to assess an individual's reported comfort with engaging with content similar to what has been described. Although this does not provide information about the past behaviour, it is indicative of current attitudes and the type of pornographic content that they would be likely to engage with (Hald et al., 2010).

We hypothesised that frequency of pornography engagement, gender, and attitudes towards sexual consent would be associated with comfort with watching nonconsensual pornography:

Hypotheses 1. Men will report greater comfort with the nonconsensual vignettes than women.

Hypotheses 2. Individuals who report higher rates of pornography consumption will also report greater perceived comfort associated with nonconsensual sexual vignettes.

Hypothesis 3a. Having less positive attitudes towards consent will be associated with greater comfort with the nonconsensual vignettes.

Hypothesis 3b. Having an indirect behavioural approach to consent will be associated with greater comfort with the nonconsensual vignettes.

Hypothesis 3c. Believing in sexual consent norms that do not require verbal consent will be associated with greater comfort with the nonconsensual vignettes.

## Method

To test these hypotheses, we conducted two studies. Study 1 involved the construction of 12 pornography vignettes to represent consensual and nonconsensual vignettes and their assessment by a panel of sexual consent experts during a three-round Delphi study. Study 2 was a cross-sectional survey that aimed to establish the most valid measurement model using a combination of exploratory factor analysis (EFA) and confirmatory factor analysis (CFA). Finally, these data from Study 2 were used to test the overall model using structural equation modelling (SEM).

### Study 1

**Recruitment.** In this study individuals who had over two years' experience working in the area of sexual consent were invited to participate as 'experts' in a three-round Delphi study. Experts were recruited via email invitation. Twelve of the invited 16 experts completed the first two rounds and eleven completed all three rounds of data collection. Data were collected online via Survey Monkey software.

**Demographics.** In total two academics who research sexual consent, three sex educators who deliver sexual consent education programmes, three legal professionals, and three psychotherapists or support workers who provide counselling to victims of sexual violence participated in the Delphi study. All experts were female and had a minimum of 5 years working in the area of sexual consent. Experts were not asked to provide additional demographic information.

**Vignette development.** The Delphi method is a research method used to establish consensus among experts in a certain field (Hsu & Sandford, 2010). In this study the method was used to establish consensus on the status of short written vignettes as representing consensual or nonconsensual sexual activity among adults. Hughes and Huby (2002) highlighted the potential of short written vignette scenarios as a potentially effective strategy for engaging participants. Short vignettes are valuable in reducing participant burden and maximising response rates (Lawrie et al., 1998). Although brief vignettes may not capture the complexity of video, they allow for the depiction of salient consensual and nonconsensual behaviours, while also protecting our participants from potential distress. We endeavoured to develop a set of vignettes to maximise participant engagement, including behavioural routines and scripts that reflect mainstream internet pornography scenes. The construct validity of vignettes is categorised by the extent to which it captures the topic under investigation (Gould, 1996). In this case, the Delphi method was used to maximise construct validity.

During each round, expert participants were asked to rate each of 12 pornography vignettes on whether they believed sexual consent was portrayed in each vignette. A consensual scenario was defined as 'a pornography vignette in which both actors appear to be consenting to every sexual behaviour described in the vignette'. An unclear scenario was defined as a 'pornography vignette in which it is not clearly evident that consent was expressed by both actors for every sexual behaviour'. A nonconsensual scenario was defined as 'a pornography vignette in which consent was not expressed, by at least one actor, for at least one of the sexual behaviours described in the vignette'.

After every round, the responses were summarised for participants in the form of a report; then, the amended questionnaire with additional clarifications was redistributed to participating experts for the next round. There were approximately five weeks between each round. An *a priori* decision was made to categorise a vignette once two-thirds (66%) or more of the 12 panel members reached consensus on which category a vignette belonged to (consensual, unclear, and nonconsensual). Because only 11 participants completed all three rounds, we then decided to reduce the percentage needed to 64%, which was 7 out of the final 11 experts (Hsu & Sandford, 2007)

**Round 1.** After Round 1 there remained five vignettes that had not been categorised. A total of three participants commented that the rating task was complicated because some of the scenarios appeared relatable to real-life relationships rather than stereotypical 'pornography settings'. Many pornography vignettes on mainstream pornography websites are often realistic in nature, therefore the vignettes in question remained without changes. To address this issue the vignettes were amended to begin with 'In this porn scene'. This was intended to remind the reader that they are to consider each scenario as a pornography scene vignette. A number of participants reported that some of the language used may influence the reader and lead them to interpret the scenario in a negative way. Wording was changed to reflect language that is more neutral.

The first round of vignettes included response options on a five-point Likert-type scale, ranging from 'extremely nonconsensual' to 'extremely consensual'. A number of participants reported that consent was either 'unclear' or 'somewhat consensual' because both actors in various vignettes appeared to be consenting at the beginning but not throughout the entire scenario; therefore, some participants were unsure how to categorise their responses for the level of consent 'overall' for each vignette. A situation that is consensual is simply regarded as consensual and not extremely consensual; for example, if it were within the eyes of the law, a nonconsensual encounter would simply be considered 'nonconsensual', rather than 'extremely nonconsensual'. Therefore, the wording was changed and response options were changed into three groups representing consensual and nonconsensual vignettes as well as vignettes that represented scenarios in which consent was unclear.

***Round 2.*** In Round 2, experts were asked to either confirm or reject their previous responses that had reached agreement and to re-appraise the vignettes that did not reach consensus, using the newly established guidelines. Agreement was not established for four of the scenarios after Round 2. Two vignettes almost reached agreement (55%; i.e., 6 experts agreed rather than 7). These vignettes were altered for the final round. Participants were informed that if after this round, a consensus of 66.6% or more had not been achieved for a vignette, then it would be categorised as 'unclear' because we could not generate a consensus on the particular vignette.

***Round 3.*** After Round 3, the 12 vignettes were categorised as representing a (1) consensual, (2) unclear, or (3) nonconsensual scenario, with two vignettes failing to reach consensus or were categorised as 'unclear'. Because our research question involved the comparison of the consensual and nonconsensual vignettes, the two vignettes that were categorised as 'unclear' by the expert participants were not included in the current analysis. The final vignette scores and categorisation are depicted in Table 1.

## Study 2

***Recruitment.*** An email invitation was sent to all students via the internal student emailing system at a public Irish university; this notification contained information about the aim of the study, the nature of the questions, approximate completion time, and a link to the online survey. A detailed study information sheet was embedded on the first page of the survey. This included the aims of the study, an overview of the study questions, information regarding confidentiality and assured anonymity, and the risks and benefits regarding participation. Information on free counselling services was provided to all study participants. Participants gave their informed consent by clicking 'Yes, I consent to participating in this study. I understand that I can participate to my own level of comfort, can stop at any time I want, and that all the information I provide will be anonymous'.

**Table 1.** Final Categorisations of Vignettes and Percentage Agreements.

|  | Nonconsensual (%) | Unclear (%) | Consensual (%) |
|---|---|---|---|
| Sam and Dan |  |  | **100** |
| Daniel and Abby |  |  | **100** |
| Rebecca and Jack |  |  | **100** |
| Jessica and Tom | **100** |  |  |
| Dee and Jack | **73** | 27 |  |
| Beth and Sandra | **91** | 9 |  |
| Kelly and Matt | **100** |  |  |
| Matt and Sarah | **100** |  |  |
| Chris and Sarah | **73** | 27 |  |
| Maria and Tom | 18 | 36 | 46 |
| Nick and Alex | **64** | 36 |  |
| Max and Meghan | 36 | **64** |  |

Numbers in bold were assigned to corresponding category.

***Participants.*** A young or 'emerging adult' (Arnett, 2007) student population was selected because previous research had found that many individuals in this population experience nonconsensual sexual contact during their time at university (Muehlenhard et al., 2016). Additionally, gender was relevant to the research enquiry. There were several non-binary or transgender identifying participants; however, these participants were too small in number for inclusion in the analysis. In addition, the current analysis focused on pornography vignettes that depicted male-female sexual scenarios, and therefore heterosexual participants. Additionally, as we were interested in the experiences of young people who engage with pornography, this inclusion criteria meant that participants who responded that they 'never' watch pornography were omitted from the current analysis. The final sample for this study consisted of 1121 heterosexual students who were aged 18–24 at the time of participation in the study. Overall, 588 identified as women and 533 as men. Of the total sample, the majority were Irish (81%). A significant proportion was single (38%) and had 1–2 sexual partners in their lifetime (31%). The dataset ($n = 1121$) were randomised and split into two datasets; the training dataset ($n = 533$) and the confirmatory dataset ($n = 588$). Data from 588 participants were analysed in the final confirmatory structural model. Information on the demographic characteristics of the sample ($n = 588$) are presented in Table 2.

***Missing data.*** A number of cases had more than 5% missing values. Tabachnick and Fidell (2007) posited that the pattern of missing data significantly affects the imputation of missing values with values of below 5% inconsequential to data imputation. Through analysing the pattern of missing data, we also found that the items were not missing at random, with the largest percentages of missing data from the last page of the online survey (i.e., missing values increased from 6% on the second last page of the survey to 15% of missing values on the last page). As such, the largest percentage of missing data was on the questions about attitudes towards sexual consent. The missing data were imputed using the Full Information Maximum Likelihood (FIML) method in AMOS.

Table 2. Sociodemographic Characteristics of Sample by Gender and Overall Sample (%).

|  | Women $n$ (%) | Men $n$ (%) | Total $n$ (%) |
| --- | --- | --- | --- |
| *Nationality* | | | |
| Irish | 252 (82) | 245 (87.5) | 497 (84.5) |
| Non-Irish | 56 (18) | 35 (12.5) | 91 (15.5) |
| *Education* | | | |
| Undergraduate education | 264 (86) | 243 (79) | 507 (86) |
| Postgraduate education | 44 (14) | 37 (21) | 81 (14) |
| *Relationship status* | | | |
| Not in a relationship | 113 (36.6) | 39.9 (39.9) | 225 (38) |
| Casual dating | 46 (15) | 48 (17) | 94 (16) |
| Single and not looking for a partner | 3 (1) | 8 (3) | 11 (2) |
| In an open relationship | 4 (1) | 5 (2) | 9 (1.5) |
| In a relationship < 6 months | 34 (11) | 17 (6) | 51 (9) |
| In a relationship > 6 months | 109 (35) | 19 (32) | 200 (34) |
| *Lifetime number of sexual partners* | | | |
| 0 | 26 (8) | 43 (15) | 69 (12) |
| 1–2 | 100 (33) | 80 (29) | 181 (31) |
| 3–5 | 77 (25) | 64 (23) | 141 (24) |
| 6–10 | 58 (19) | 43 (15) | 101 (17) |
| 11–15 | 23 (7) | 15 (5) | 38 (6.5) |
| 16–20 | 7 (2) | 11 (4) | 41 (7) |
| 21+ | 17 (5) | 24 (9) | 41 (7) |
| Total | 308 (100) | 280 (100) | 588 (100) |

## Measures

### Pornography engagement

Pornography engagement was assessed by asking participants how often they watch internet pornography, which was defined as 'Websites that have descriptions, pictures, movies, or audio of people having sex or engaging in other sexual behaviours'. Response options were on a six-point scale: (1) Never, (2) A few times per year, (3) A few times per month, (4) Once-twice per week, (5) Daily, and (6) A few times per day. Across the entire sample, response option 'once-twice per week' was reported most often (29%) as presented in Table 5.

Participants were asked to read each vignette sequentially and report how comfortable they would feel in watching the porn vignette described. All pornography vignette questions had five response options (Very uncomfortable; uncomfortable; neither comfortable nor uncomfortable; comfortable; very comfortable).

### Attitudes towards sexual consent

Attitudes towards sexual consent were measured using the three subscales of the revised version of the Sexual Consent Scale (Humphreys & Brousseau, 2010) that assessed (1) positive attitudes towards establishing sexual consent, which included items like 'I feel that sexual consent should always be obtained before the start of any sexual activity', (2) indirect behavioural approaches to consent; for example, 'typically I communicate sexual consent to my partner using nonverbal signals and body language', and (3) sexual consent norms; for example, 'I believe it is enough to ask for sexual consent at the beginning of a sexual encounter'. All items were measured using a seven-point Likert scale ranging from 1 ('strongly disagree') to 7 ('strongly agree'). The scale has previously been shown to be reliable and valid among a sample of 372 undergraduate students (Humphreys & Brousseau, 2010). Cronbach's α indicated high internal consistency within subscale 1 (positive attitudes towards establishing consent; α =.887), subscale 2 (indirect behavioural approach to consent; α = .746), and subscale 3 (consent norms; α = .779).

### Procedure

The questionnaire was piloted with 10 university students to identify ambiguities or difficult questions and to ensure question and instruction clarity. Completion time of approximately 15 minutes was recorded and was used as an approximate time completion guideline for subsequent participants. The survey was then administered via the internal university student email system. Every participant read all of the scenarios. In an effort to reduce bias the order of presentation was randomised for each participant. The study received approval from the Research Ethics Committee of the university.

### Analysis

We began by randomising the dataset (n = 1121) by using the random number generator function in SPSS and allocating a 1 or 2 to each participant. Analyses of the training dataset (n = 542) data began by conducting an exploratory factor analysis (EFA) of the self-reported comfort items in response to the consensual, unclear and nonconsensual pornography vignettes using IBM SPSS Statistics 23 (IBM Corp, IBM Corp, N, 2013). Under the central limit theorem, normality was assumed, and results from a Kaiser-Meyer-Olkin test of sampling adequacy (KMO) indicated that the sample size was sufficiently large (KMO = .870) with a ratio of 54 participants to each item (Costello & Osborne, 2005), confirming that the data were appropriate for the application of EFA (Tabachnick & Fidell, 2007). EFA was used to examine whether the categories developed with the consent experts were validated by the student sample. Maximum likelihood (ML) was used for data extraction. Correlations between factors were assumed and therefore an oblique promax rotation with Kaiser normalisation was used, which is also appropriate for use on large datasets (Byrne, 2016).

Exploratory factor analyses of the training dataset ($n = 533$) were conducted using the 10 vignettes (3 consensual and 7 nonconsensual vignettes) developed in the Delphi phase to assess the reliability of the nonconsensual and consensual latent constructs. In addition, confirmatory factor analyses of the Sexual Consent Scale – Revised (Humphreys & Brousseau, 2010) were used to assess the reliability of responses for use in subsequent analyses.

Based on the measurement models constructed the next set of analyses involved using structural equation modelling to evaluate the relationships between the comfort with the pornography vignettes, attitudes towards sexual consent, and frequency of engagement. Bivariate correlations are presented in Table 3. Mean values, standard deviations, and tests of normality are presented in Table 4. This was an appropriate method for analysis because we had multiple indicators for each of the latent constructs, which were based on theoretical considerations. Descriptive statistics, correlation analyses, reliability tests, and exploratory factor analysis were carried out using IBM SPSS Statistics 22 (2013). CFA and SEM (n = 588) were carried out in AMOS Version 24 (Arbuckle, 2016), using maximum likelihood estimation. The FIML function was used to impute missing data.

## Results

### Exploratory factor analysis

Anti-image covariance matrices showed that partial correlations between the variables were small, with diagonals ranging between .373 and .584. Theory, scree plot illustrations, and eigenvalues were used to determine the number of factors to be retained. Factors with eigenvalues larger than 1 were retained (Hair et al., 1987). This resulted in two factors, which explained 64.24% of the variance; Factor 1 explaining 45.43% and Factor 2 explaining 18.81%. An *a priori* decision was made to retain item loadings above .30 (Costello & Osborne, 2005). All of the vignettes categorised as nonconsensual during the Delphi process loaded on to Factor 1, while the consensual vignettes identified in the Delphi process loaded on to Factor 2 – with high factor loadings across both factors (see Table 6). Given that, the vignettes varied not only by the degree of consent depicted but also on actor gender, sexual orientation of each actor, and relationship status portrayed, i.e no relationship versus committed relationship, a decision was made to retain three consensual and three nonconsensual vignettes for analysis. These three pairs of vignettes each depicted similar sexual behaviours among

**Table 3.** Bivariate Correlations.

| | Consensual vignettes | Positive attitude | Indirect behavioural | Consent norms | Pornography frequency |
|---|---|---|---|---|---|
| Comfort with nonconsensual vignettes | .308** | −.244** | .150** | .260** | .171** |
| Comfort with consensual vignettes | | −.059 | .145** | .070 | .090* |
| Positive attitude to establishing consent | | | −.272** | −.267** | −.007 |
| Indirect behavioural approach to consent | | | | .388** | −.103* |
| Consent norms | | | | | −.050 |

** $p < .01$  * $p < .05$

**Table 4.** Mean, Standard Deviation, Skewness, and Kurtosis.

| | Mean | SD | Skewness | Kurtosis |
|---|---|---|---|---|
| Nonconsensual vignettes | 2.48 | .99 | .52 | −.05 |
| Consensual vignettes | 3.97 | .90 | −1.03 | 1.35 |
| Positive attitudes towards consent | 5.50 | 1.04 | −.74 | .73 |
| Indirect behavioural approach | 5.02 | 1.14 | −.60 | .59 |
| Consent norms | 4.59 | 1.09 | −.49 | .12 |

**Table 5.** Pornography Engagement by Gender and Overall n (%).

| | Women n (%) | Men n (%) | Total n (%) | $X_2$ (Cramers V) |
|---|---|---|---|---|
| Frequency of pornography use | | | | 311.80 (.72) ** |
| A few times per year | 104 (34) | 15 (5) | 119 (20) | |
| A few times per month | 74 (24) | 48 (17) | 122 (21) | |
| Once-twice per week | 22 (7) | 150 (54) | 172 (29) | |
| Daily | 4 (1) | 57 (20) | 61 (10) | |
| Few times per day | 1 (.3) | 7 (2.5) | 8 (1) | |
| Total | 205 | 277 | 482 | |

**p < .01

heterosexual couples who all appeared to be in relationships with each other. This was to ensure that participants reported levels of comfort with each of the vignettes pertained to the degree of consent depicted. The final two factors, each containing three vignettes, represent the latent constructs used in the development of the model. Factor solutions for the two latent constructs are presented in Table 6. Cronbach's Alpha test results indicated high internal consistency within the consensual (.797) and nonconsensual vignettes (.882). For full information on the contents of the vignettes see the appendix.

### *Confirmatory factor analysis*

In the construction of our models, we first conducted confirmatory factor analysis (CFA) of the two factors generated during EFA on our confirmatory dataset (n = 588) using AMOS 24 (Arbuckle, 2016). An *a priori* decision was made to retain any items with loadings greater than 0.30. Regarding the model fit, we chose *a priori* to interpret the comparative fit index (CFI), the Tucker-Lewis index (TLI), and incremental fit index (IFI), which should each be greater than .90 and the root mean square error of approximation (RMSEA), which should be less than .06. The model indicated good fit with a CFI of .98 TLI of .966, IFI value of .98, and RMSEA of .06, with a significant $\chi^2$ test (3.33, $p < .001$).

We then conducted CFA of the three subscales from the Sexual Consent Scale – Revised (Humphreys & Brousseau, 2010). We hypothesised a three-factor model to be confirmed in the measurement proportion of the model, reflecting the three subscales. CFA on the scale items resulted in a poor model fit with a CFI of .76, TLI of .73, IFI of .76 and RMSEA of .10. However, this may be due to the fact that the SCS-Revised was originally a five-factor scale, three of which were used in the current analysis because this study was concerned with consent-related attitudes, behavioural intentions and norms.

### *Measurement Invariance*

To ensure that these items functioned similarly across gender measurement invariance was investigated for the female and male genders. There was excellent model fit for the configural invariant model, suggesting that the factorial structure was equivalent across these groups. The evidence for invariance of factor loadings, item intercepts and residuals across these groups was weaker. Chi-square difference tests suggested that there was no difference in fit between the unconstrained

**Table 6.** Promax Rotated Factor Loadings for 2 Factor Solution ML of Porn Vignettes.

| Vignettes (category) | Mean | SD | F1 | F2 |
|---|---|---|---|---|
| Jessica and Tom (NC) | 2.56 | 1.11 | **.010** | .842 |
| Dee and Jack (NC) | 2.68 | 1.10 | **.025** | .841 |
| Matt and Sarah (NC) | 2.23 | 1.15 | **−.030** | .858 |
| Sam and Dan (C) | 4.04 | .93 | .937 | **−.059** |
| Rebecca and Jack (C) | 4.03 | .94 | .895 | **.024** |
| Dan and Abby (C) | 3.85 | .97 | .829 | **.043** |

model and the configural invariance model but that there were differences between these models and the subsequent measurement invariance models. These results are presented in Table 7.

## Structural models

The data for our hypothesised model came from assessments of self-reported comfort with the six vignettes discussed above. These data loaded on two latent variables, respectively, corresponding to the nature of the vignette. A total of 24 questions from three subscales of the revised version of the Sexual Consent Scale – Revised (Humphreys & Brousseau, 2010) made up three latent variables: 'Positive attitudes towards establishing consent', 'indirect behavioural approach to consent' and 'sexual consent norms'. Gender and a single item indicator representing frequency of pornography engagement were also included in the model. Our hypothesised models are illustrated below. In each model, circles represent latent variables and rectangles represent measurement variables. We used maximum likelihood parameter estimation because of our large sample size and reliable indicators for each latent construct (Wen, Marsh & Hau, 2010). For the predicted paths, we reported unstandardised coefficients (β), standard errors (SE), and significance of the unstandardised coefficients.

## Self-reported comfort with vignettes

Although gender differences were evident in reported comfort with each of the vignettes, larger gender differences were observed on three nonconsensual vignettes. Depictions of nonconsensual manual or digital sex vignettes had higher scores on self-reported comfort than vaginal and anal sex vignettes. See Table 8 for gender differences reported on each vignette.

## Hypothesis 1 (Model 1)

Model 1 explored differences between men and women on their reported comfort with the consensual and nonconsensual vignettes. Model 1 resulted in poor model fit with a CFI of .932, TLI of .854, of IFI .933, RMSEA of .11 and significant chi-square statistic (9.20, $p < .001$). Results of model 1 show men are more comfortable with both consensual vignettes ($\beta = .345$, $p < .001$) and nonconsensual vignettes ($\beta = .636$, $p < .001$) than women. The gender effect was slightly stronger for nonconsensual vignettes.

## Hypothesis 2 (Model 2)

Model 2 tested the hypothesis that more frequent pornography users reported being more comfortable with the nonconsensual vignettes in comparison with less frequent pornography users. Model 2 resulted in a poor model fit with a CFI of .945, TLI of .882, IFI of .946, RMSEA of .10, and significant chi-square statistic (7.35, $p < .001$). More frequent pornography users are more comfortable with both consensual vignettes ($\beta = .323$, $p < .001$) and nonconsensual vignettes ($\beta = .486$, $p < .001$). Standardised regression weights show there is essentially no difference in the strength of the relationships between the consensual ($\beta = .228$, $p < .001$) and nonconsensual ($\beta = .279$, $p < .001$) vignettes.

Table 7. Model Fit for Unconstrained and Measurement Invariant Models.

| Model | CFI | TLI | IFI | RMSEA | $\chi^2$ difference test |
|---|---|---|---|---|---|
| Unconstrained Model | .99 | .99 | .99 | .03 [.00, .05] | n/a |
| Configural Invariance | .99 | .98 | .99 | .03 [.00, .05] | $\chi^2(4) = 8.32$, p = .08 |
| Metric Invariance | .89 | .82 | .89 | .10 [.08, .11] | $\chi^2(6) = 138.00$, p < .001 |
| Scalar Invariance | .88 | .82 | .88 | .10 [.09, .11] | $\chi^2(3) = 24.55$, p < .001 |
| Residual Invariance | .86 | .83 | .86 | .10 [.08, .11] | $\chi^2(6) = 25.41$, p < .001 |

The χ2 difference test examines the difference in fit between each model and the previous model.

**Table 8.** Mean, Standard Deviations (SD) and Chi-Square Results by Gender.

|  | Female | | Male | | |
| --- | --- | --- | --- | --- | --- |
|  | Mean | SD | Mean | SD | $X^2$ (Cramer's V) |
| Consensual (Total) | 11.33 | 2.68 | 12.57 | 2.11 | 44.59** (.28) |
| Dan & Abby | 3.56 | 1.03 | 4.18 | .79 | 30.06** (.16) |
| Samantha & Dan | 3.89 | 1.01 | 4.18 | .821 | 2.05 (.04) |
| Rebecca & Jack | 3.85 | 1.02 | 4.23 | .802 | 6.73* (.07) |
| Nonconsensual (Total) | 6.61 | 2.49 | 8.42 | 2.91 | 72.64** (.35) |
| Jessica & Tom | 2.18 | .96 | 3.00 | 1.12 | 160.31** (.38) |
| Dee & Jack | 2.48 | 1.07 | 2.90 | 1.11 | 27.73** (.15) |
| Matt & Sarah | 1.95 | 1.01 | 2.53 | 1.22 | 40.55** (.19) |

**p < .01 *p < .05 (C) represents a consensual vignette (NC) represents a nonconsensual vignette.

*Hypothesis 3 (Model 3)*

Model 3 explored the relationships between reported comfort with the vignettes and a person's attitudes towards establishing consent, their indirect behavioural approach to consent, and one's sexual consent-related norms. Standardised direct effects for the models are presented in Table 9. Model 3 resulted in poor model fit with a CFI of .840, TLI of .811, IFI of .842, RMSEA of .07, and significant chi square statistic (3.74, $p < .001$). Results of model 3 are as follows:

*Hypothesis 3a. Positive attitude towards establishing consent.* Comfort with the nonconsensual vignettes was negatively associated with having positive attitudes towards sexual consent ($\beta = -.923$, $p = .012$), but not associated with the consensual vignettes ($\beta = -.084$, $p = .602$).

*Hypothesis 3b. Indirect behavioural approach to consent.* Scores on the indirect behavioural approach to sexual consent subscale were not significantly associated with being comfortable with the nonconsensual vignettes ($\beta = .064$, $p = .073$), or with the consensual vignettes ($\beta = .011$, $p = .713$).

*Hypothesis 3c. Sexual consent norms.* Level of endorsement of sexual consent norms was associated with comfort with nonconsensual vignettes ($\beta = .138$, $p = .003$) but not with the consensual vignettes ($\beta = .057$, $p = .128$).

## Discussion

Based on previous research we hypothesised that gender, frequency of pornography engagement, and attitudes towards sexual consent would predict participants' comfort with the pornography vignettes. Our findings indicate that underlying these associations is schemas and scripts into which the interpretation of nonconsensual and consensual vignettes fall. How likely a person is to engage

**Table 9.** Standardised Direct Effects for Full Path Model, with Standard Errors (SE), Beta Coefficients ($\beta$), and Significance Values (p).

| Direct effect | SE | $\beta$ | p |
| --- | --- | --- | --- |
| Frequency – > Comfort with consensual vignettes** | .06 | .32 | <.001 |
| Frequency -> Comfort with nonconsensual vignettes** | .08 | .49 | <.001 |
| Gender -> Consensual vignettes** | .06 | .34 | <.001 |
| Gender -> Nonconsensual vignettes** | .08 | .64 | <.001 |
| Sexual consent norms -> Comfort with consensual vignettes | .04 | .06 | .128 |
| Indirect behavioural approach to consent -> Comfort with consensual vignettes | .03 | .01 | .713 |
| Positive attitudes to consent -> Comfort with consensual vignettes | .16 | −.08 | .602 |
| Sexual consent norms -> Comfort with nonconsensual vignettes** | .05 | .14 | .003 |
| Indirect behavioural approach to consent -> Comfort with nonconsensual vignettes | .04 | .06 | .073 |
| Positive attitudes to consent -> Comfort with non- consensual vignettes* | .37 | −.92 | .012 |

** p < .01 *p < .05

with nonconsensual pornography may depend on how closely the observed scenarios match their existing understanding of normal behaviour. Less positive attitudes towards establishing verbal consent were associated with greater comfort with the nonconsensual vignettes. Our findings support others who have found that nonconsensual pornography engagement is associated with negative consent attitudes (e.g., Romito & Beltramini, 2015); however, because of the cross-sectional nature of the data, the causal direction of such associations is beyond the scope of this study.

Hypothesis 1 is supported; men reported greater comfort with the consensual or nonconsensual vignettes than women. We observed differences between women and men on their comfort with the consensual and nonconsensual vignettes. Engagement rates also differed greatly between women and men in that men were more likely to report regular engagement with pornography. These findings are consistent with others (Lim et al., 2017). This indicated that women and men experience different drives to engage with pornography, and they may also differ in their interpretation or acceptance with pornographic content. Vignette. A minority of participants overall reported that they would be comfortable watching the nonconsensual vignettes. Such findings support those of Shor and Seida (2018) who found that engaging with nonconsensual pornography, which involved 'explicit verbal requests to stop or avoid a certain act, nonverbal signs of resistance (e.g., pushing away), attempts to avoid the act, and/or evident unhappiness at being in the situation or performing a certain act, which were nevertheless ignored by the sexual partner' (p. 6), has not increased over time and in fact was found to be unpopular; only 1.4% of the most viewed videos on PornHub featured nonconsensual content.

Hypothesis 2 is not supported; more frequent engagement with pornography was associated with greater comfort with the consensual vignettes; however, it was not associated with the nonconsensual vignettes. More frequent pornography viewers were no more comfortable with nonconsensual content in comparison with less frequent viewers. This indicates that there is no difference in terms of comfort associated with increased frequency for consensual and nonconsensual vignettes. These findings contradict those who have argued that pornography is contributing to a culture of callousness (Zillmann & Bryant, 1982) whereby individuals are increasingly demanding nonconsensual or aggressive content. What is often at the centre of this argument is that more frequent engagement results in individuals becoming desensitised to aggressive content and in turn prefer it (Dines, 2010). Following this logic, we would expect to find aggressive or nonconsensual content to be more popular (Shor & Seida, 2018) or for frequent pornography engagement to be associated with greater comfort with the nonconsensual vignettes in comparison to the consensual vignettes.

Hypothesis 3 is supported; Those who report less positive attitudes towards establishing sexual consent were more likely to report being comfortable with the nonconsensual vignettes. In other words, those with higher positive attitude scores were less tolerant of the nonconsensual vignettes. It could be that those with particularly positive attitudes see explicit or verbal communication as part of their existing script and may therefore be more likely to want to see explicit consent in the pornography that they would engage with. On the other hand, those who engage with nonconsensual content may develop or reinforce previously held beliefs around the acceptability of nonconsensual sex. Because explicit verbal consent is uncommon in mainstream pornography (Willis et al., 2019), it may also be that those who are comfortable with nonconsensual pornography may not realise the importance of consent in sexual activity. Similarly, those who have more positive attitudes towards consent may have received more information about sexual consent or attended sexual consent workshops and have a more critical understanding regarding the interpretation of consent in different scenarios.

Hypothesis 4 is not supported; having an indirect behavioural approach to sexual consent was not significantly associated with reporting comfort with the nonconsensual vignettes. Hypothesis 5 is partially supported; level of endorsement of sexual consent norms was associated with comfort with the nonconsensual vignettes but not with the consensual vignettes. Those who endorsed sexual consent norms were more likely to report comfort with the nonconsensual vignettes. Those who believe sexual consent to be an unnecessary component of sexual interaction may be more comfortable with or tolerant of the nonconsensual vignettes as it may more closely coincide with their existing attitudes, in comparison to those whose existing sexual scripts include explicit verbal communication of consent. Additionally, pornography typically may not feature ongoing consent, as this is something that is established by actors beforehand or may be dictated by directors and is omitted from view. Some participants may have acquired beliefs about sexual consent from watching pornography, which in turn could have influenced their sexual scripts and beliefs around acceptable sexual behaviour; however, the causal direction cannot be inferred by our data. In contrast, some people enjoy rape fantasies (Bivona et al., 2012), but this may not reflect their desires for real-life experiences or influence their behaviour; what an individual feels comfortable in watching may also not reflect their desired behaviours in their own relationships. For instance, one study showed 62% of young women have had sexual fantasies about rape (Bivona & Critelli, 2009). However, studies also show that most women do not want to act out a realistic rape fantasy (Bond & Mosher, 1986; Gold & Clegg, 1990).

## Limitations and recommendations

Although critical improvements have been made within the literature, simply providing participants with definitions regarding nonconsensual pornography (e.g., Davis et al., 2018) may not be sufficient and indeed may not reflect the true nature of the content that people engage with. The vignettes developed in this study demonstrated construct validity as well as reliability and provided greater clarity regarding the exploration of the types of pornography that people are comfortable with. Although this study has several strengths, there are also a number of limitations that warrant discussion. First, all expert participants in the Delphi component were female. Although the expert group was recruited based on their professional experience in the area of consent, we cannot guarantee that their experiences as women did not influence their interpretation of the vignettes. Second, it was based on cross-sectional data from a convenience sample of young adult university students; the demographic characteristics, including low numbers of sexual partners, mean that our findings may apply specifically to the models that young adults apply in their first sexual encounters. People with more sexual partners and greater sexual experience may have different beliefs about consent-related norms and approaches to sex. Therefore, the findings cannot be considered as representative of the general population. However, the findings may be applied to the specific types of scripts that young adults have during their early sexual experiences. In addition, university students may have more experience with pornography than other adults and have grown up in an age where pornography engagement is becoming increasingly normalised (Carroll et al., 2008). The sexual socialisation of this cohort may therefore differ compared with adults in older generations, which again limits its potential for generalisability. Nevertheless, this study provided interesting insight into the experiences of one of the first cohorts of young people to have gone through adolescence living in an environment where pornography is accessible and frequently used by young people.

Third, the external validity of the written vignettes as an alternative to viewing a pornography video is unknown. Although participants reported that they would feel comfortable watching the vignettes described, we do not know if those who were comfortable with the nonconsensual vignettes have watched nonconsensual pornography in the past or indeed if it was their preferred type of pornography to watch. We also do not know how the participants interpreted the vignettes with regard to sexual consent. Some participants may see the nonconsensual nature of the vignettes and still report being comfortable watching them. Others may interpret the vignettes as depictions of encounters which are entirely consensual. If this is the case, there may be important differences between these two groups with regard to the attitudinal variables measured in this study.

Further validation comparing responses to vignettes and video content would be valuable. Subtle cues that are exchanged between two people when being sexually intimate are not described with the written narratives. More detailed descriptions may have provided clearer indications of the context of each of the vignettes. In addition, depictions of nonconsensual manual or digital sex vignettes had higher scores on self-reported comfort than vaginal and anal sex vignettes. It may be that apparently nonconsensual behaviours that are considered less severe may be more acceptable to some participants than more intimate behaviours like vaginal or anal sex. Additionally, it may be that some participants are more comfortable with these particular vignettes because of the behaviours portrayed. In other words, some people might only feel comfortable watching manual sex vignettes. We also used a within-subject design. In an effort to reduce bias, where participants recognise the differences between each vignette, the order in which participants read vignettes were randomised. However, some bias may remain.

Fourth, cognitive scripting theorists have argued that the nonconsensual scripts that are more likely to be learned and applied by individuals are those that feature nonconsensual behaviour being rewarded. We urge future researchers to use vignettes that describe nonconsensual behaviours being rewarded or punished to get a clearer understanding of the acceptability of nonconsensual content and how they might be related to sexual consent attitudes. The use of the term 'comfort' to establish a participant's likelihood to engage with the content provided speaks to attitudinal, and less so behavioural intentions. Some people may be aroused by, and therefore engage with, content that may make them uncomfortable, such as erotic humiliation or masochism. Future research should replicate this study by asking participants whether the vignette described resembles the type of content that a person normally engages with – or that they hypothetically would engage with. Such studies should be conducted using longitudinal methodologies to obtain a more robust understanding of the direction of the relationships between pornography content choices and individual consent attitudes. Finally, porn literacy interventions for youth that aim to challenge representations of violent sex in pornography (e.g., K. Dawson, Nic Gabhainn et al., 2019) should promote critical awareness of the differences between aggressive and nonconsensual and aggressive and consensual pornography.

## Conclusion

Previous research has relied on broad categories or individual beliefs about whether they had watched nonconsensual pornography, which may have provided unreliable information about the type of content that people engage with. This study provides a more objective measure for assessing people's comfort with nonconsensual pornography. Findings suggest that a person's existing attitudes to sexual consent may be a more reliable indicator for the type of content that people engage with than frequency of pornography engagement alone.

## Disclosure statement

No potential conflict of interest was reported by the authors.

## Funding

This study was not supported by any funding body.

## ORCID

Chris Noone http://orcid.org/0000-0003-4974-9066

## References

Aguinis, H, & Bradley, K. J. (2014). Best practice recommendations for designing and implementing experimental vignette methodology studies. *Organizational Research Methods, 17,* 351-371.

Allen, M., D'alessio, D. A. V. E., & Brezgel, K. (1995). A meta-analysis summarizing the effects of pornography II: Aggression after exposure. *Human Communication Research, 22*(2), 258–283. https://doi.org/10.1111/j.1468-2958.1995.tb00368.x

Arbuckle, J. L. (2016). *Amos (Version 24.0) [Computer Program].* SPSS.

Arnett, J. J. (2007). Emerging adulthood: What is it, and what is it good for? *Child Development Perspectives, 1*(2), 68–73. https://doi.org/10.1111/j.1750-8606.2007.00016.x

Bandura, A. (1986). *Social foundations of thought and action.* SAGE Publications. https://doi.org/10.4135/9781446221129.n6

Bauserman, R. (1996). Sexual aggression and pornography: A review of correlational research. *Basic and Applied Social Psychology, 18*(4), 405–427. https://doi.org/10.1207/s15324834basp1804_4 https://doi.org/10.1080/00224490802398381

Bivona, J., & Critelli, J. (2009). The nature of women's rape fantasies: An analysis of prevalence, frequency, and contents. *Journal of Sex Research, 46*(1), 33–45. https://doi.org/10.1080/00224490802624406

Bivona, J. M., Critelli, J. W., & Clark, M. J. (2012). Women's rape fantasies: An empirical evaluation of the major explanations. *Archives of Sexual Behavior, 41*(5), 1107–1119. https://doi.org/10.1007/s10508-012-9934-6

Blunt-Vinti, H., Jozkowski, K. N., & Hunt, M. (2019). Show or tell? Does verbal and/or nonverbal sexual communication matter for sexual satisfaction? *Journal of Sex & Marital Therapy,45*(3), 206-217. https://doi.org/10.1080/0092623X.2018.1501446

Bond, S. B., & Mosher, D. L. (1986). Guided imager of rape: Fantasy, reality, and the willing victim myth. *Journal of Sex Research, 22*(2), 162–183. https://doi.org/10.1080/00224498609551298

Boone, T. L, & Lefkowitz, E. S. (2004). Safer sex and the health belief model: considering the contributions of peer norms and socialization factors. *Journal Of Psychology & Human Sexuality, 16,* 51-68.

Bridges, A. J., Wosnitzer, R., Scharrer, E., Sun, C., & Liberman, R. (2010). Aggression and sexual behavior in best-selling pornography videos: A content analysis update. *Violence against Women, 16*(10), 1065–1085. https://doi.org/10.1177/1077801210382866

Brown, J. D, & L'Engle, K. L. (2009). X-rated: sexual attitudes and behaviors associated with u.s. early adolescents' exposure to sexually explicit media. *Communication Research, 36,* 129–151.

Buunk, B. P, van den Eijnden, R. J, & Siero, F. W. (2002). The double- edged sword of providing information about the prevalence of safer sex 1. *Journal Of Applied Social Psychology, 32,* 684-699.

Byrne, B. M. (2016). *Structural equation modeling with AMOS: Basic concepts, applications, and programming.* Routledge. 227. https://doi.org/10.4324/9781410600219

Carroll, J. S., Padilla-Walker, L. M., Nelson, L. J., Olson, C. D., McNamara Barry, C., & Madsen, S. D. (2008). Generation XXX: Pornography acceptance and use among emerging adults. *Journal of Adolescent Research, 23*(1), 6–30. https://doi.org/10.1177/0743558407306348

Costello, A. B., & Osborne, J. W. (2005). Best practices in exploratory factor analysis: Four recommendations for getting the most from your analysis. *Practical Assessment, Research & Evaluation, 10*(1), 7, 1–9. https://doi.org/10.4135/9781412995627.d8

Davis, A. C., Carrotte, E. R., Hellard, M. E., & Lim, M. S. (2018). What behaviors do young heterosexual Australians see in pornography? A cross-sectional study. *Journal of Sex Research, 55*(3), 310–319. https://doi.org/10.1080/00224499.2017.1417350

Dawson, K., Nic Gabhainn, S., & MacNeela, P. (2019). Toward a Model of Porn Literacy: Core Concepts, Rationales, and Approaches. *The Journal of Sex Research, 57*(1) 1–15. https://doi.org/10.1080/00224499.2018.1556238

Dawson, K., Tafro, A., & Štulhofer, A. (2019). Adolescent sexual aggressiveness and pornography use: A longitudinal assessment. *Aggressive Behavior, 45*(6), 587–597. https://doi.org/10.1002/ab.21854

Diamond, M., Jozifkova, E., & Weiss, P. (2011). Pornography and sex crimes in the Czech Republic. *Archives of Sexual Behavior, 40*(5), 1037–1043. https://doi.org/10.1007/s10508-011-9871-9

Dines, G. (2010). *Pornland: How pornography has hijacked our sexuality.* Beacon.

D'abreu, L. C. F.&Krahé, B. (2014). Predicting sexual aggression in male college students in Brazil. Psychology of Men & Masculinity, 15, 152

Ferguson, C. J., & Hartley, R. D. (2009). The pleasure is momentary ... the expense damnable?: The influence of pornography on rape and sexual assault. *Aggression and Violent Behavior, 14*(5), 323–329. https://doi.org/10.1016/j.avb.2009.04.008

Fisher, W. A., & Grenier, G. (1994). Violent pornography, antiwoman thoughts, and antiwoman acts: In search of reliable effects. *Journal of Sex Research, 31*(1), 23–38. https://doi.org/10.1080/00224499409551727

Foubert, J. D. (2000). The longitudinal effects of a rape-prevention program on fraternity men's attitudes, behavioral intent, and behavior. *Journal of American College Health, 48*(4), 158–163. https://doi.org/10.1080/07448480009595691

Gagnon, J. H., & Simon, W. (1973). *Sexual conduct: The social origins of human sexuality.* Routledge

Gidycz, C. A., Warkentin, J. B., & Orchowski, L. M. (2007). Predictors of perpetration of verbal, physical, and sexual violence: A prospective analysis of college men. *Psychology of Men & Masculinity, 8*(2), 79. https://doi.org/10.1037/1524-9220.8.2.79

Gold, S. R., & Clegg, C. L. (1990). Sexual fantasies of college students with coercive experiences and coercive attitudes. *Journal of Interpersonal Violence, 5*(4), 464–473. https://doi.org/10.1177/088626090005004003

Gould, D. (1996). Using vignettes to collect data for nursing research studies: How valid are the findings? *Journal of Clinical Nursing, 5*(4), 207–212. https://doi.org/10.1111/j.1365-2702.1996.tb00253.x

Hair, J., Anderson, R. O., & Tatham, R. (1987). *Multidimensional data analysis.*

Hald, G. M., Malamuth, N. M., & Yuen, C. (2010). Pornography and attitudes supporting violence against women: Revisiting the relationship in nonexperimental studies. *Aggressive Behavior: Official Journal of the International Society for Research on Aggression, 36*(1), 14–20. https://doi.org/10.1002/ab.20328

Hayes, R. M., Abbott, R. L., & Cook, S. (2016). It's her fault: Student acceptance of rape myths on two college campuses. *Violence against Women, 22*(13), 1540–1555. https://doi.org/10.1177/1077801216630147

Hsu, C. C., & Sandford, B. A. (2007). The Delphi technique: Making sense of consensus. *Practical Assessment, Research & Evaluation, 12*(10), 1–8.

Hickman, S. E., & Muehlenhard, C. L. (1999). "By the semi–mystical appearance of a condom": How young women and men communicate sexual consent in heterosexual situations. *Journal of Sex Research, 36,* 258–272.

Hsu, C. C., & Sandford, B. A. (2010). Delphi technique. *Encyclopedia of Research Design,* 344–347.3.

Hughes, R., & Huby, M. (2002). The application of vignettes in social and nursing research. *Journal of Advanced Nursing, 37*(4), 382–386. https://doi.org/10.1046/j.1365-2648.2002.02100.x

Humphreys, T, & Herold, E. (2007). Sexual consent in heterosexual relationships: development of a new measure. *Sex Roles, 57*(), 305-315.

Humphreys, T. P., & Brousseau, M. M. (2010). The sexual consent scale–revised: Development, reliability, and preliminary validity. *Journal of Sex Research, 47*(5), 420–428. https://doi.org/10.1080/00224490903151358

Humphreys, T. P. (2004). Understanding sexual consent: An empirical investigation of the normative script for young heterosexual adults. Making sense of sexual consent, 209–225.

IBM Corp, N. (2013). *IBM SPSS Statistics for Windows, Version 22.* IBM Corp.

Jozkowski, K. N, Peterson, Z. D, Sanders, S. A, Dennis, B, & Reece, M. (2014). Gender differences in heterosexual college students' conceptualizations and indicators of sexual consent: implications for contemporary sexual assault prevention education. *Journal Of Sex Research, 51*(), 904-916.

Jozkowski, K. N, & Wiersma, J. D. (2015). Does drinking alcohol prior to sexual activity influence college students' consent?. *International Journal Of Sexual Health, 27*(), 156-174.

Kingston, D. A., Malamuth, N. M., Fedoroff, P., & Marshall, W. L. (2009). The importance of individual differences in pornography use: Theoretical perspectives and implications for treating sexual offenders. *Journal of Sex Research, 46*(2–3), 216–232. https://doi.org/10.1080/00224490902747701

Koletić, G, Kohut, T, & Štulhofer, A. (2019). Associations between adolescents' use of sexually explicit material and risky sexual behavior: a longitudinal assessment. *Plos One, 14,* e0218962.

Koopman, E. M., Hilscher, M., & Cupchik, G. C. (2012). Reader responses to literary depictions of rape. Psychology of Aesthetics. *Creativity, and the Arts, 6*(1), 66. https://doi.org/10.1037/a0024153

Krafka, C., Linz, D., Donnerstein, E., & Penrod, S. (1997). Women's reactions to sexually aggressive mass media depictions. *Violence against Women, 3*(2), 149–181. https://doi.org/10.1177/1077801297003002004

Landripet, I., Buško, V., & Štulhofer, A. (2019). Testing the content progression thesis: A longitudinal assessment of pornography use and preference for coercive and violent content among male adolescents. *Social Science Research, 81,* 32–41. https://doi.org/10.1016/j.ssresearch.2019.03.003

Lawrie, S. M., Martin, K., McNeill, G., Drife, J., Chrystie, P., Reid, A., WU, P., NAMMARY, S., & Ball, J. (1998). General practitioners' attitudes to psychiatric and medical illness. *Psychological Medicine, 28*(6), 1463–1467. https://doi.org/10.1017/S0033291798007004

L'Engle, K. L, & Jackson, C. (2008). Socialization influences on early adolescents' cognitive susceptibility and transition to sexual intercourse. *Journal Of Research on Adolescence, 18*, 353-378.

Lim, M. S., Agius, P. A., Carrotte, E. R., Vella, A. M., & Hellard, M. E. (2017). Young Australians' use of pornography and associations with sexual risk behaviours. *Australian and New Zealand Journal of Public Health, 41*(4), 438–443. https://doi.org/10.1111/1753-6405.12678

MacNeela, B., Byrnes, O., & Seery, S. (2017). "Development, Implementation, and Evaluation of the SMART Consent Workshop on Sexual Consent for Third Level Students". National Universtiy of Ireland, Galway. Retrieved from: http://www.nuigalway.ie/media/studentservices/SMART-Consent-Workshop-Report-WEB.pdf

Malamuth, N. M., & Check, J. V. P. (1980). Sexual arousal to rape and consenting depictions: The importance of the woman's arousal. *Journal of Abnormal Psychology, 89*(6), 763–766. https://doi.org/10.1037/0021-843X.89.6.763

Malamuth, N. M, Heim, M, & Feshbach, S. (1980). Sexual responsiveness of college students to rape depictions: inhibitory and disinhibitory effects. *Journal Of Personality and Social Psychology, 38*, 399.

Muehlenhard, C. L., Humphreys, T. P., Jozkowski, K. N., & Peterson, Z. D. (2016). The complexities of sexual consent among college students: A conceptual and empirical review. *The Journal of Sex Research, 53*(4–5), 457–487. https://doi.org/10.1080/00224499.2016.1146651

Muehlenhard, C. L, Peterson, Z. D, Humphreys, T. P, & Jozkowski, K. N. (2017). Evaluating the one-in-five statistic: women's risk of sexual assault while in college. *The Journal Of Sex Research, 54*, 549-576.

Norris, J., Davis, K. C., George, W. H., Martell, J., & Heiman, J. R. (2004). Victim's response and alcohol-related factors as determinants of women's responses to violent pornography. *Psychology of Women Quarterly, 28*(1), 59–69. https://doi.org/10.1111/j.1471-6402.2004.00123.x

Parvez, Z. F. (2006). The labor of pleasure: How perceptions of emotional labor impact women's enjoyment of pornography. *Gender & Society, 20*(5), 605–631. https://doi.org/10.1177/0891243206291109

Paul, P. (2010). From pornography to porno to porn: How porn became the norm. In *The social costs of pornography: A collection of papers* (pp. 3–20). Princeton: Witherspoon Institute.

Romito, P., & Beltramini, L. (2015). Factors associated with violent or degrading pornography. *The Journal of School Nursing, 31*(4), 280–290. https://doi.org/10.1177/1059840514563313

Shor, E., & Seida, K. (2018). "Harder and Harder"? Is Mainstream Pornography Becoming Increasingly Violent and Do Viewers Prefer Violent Content? *Journal of Sex Research*, 1–13. 1. https://doi.org/10.1080/00224499.2018.1451476

Short, M. B., Black, L., Smith, A. H., Wetterneck, C. T., & Wells, D. E. (2012). A review of Internet pornography use research: Methodology and content from the past 10 years. *Cyberpsychology, Behavior and Social Networking, 15*(1), 13–23. https://doi.org/10.1089/cyber.2010.0477

Suarez, E., & Gadalla, T. M. (2010). Stop blaming the victim: A meta-analysis on rape myths. *Journal of Interpersonal Violence, 25*(11), 2010–2035. https://doi.org/10.1177/0886260509354503

Sun, C. (2011). The Price Of Pleasure: Pornography, Sexuality, And Relationships: 507. *The Journal of Sexual Medicine, 8*, 209.

Tabachnick, B. G., & Fidell, L. S. (2007). *Using multivariate statistics*. Allyn & Bacon/Pearson Education.

Tomaszewska, P., & Krahé, B. (2018). Predictors of sexual aggression victimization and perpetration among Polish university students: A longitudinal study. *Archives of Sexual Behavior, 47*(2), 493–505. https://doi.org/10.1007/s10508-016-0823-2

Vega, V., & Malamuth, N. M. (2007). Predicting sexual aggression: The role of pornography in the context of general and specific risk factors. *Aggressive Behavior: Official Journal of the International Society for Research on Aggression, 33*(2), 104–117. https://doi.org/10.1002/ab.20172

Wallace, S. A, Miller, K. S, & Forehand, R. (2008). Perceived peer norms and sexual intentions among african american preadolescents. *Aids Education & Prevention, 20*, 360-369.

Wen, Z, Marsh, H. W, & Hau, K. T. (2010). Structural equation models of latent interactions: an appropriate standardized solution and its scale-free properties. *Structural Equation Modeling, 17*, 1-22.

Wilks, T. (2004). The use of vignettes in qualitative research into social work values. *Qualitative Social Work, 3*(1), 78–87. https://doi.org/10.1177/1473325004041133

Willis, M., Canan, S. N., Jozkowski, K. N., & Bridges, A. J. (2019). Sexual consent communication in best-selling pornography films: A content analysis. *Journal of Sex Research, 57*(1) 1–13. https://doi.org/10.1080/00224499.2019.1655522

Willoughby, B. J., Carroll, J. S., Nelson, L. J., & Padilla-Walker, L. M. (2014). Associations between relational sexual behaviour, pornography use, and pornography acceptance among US college students. *Culture, Health & Sexuality, 16*(9), 1052–1069. https://doi.org/10.1080/13691058.2014.927075

Wright, P. J. (2011). Mass media effects on youth sexual behavior assessing the claim for causality. *Annals of the International Communication Association, 35*(1), 343–385. https://doi.org/10.1080/23808985.2011.11679121

Wright, P. J. (2013). A three-wave longitudinal analysis of preexisting beliefs, exposure to pornography, and attitude change. *Communication Reports, 26*(1), 13–25. https://doi.org/10.1080/08934215.2013.773053

Wright, P. J, & Štulhofer, A. (2019). Adolescent pornography use and the dynamics of perceived pornography realism: does seeing more make it more realistic?. *Computers in Human Behavior, 95,* 37-47.

Wright, P. J., & Tokunaga, R. S. (2016). Men's objectifying media consumption, objectification of women, and attitudes supportive of violence against women. *Archives of Sexual Behavior, 45*(4), 955–964. https://doi.org/10.1007/s10508-015-0644-8

Wright, P. J., Tokunaga, R. S., & Kraus, A. (2015). A meta-analysis of pornography consumption and actual acts of sexual aggression in general population studies. *Journal of Communication, 66*(1), 183–205. https://doi.org/10.1111/jcom.12201

Ybarra, M. L, Mitchell, K. J, Hamburger, M, Diener-West, M, & Leaf, P. J. (2011). X-rated material and perpetration of sexually aggressive behavior among children and adolescents. *Is There a Link? Aggressive Behavior, 37,* 1–18.

Ybarra, M. L, & Thompson, R. E. (2018). Predicting the emergence of sexual violence in adolescence. *Prevention Science, 19* 403–415.

Zillmann, D., & Bryant, J. (1982). Pornography and sexual callousness, and the trivialization of rape. *Journal of Communication, 32*(4), 10–21. https://doi.org/10.1111/j.1460-2466.1982.tb02514.x

Zinzow, H. M., & Thompson, M. (2011). Barriers to reporting sexual victimization: Prevalence and correlates among undergraduate women. *Journal of Aggression, Maltreatment & Trauma, 20*(7), 711-725. https://doi.org/10.1080/10926771.2011.613447

# Appendix

Porn scene vignette survey
Please read each of the scenes below and report how comfortable you would feel in watching the porn scene described.
Chris and Sarah (Nonconsensual manual sex scene)
Chris is a friend of Sarah's brother, Rob. One evening the three are watching TV. Rob gets up and leaves the room to take a phone call. Chris looks at Sarah, moves closer to her and leans in to kiss her. Sarah laughs and pushes him away playfully. Chris starts to rub Sarah's thigh, takes her hand and moves it towards his crotch. Sarah blushes.

- Very uncomfortable
- Uncomfortable
- Neither comfortable nor uncomfortable
- Comfortable
- Very comfortable

Nick and Alex (Nonconsensual vaginal sex scene)
In this scene, Nick has invited Alex back to his apartment. Nick goes to the kitchen to make two cups of coffee. When he returns to the living room, Alex is lying naked on the sofa. 'What are you doing', Nick asks, seeming slightly shocked. She begins to unbuckle Nick's belt and stroke his penis until he gets an erection. She guides him by the arm, down onto the sofa and straddles his lap, slipping his penis inside her vagina. 'I don't know if we should do this', says Nick.

- Very uncomfortable
- Uncomfortable
- Neither comfortable nor uncomfortable
- Comfortable
- Very comfortable

Samanta and Dan (Consensual digital sex scene)
In this porn scene, Samantha and Dan are alone in a bedroom. They start kissing and Dan begins to run his hand up Samantha's thigh; she smiles at him and giggles. Dan whispers in her ear that he wants to touch her body. Samantha nods her head. Dan continues to open her trousers and inserts his finger into her vagina. 'That feels really good', murmurs Samantha.

- Very uncomfortable
- Uncomfortable
- Neither comfortable nor uncomfortable
- Comfortable
- Very comfortable

Dan and Abby (Consensual oral sex scene)

In this porn scene, Daniel and Abby are passionately kissing in a bedroom. Abby pulls Daniel's belt, undoing the buckle and buttons, pulling his erection out of his trousers. 'Do you like that', Abby asks. 'I do', he replies. 'Do you want me to keep going, then', ask Abby. Daniel nods. She puts his penis inside her mouth and gives him oral sex.

- Very uncomfortable
- Uncomfortable
- Neither comfortable nor uncomfortable
- Comfortable
- Very comfortable

Rebecca and Jack (Consensual vaginal sex scene)
In this porn scene, Rebecca and Jack are watching a movie, on the sofa. Jack begins to caress Rebecca's thigh. She smiles, leans in, and pulls him closely to her while opening her legs. Jack raises her skirt and notices that she is not wearing any underwear. Jack removes his trousers. He has an erection. Rebecca guides Jack's penis slowly inside her vagina.

- Very uncomfortable
- Uncomfortable
- Neither comfortable nor uncomfortable
- Comfortable
- Very comfortable

Jessica and Tom (Nonconsensual digital sex scene)
In this porn scene, Jessica and Tom are sitting on a sofa, flirting. Jessica begins to run her hand over Tom's chest, kisses him deeply and moves her hand down further and strokes his penis, through his trousers. Tom seems hesitant, 'I'm not in the mood', but Jessica continues to kiss him and slides her hand inside his boxer shorts and pulls his penis out. Despite his protestations, Tom continues to get an erection.

- Very uncomfortable
- Uncomfortable
- Neither comfortable nor uncomfortable
- Comfortable
- Very comfortable

Dee and Jack (Nonconsensual oral sex scene)
In this porn scene, Dee and Jack are naked in a bedroom. Dee is kneeling on the ground, sucking Jack's penis. Jack then reaches down and winding her hair around his fingers, pulls Dee off her knees, pushing her backward on to the bed. Jack kneels down in front of her. Dee is hesitant, 'Actually ...' Dee says, but before she could object, Jack puts his face in between her thighs and kisses her vagina. Jack pulls back, looks at Dee and smiles, saying, 'That was so nice, I've wanted to do that for such a long time'.

- Very uncomfortable
- Uncomfortable
- Neither comfortable nor uncomfortable
- Comfortable
- Very comfortable

Beth and Sandra (Nonconsensual oral sex scene)
In this porn scene, Beth and Sandra are standing at the front door of an apartment block. Both are acting flirtatious. Beth pulls Sandra in through the door and upstairs to her bedroom. 'I've never gone this far with a girl before', says Sandra. 'Don't worry, I'll show you what to do', Beth replies. Beth kisses Sandra, widening her mouth and pushing her tongue into Sandra's mouth. 'Can we slow down for a second', says Sandra. Beth smiles, 'Trust me, I know what I'm doing'. She summons Sandra to the bed, climbs on top of her and sits on Sandra's face.

- Very uncomfortable
- Uncomfortable
- Neither comfortable nor uncomfortable
- Comfortable
- Very comfortable

Kelly & Matt (Nonconsensual anal sex scene)

In this scene, Kelly and Matt are naked in a hotel room. Kelly is sitting on top of Matt, straddling his penis. 'What would you like to do to me', Kelly asks. Without answering, he pulls out, flips her onto her stomach, and pushes his penis inside her anus. Kelly lets out an aching moan, catching her breath in her throat. Matt, putting his hands on Kelly's hips, thrusts harder, saying, 'you feel so good'.

- Very uncomfortable
- Uncomfortable
- Neither comfortable nor uncomfortable
- Comfortable
- Very comfortable

Matt and Sarah (Nonconsensual vaginal sex scene)
Matt and Sarah are in bed. They begin to kiss, nuzzling into each other's necks. Without saying anything, Matt quickly pulls her on top of him and pushes his penis inside her vagina. Sarah gasps, digging her nails into his skin, 'Ouch!', Sarah shouts. Matt laughs and pulls her closer to him.

- Very uncomfortable
- Uncomfortable
- Neither comfortable nor uncomfortable
- Comfortable
- Very comfortable

**The following vignettes were categorised as representing scenes in which the depiction of sexual consent was unclear and were not included in the analysis.**
Maria and Tom (Unclear vaginal sex scene)
Maria has hired Tom to fix a fault in her kitchen. As Tom is working, Maria tiptoes up behind him, slipping her arms around his body and runs her hand down his chest. Tom quickly turns around, 'What do you think you are doing', he asks. Maria turns around, pushing her backside into his crotch. Tom pushes Maria's jeans down around her hips and slips his penis inside her anus. 'Keep going?' he asked. She murmured her approval.

- Very uncomfortable
- Uncomfortable
- Neither comfortable nor uncomfortable
- Comfortable
- Very comfortable

Max and Meghan (Unclear anal sex scene)
In this scene Max and Meghan are in the shower together, washing each other's bodies. Max reaches down, grabbing Meghan's thigh, pulling her towards him. Meghan moans, pressing her lips to his. Max, kissing her fiercely, holds both Meghan's arms behind her back. Meghan, without any determination, moans and tries to tug free. Max, then bending her forward, pushes his penis inside of her vagina, with forceful thrusts.

- Very uncomfortable
- Uncomfortable
- Neither comfortable nor uncomfortable
- Comfortable
- Very comfortable

# Sexual consent and sexual agency of women in healthy relationships following a history of sexual trauma

Kristen P. Mark and Laura M. Vowels

**ABSTRACT**
Sexual consent is a crucial component of any healthy sexual relationship. Women who have experienced sexual trauma are uniquely positioned to provide insight into sexual consent given that they have lived through sexual violence in the form of non-consensual sex and can reflect upon the importance of consent. Forty-one women completed an in-depth semi-structured phone interview and their responses were analyzed using reflexive thematic analysis. The analytic process resulted in the identification of nine themes in total; three related to consent in their current relationship and six related to the communication of needs and wants. Participants were divided between consent within their relationship as 1) explicit; 2) non-explicit; and 3) evolving. In their experience of feeling empowered to voice their needs and wants, participants indicated this to be 1) evolving; 2) requiring vulnerability and safety; 3) a non-negotiable requirement; 4) inherently interpersonal; 5) something that takes work; and 6) involves echoes of shame and trauma. These results highlight the complicated nature of negotiating consent and finding sexual agency. They also provide unique insight into consent and agency in a sample of women who have experienced sexual violence and have shown resilience in their pursuit of a healthy relationship post-sexual trauma.

There has been a notable shift in the importance society has placed on sexual consent and the notoriety it has received in recent years – in part due to campaigns such as #MeToo or #TimesUp and an increased number of women feeling empowered to voice their experiences. This has highlighted the significance of studying sexual consent to better understand what sexual consent means and how it should be expressed in and out of relationships. Sexual consent is a crucial component of healthy relationships and sexual encounters (Carmody, 2003). Definitions of sexual consent vary (Jozkowski, Peterson et al., 2014) and there is often ambiguity in what constitutes consent, but it is generally defined as 'one's voluntary, sober, and conscious willingness to engage in a particular sexual behaviour with a particular person within a particular context' (Willis & Jozkowski, 2019, p. 1723). The majority of existing sexual consent research has focused specifically on college students due to the large number of sexual assaults that occur on college campuses (Muehlenhard et al., 2016; Willis, Blunt-Vinti et al., 2019). Although the experience of college students' consent is crucial to understanding consent during a formative sexual time, it does not provide a comprehensive understanding of sexual consent beyond those years. In the present study, we addressed the question of what healthy sexual consent communication looks like in a community sample of women ranging in age who have a history of sexual trauma but are now in a healthy consensual sexual relationship. These women are uniquely positioned to provide insights into sexual consent given that they have lived through the result of nonconsensual sex and can reflect upon what makes consent particularly important to them in their relationships post-sexual trauma.

Communicating sexual consent is crucial for a healthy sexual relationship, and the effects of nonconsensual sex can be far-reaching. Estimates of the frequency of sexual assault varies somewhat but overall somewhere between one in three to one in five women have experienced sexual assault (Katz et al., 2019; Novack, 2017; Smith et al., 2018). Many survivors of sexual assault experience symptoms of trauma as a result (Frazier et al., 2009; Paquette et al., 2019; Tansill et al., 2012). The sexual trauma symptoms, in turn, are associated with negative outcomes such as poorer mental health (Christopher & Kisler, 2012; Frazier et al., 2009; Jordan et al., 2010; Mengo & Black, 2016), lower academic performance (Paolucci et al., 2001), unhealthy sexual behaviour (Paolucci et al., 2001), marital difficulties (Godbout et al., 2009), and issues with parenthood (Zvara et al., 2015). Some research has examined the effect sexual trauma may have on romantic relationships post-trauma. For example, O'Callaghan et al. (2019) found that sexual experiences change after sexual assault and potentially impact future relationships. In the current study, we also addressed how the women in our sample have managed the consequences of their experiences and moved towards being able to express their consent, needs, and desires in their current relationships.

There are various ways to communicate sexual consent. Many state legislations in the US now require affirmative consent, which means providing a conscious and voluntary agreement to engage in sexual activity and explicitly states that lack of protest, resistance, or silence does not mean a person is consenting to sexual activity (e.g. California State Legistlature, 2014). Affirmative consent goes one step further from 'no means no' to 'yes means yes;' for consent to be affirmative, one must provide a clear 'yes' rather than rely on an absence of a 'no' (Novack, 2017). Best practice requires both parties to communicate their consent to sexual activity (Beres, 2007; Muehlenhard et al., 2016), which can be communicated verbally or nonverbally, explicitly or implicitly (Willis & Jozkowski, 2019). While affirmative consent requires individuals to express consent verbally, research has shown that people are more likely to use non-verbal cues to express their consent (Beres, 2010, 2014; Beres et al., 2004; Hickman & Muehlenhard, 1999; Jozkowski, Peterson et al., 2014; Jozkowski, Sanders et al., 2014).

The sexual precedent theory posits that sexual consent becomes expected once partners engage in consensual sex (Livingston et al., 2004; Shotland & Goodstein, 1992; Willis & Jozkowski, 2019). In fact, many studies have found that a history of sexual relationship is associated with the assumption that a partner is interested and consents to future sexual activity (Beres, 2010, 2014; Humphreys & Brousseau, 2010; Humphreys & Herold, 2007; Muehlenhard et al., 2016), and partners are more likely to assume consent and less likely to explicitly ask for consent as the number of sexual events increases (Livingston et al., 2004; Shotland & Goodstein, 1992; Willis & Jozkowski, 2019). However, nonconsensual sex can also occur in relationships (e.g. marital rape, forced marriages, coercive relationships) highlighting the importance of consent in romantic relationships and not only in casual encounters.

Furthermore, researchers have suggested that consent can be viewed as a discrete event that occurs in the beginning of sexual activity or even in the beginning of a relationship or as a continuous, ongoing negotiation at each stage of the sexual activity (Beres, 2010, 2014; Muehlenhard et al., 2016). Because of the existence of nonconsensual sex in relationships as well as in casual encounters (Willis & Jozkowski, 2019), ongoing sexual consent and open communication around sexual consent and needs is important at every stage of a relationship, but the way in which these are communicated may change over the course of the relationship. For example, some couples may have a conversation about their preferences, needs, and boundaries in the beginning of their relationship and adjust as and when needed, whereas other couples may prefer to negotiate each sexual encounter separately. Additionally, Burkett and Hamilton (2012) argued that many standard models of sexual consent fail to address women's experiences of implicit pressure during sexual encounters that can disrupt their ability to negotiate consent. Feeling truly sexually empowered can enable women to shed the implicit pressure and to express sexual consent as well as their wants and needs in sexual relationships. The role of sexual agency, where one not only consents to sexual behaviour but feels empowered to ask for their sexual needs to be met (Burkett & Hamilton, 2012; Curtin et al., 2011), may be particularly salient in the context of relationships post-sexual trauma.

Women who have experienced sexual trauma are uniquely positioned to have a clearer understanding of consent and, importantly, the impact of the absence of consent. Previous research has addressed what sexual consent looks like in relationships (e.g. Muehlenhard et al., 2016; O'Callaghan et al., 2019; Willis & Jozkowski, 2019) but we are aware of no studies to date that have addressed how women with a history of sexual trauma navigate sexual consent, safety, and agency in their subsequent healthy relationships. In the current study, we aimed to understand the extent to which women who have previously experienced sexual trauma but are now in a healthy relationship understand and navigate consent and feel empowered to voice their needs and wants in their relationship.

## Method

### Participants

In this study, we recruited 41 women to participate in a semi-structured phone interview that lasted an average of 42 minutes (range of 28 to 78 minutes). Data were collected during late 2018 into early 2019, and we stopped recruitment once data saturation was reached. Participants were recruited primarily through online advertisements placed on Twitter and Facebook relying on social network snowball sampling, with some advertisements posted in cafes and around a mid-sized university campus in a medium sized city in the United States. The majority of participants resided in the United States ($n = 35$; 85.4%), with a minority residing in Canada ($n = 3$; 7.4%), Australia ($n = 1$; 2.4%), England ($n = 1$, 2.4%), and New Zealand ($n = 1$, 2.4%). Participants were eligible to participate in the study if they identified as a woman, were over the age of 18, had a history of sexual trauma, and were currently in what they considered a healthy sexual relationship. Both history of sexual trauma and healthy sexual relationship were self-defined by participants. In the recruitment process, we screened for sexual violence in their current relationship by asking participants if the sexual trauma they experienced happened within their current relationship and if they have ever felt unsafe in their current relationship. None of the participants indicated sexual violence in their current relationship.

Participant ages ranged from 18 to 55, with an average age of 28.9 ($SD = 7.58$). The majority of the sample identified as heterosexual ($n = 27$; 65.8%), with a minority of participants identifying as bisexual ($n = 5$, 12.2%), lesbian ($n = 1$; 2.4%), pansexual ($n = 2$; 4.9%), queer ($n = 4$; 9.8%), and questioning ($n = 2$; 4.9%). All but two of the participants were in a relationship with a man at the time of data collection (one participant was in a relationship with another woman and the other was in a relationship with a non-binary partner), and the average relationship length was 50.78 months (4.23 years) with a range from 3 months to 29 years. A minority of our participants ($n = 3$, 7.3%) indicated that they were in a polyamorous relationship. Only one participant was an undergraduate college student at the time of data collection; two were graduate students and the rest were non-students. Most of the participants were self-described as White ($n = 33$, 80.5%), though 8 (19.5%) self-identified as a racial or ethnic minority (self-described as one of the following: AfroLatina, Asian, Black, Filipino, Jewish, Hispanic). Most of the participants experienced sexual trauma after the age of 12 (71%), with 25% having experienced sexual trauma before the age of 12 and 4% who reported sexual trauma having happened both before and after the age of 12.

*Measures*

The current paper was part of a larger study aimed at understanding how prior sexual trauma experience informs navigating communication, consent, sexual pleasure, and other aspects of romantic relationships in women. The current paper aimed to understand sexual consent and sexual agency in the context of women who had experienced sexual trauma and were in healthy sexual relationships at the time of the study through the iterative analysis of answers to the following questions: 'What does sexual consent look like in your current relationship?' and 'Do you feel safe voicing your sexual wants and needs?'

*Procedure*

When participants were exposed to the advertisement for the study, they were instructed to email the first author to schedule an interview where they were screened for eligibility. If the participant met eligibility criteria, they were informed the interview would be recorded for later verbatim transcription with any identifying information masked; they then provided verbal informed consent. All interviews were conducted by the first author over the phone regardless of geographical location to provide methodological consistency. Participants were free to skip any question that made them uncomfortable or that they did not feel prepared to answer. At the end of the interview, participants were provided with a 20 USD online gift card as a token of appreciation for their participation and were provided the opportunity to access resources in case the interview brought up any feelings for them that needed to be further processed. All interviews were audio recorded and transcribed verbatim. Any identifying information from participants were removed from the transcripts, and names were replaced with pseudonyms. All protocol were approved by the first author's institutional research ethics board.

*Analytical approach*

In this study, we followed reflexive thematic analysis taking an inductive approach based on Clarke and Braun (2013) to reflect the explicit content of the data provided by the women. Both authors familiarised themselves with the data before creating a series of codes that were identified from the interviews to provide insight to the research questions of interest. These codes were then classified into themes and an iterative process was followed between both coders in generating, reviewing, defining, and naming themes from the codes generated by the data. Any disagreements regarding the classification of codes were discussed until 100% agreement could be reached. Although the transcripts were taken and analysed as a whole, the classification of codes into themes was conducted separately for our two research questions. The analytic process resulted in the identification of three themes on the function of sexual consent in their current relationship and six themes on the evolution of the sexual agency to communicate needs and wants. We also had an auditor familiar with the study and thematic analytic technique but not familiar with this particular research question read through the results and assess any inconsistencies with the themes or thematic representative quotes. We used '[…]' signals to remove unnecessary detail or provide needed additional information in the quoted data provided. All identifying information was masked in the quotes provided to support the themes. Additionally, spelling, grammatical, and typographical errors were all corrected to aid readability in the quoted data.

## Results

The analytic process resulted in the identification of nine themes in total: three related to sexual consent in their current relationship and six related to sexual agency and the communication of needs and wants. Participants were divided between consent within their relationship as (1) explicit,

(2) non-explicit, and (3) evolving. In their experience of feeling empowered to voice their needs and wants, participants indicated this to be (1) evolving, (2) requiring vulnerability and safety, (3) a non-negotiable requirement, (4) inherently interpersonal, (5) something that takes work, and (6) involving echoes of shame and trauma.

## Sexual consent in healthy relationships post-trauma

### As explicit

Participants indicated that consent was explicit in their relationships; some found it to be enthusiastic, where consent communicated pleasure or consent was seen as sexy. This pleasure and the importance of verbal communication as it contributes to pleasure is stated by Lucy, a 25-year-old participant, who said 'I have had relationships before where, and I really loved it when they asked like every time [...] that's really hot.' Or as expressed by Heather, a 42-year-old participant:

> Yeah, there's a whole lot of verbal communication. Even after us being together for eight years. We're fucking a lot. Even if we've done an act a hundred times, so moving in slowly, and how do you feel about that? And how's the position? And I mean, it's not always that much talk, but it's still pretty regular. That's what makes it feel so good; it makes it pleasurable. And I feel like that is because of past trauma. [...] So yeah, the verbal communication is big.

Others experienced consent in their relationships as verbally explicit, but expressed this as a form of respect that is necessary and not explicitly tied to pleasure. Or they discussed sexual consent as ongoing in their relationship. For example, Jess, a 26-year-old participant, stated:

> [Consent] definitely, definitely has a different definition than it used to have. It is explicit. One thing that makes me have a great deal of, not just love, but yeah, just respect, simply, is before I even told him about my sexual trauma, he was always big on consent. I don't know if it was because of dealing with someone prior that had sexual trauma, but things like he absolutely, if I've had too much to drink he will not, no matter how long we've been together, have sex with me. I know a lot of couples, or at least on the movies, they just start to kiss and then clothes come off, and then they have this romantic experience. But we have never had intercourse without one person saying, 'Are you okay with this? Do you want to have sex?' That was something prior to him ever learning about my trauma. Yeah, so that's been really big to me with consent.

Another example of this was provided by 37-year-old Kate: 'Yeah, it's very verbal. It's very careful as well. I talk out whatever is going on and depending on how I'm feeling, either we'll continue or we'll stop for the night and watch a movie or something or just be together.'

Explicit consent was also articulated by 22-year-old Cait, 'We straight up ask each other, because that's a huge thing for me and for him. Yeah, we ask. We say, "Is this okay?"'

Sexual consent as ongoing and as something that some women had to educate their partners on was stated by Emily, a 26-year-old participant:

> Everybody that I date has given me the feedback that I'm very good about consent. It is always voiced every step along the way. It is asked about. If it's not, then I leave. So, consent is a really active ongoing process that takes practice. I have definitely made my girlfriend role play with me just because neither of us as women are good at asking for what we want or moving things along. So, sometimes you've just got to sit down and get used to the way that words feel in your mouth and role play a little bit. I guess there's like sexual role playing or whatever, but not like, just like we are going to practice having this conversation right now. Like you're getting a class on consent whether you like it or not. Complete with handouts. I'm not fucking around.

Explicit consent was also something that participants expressed being educated on by partners, as expressed by Katarina, a participant in a polyamorous relationship, age 22:

> And then in the other relationship that I'm in, the triad, that was a little bit different. So, the negotiation that they preferred around consenting to things was more of everything is on the table except for what you put off the table, which was different for me and I wasn't sure if I liked that idea. But we literally took out a big, long list, like a packet of various activities and I went through it and filled it out extensively and put little notes next to things. Yeah, like color coded what I was super into and color coded what I really didn't want or was like on the fence about. So when I go up and visit them, I literally bring the packet. And stuff has changed in the last few months, so I went through it and I filled it out again. So I bring my packet and it has everything in there and if there's

something specific we're going to do that maybe I haven't done before, we'll have a conversation about it beforehand. It's like so obnoxious and extensive but it's useful.

Or in the example of 24-year-old Corrine:

> He had said, you know, 'I don't want to have sex with you unless you can look me in the eye and tell me that you genuinely want to have sex with me. And want you to just actively say it and not be weird about it.' Like, 'I want you to be as open and comfortable with the idea to the point where you can look at me and say it yourself.' Which was something that I had never heard before in my life. And I really thought that that was pretty incredible, actually.

Sometimes the women expressed that they relied on their partners to get explicit consent, like in the case of 30-year-old participant Beth, who said 'I think he's much more comfortable with going like, "Hey, do you want to have sex tonight? I'm going to go take a shower and then we can get into bed." He's a lot freer to ask it explicitly and to not pursue anything if it's not asked explicitly.'

Lessons about how explicit consent can be communicated without someone taking it personally was also common in the interviews. This is highlighted nicely by 28-year-old participant Mel:

> Yeah, so we talked about explicit consent and he was just like, 'You know, if at any point you're ever uncomfortable, just tell me.' I feel in past relationships when I would be feeling really awful or not in the mood to be sexual, if I told them no, they would internalize that and blame themselves or blame me. And now I feel like if you want to go for it, you want to initiate sex or something, go for it. And if I'm reciprocating those things, then I'm all for it, and if not, I'll tell you and I'll stop you and just be like, 'I love you and I think you're super attractive and I want to have sex with you but right now I'm just not in the mood.' And think that that works really well with us especially.

### *As non-explicit*

Consent as non-explicit was expressed by the women in this study exclusively in the context of a long-term relationship, with explicit consent becoming unnecessary over time. There were not any women in the sample who expressed non-explicit consent as nonconsensual in any way. In fact, overwhelmingly, the women indicated non-explicit consent was very clear in their relationships, such as with 26-year-old Cindy: '[showing consent] is more behavioural really, like, reciprocating. He's kissing me, I'll kiss him back, and I feel like that's consent enough for us at this point, or we know that this is okay, that this behaviour is okay.' Body language was reported as being used as a clear indicator of consent, such as with 27-year-old Mia, 'we understand body language and how things are going' or with 42-year-old Clare, 'I mean, it depends, you know? Sometimes it's raised eyebrows, raised eyebrows. Okay – that's consent.' Allie, a 22-year-old participant, stated 'But for us, we know each other's body language well enough that we don't necessarily have to verbalise it.' And from 22-year-old Katarina: 'I still trust him to read my body language. Like if I'm being grumpy, I trust him to not do the thing [sex].' The mutual agreement between partners was also clearly articulated by 24-year-old Amy, who stated:

> I don't think that we've ever had to say, or ask for consent really. I think that we have just like a mutual agreement of consent whenever we start to feel sexual, or we go into the bedroom and start to have foreplay. We don't ever actually say, 'Do you want to have sex?' Or anything. We kind of just as we're kissing and everything, it kind of just happens.

The reliance on non-verbal cues can also amount to a scaffolding of a variety of signs, as expressed here by 27-year-old Kristy:

> So there's a lot of overlapping actions, and I think more recently it has developed into verbal cues or physical shifts in body position or body language, that kind of thing that we have agreed as this means that I want to continue, or this means that I want to stop. I think that really central to that is eye contact and just checking in with each other.

### *As evolving*

For some participants, consent is constantly evolving in their relationship and can be complicated, especially as it relates to their prior experiences of sexual trauma. For example, as Stef, a 26-year-old participant stated:

> He waits for a direct yes. I think it's good because he respects the fact that I have consent issues, but it sucks sometimes, because I guess it kills the mood kind of. Because then I think like, 'Well, if I wouldn't have told him [about prior sexual trauma] then he wouldn't ask me, but then I want him to ask me, but I don't because it reminds me of why he has to ask me in the first place.

The evolution of consent in relationships was also regularly expressed as an ongoing discussion of boundaries. This is articulated by 25-year-old Alicia, who stated:

> I've never felt that I couldn't, that we couldn't discuss it, about different sexual activities. And we definitely have conversations about our own boundaries for different activities and what we're comfortable with and not. And those are verbal conversations we'll have outside of a sexual context so I think that's part of it. So my partner knows my boundaries and I'm aware of their boundaries for future interactions but I would say consent at the time, it's not that perfect image of 'you consent to xyz' but I feel positive that I can provide my consent and it is ongoing and checked in.

Discussing consent to specific sexual behaviours was also clearly articulated by 24-year-old Callie:

> We've walked through some scenarios that we're okay with and not okay with. I've explicitly told him even though he's never requested this of me, I just explicitly let him know I'm never going to want to do anal. This is never going to be something I'm ever going to want. I've also told him conditions in which I'm okay with him trying to engage with me while I'm asleep, essentially telling him that I'm okay with a lot of stuff as long as he just doesn't try [penis in vagina]. So, we have talked about things in which we are okay with and not okay with. Yeah, often times that's before anyone even makes a request for it to happen.

A minority of the women expressed how it was sometimes difficult to develop a clear pattern of consent and this evolution of consent is still something that can be hard to navigate. Take Patti, an 18-year-old participant, who said:

> There have been times at the beginning [of our relationship] where I haven't said no, but I will just lay there. Instead of speaking up, it makes me so uncomfortable to speak up that I would rather just be quiet and let it finish instead of speaking up or saying anything ... things are better now, but it can be hard.

Or from 42-year-old Heather: 'Early on in our relationship maybe there was actually less talking, and I was holding it in trying to act like I was fine, but I wasn't. And at some point, whether his therapy or my therapy recognised that's not helping us to progress.'

### *Empowerment to voice sexual needs and wants*

#### *As evolving*

There was also an evolution to the ability to voice needs and wants in the women in this sample. As 25-year-old Lucy expressed: 'I think really for me, getting [comfortable voicing needs and wants] was about making enough mistakes to realise that I needed to be up front with how I felt about things, and not let myself get walked on. That's definitely something that I'm still growing with.' Or as 28-year-old Mel indicated:

> A long time ago I wouldn't. I felt like I disliked myself so much that the bad things that were happening to me or the awful things in my relationships that were happening to me is what I deserved, and that that's how it was and that's how it was going to be, and I just had to accept that. I think through therapy I've learned that I am important too and my needs are important, and if those needs aren't being met, I can say that to my partner and they can choose to either try to meet those needs or tell me that that's out of the question and move on.

The evolution of empowerment to voice needs and wants was also expressed by some as having to evolve from non-sexual to sexual contexts, as demonstrated by this quote from 34-year-old Kate:

> So, I have always generally felt safe voicing general needs and wants. 'I want this for dinner, or it's your turn to do the laundry.' But, in terms of sexual or intimate needs, I had always theoretically felt comfortable, like in theory. I would, be comfortable voicing my needs, but I was a little bit more willing to be like 'oh if that's not what you want, then that's okay.' And it took able time to be able to say 'well, I'm glad that's what you want and I'm happy to acquiesce, but this is what I want too.' And be able to voice those needs.

Our data showed that it was empowering for women when they did see the evolution of voicing their needs and wants come to fruition, as expressed here by 33-year-old Angela:

> I would say for many years of my life as being a sexually active woman, I probably did not ask for what I wanted, or maybe didn't even know what I wanted or what to ask for, and maybe on some level didn't think that my needs were even that important, and I think that honestly, experiencing true loving relationships are what I have considered to be true loving relationships, have I guess empowered me more to ask for what I want and made me feel safe like I could do that and I was worth doing that, and that kind of thing. I think that I have just as a person, grown to know myself and my own needs more, and have gotten more comfortable voicing those to other people and knowing when to take care of myself, honestly. I feel like I'm more in tune with that now, more aligned with my own needs and wants, and when you're more aware of those, you're more capable of voicing that or setting boundaries or that kind of stuff.

### *As requiring vulnerability and safety*
In addition to the ability to voice needs and wants being an evolving process, many women talked about the importance of safety to be able to be vulnerable with someone. This experience was articulated by 26-year-old Mandy:

> In this relationship [I can voice my needs and wants]. I haven't always, but I also think maybe in the past I haven't always felt safe. I guess it was about not wanting to be vulnerable or open up to those people because I didn't care about them or feel safe […] I am willing to be vulnerable in this relationship.

Similarly, 25-year-old Holly said:

> Yeah, I think feeling safe voicing needs and wants is totally critical and I think that's something that I didn't necessarily have in previous relationships and not being able to voice things. I really respect the insecurity of the person that I'm with, so if I'm saying something is not working for me, I'm not making a judgment. I'm not saying you're terrible in bed. You know, but some people will take it that way. I think it just goes back to maybe that we are in this relationship where I showed all my cards right away and so, from the very beginning I've been able to say, you know, like yes [I can voice my needs and wants].

The ability to trust a partner in order to open up was also really important for 24-year-old Sarah, who said:

> You know if we were going to really kind of commit to this, then we were probably going to be in it for the long run, and I think that kind of provided the space to feel safe in voicing my needs and wants and giving me kind of the autonomy. Because I felt like I had a true partner now, not just a boyfriend and not just kind of someone who's there sometimes. I felt like I had a true partner, which gave me the safety to voice my needs and wants. This is the longest relationship I've been in to date, so I think that helps with becoming more and more comfortable with each other, especially since he's the first that I was able to talk to about my trauma. So things like that have contributed to me feeling safe and open and this is probably the most open relationship I've been in and I'm really grateful for that.

### *As a non-negotiable requirement*
Given the history of sexual trauma in the sample of women, the ability to voice wants and needs was a non-negotiable requirement for many of the women. This sentiment is summed up nicely by 24-year-old Callie, who said:

> I realize that if I don't express [needs and wants] I'm going to get used in a way that is traumatizing. And if I express them quietly I may or may not have those wishes respected, but if I express them loudly and with clear intent in my voice there can be no argument – this is not up for debate.

Participants also made this requirement clear to their partners early on in the relationship, articulated here by 27-year-old Mia:

> …It was back when I started to take the power back, of my own body and my own life. I can't recall exactly what it was that made me feel like I wanted to take the power back of my own life and my body. […] When I decided to take that power back in my life, I decided that I would communicate everything that I wanted. The importance of

> making sure that I was happy and I felt good in relationships. Nobody's a mind reader, so it was about explaining this is what I want and this is what I would like. I do that from the outset now. It is a requirement.

Placing the importance on voicing needs and wants as non-negotiable was something learned over time, as expressed by 25-year-old Holly, who said:

> When I was in high school and even starting in middle school, I did not have any boundaries. I just said yes to anything if someone showed any remote interest in me, I did whatever they asked. [...] My needs were not considered and definitely not voiced. That isn't acceptable now.

### *As inherently interpersonal*

The women in this study also discussed how gaining the empowerment to voice their needs and wants relied on support from others, specifically through partners and friends. For example, 21-year-old Hannah reported struggling with expressing her needs and wants to her partner, so she relies on a go-to friend for support:

> There's always that anxiety that comes with [expressing needs and wants to him] and I think that's just almost inherent now. It's not going to go away that easily, no matter how much I trust him. There's always that nervousness that comes up at first. I do have a friend that I talk to beforehand to help get that nervousness out almost start the talk in advance with her so that I can then talk with him later.

For 33-year-old Angela, partners were crucial to helping her get to a point of feeling safe voicing needs and wants: 'I think that honestly, experiencing true loving relationships have empowered me to ask for what I want and made me feel safe.' This was also the case for 37-year-old Ariel, because she didn't feel like others in her life had allowed for the space to really express needs and wants before her current partner:

> In my current relationship, he is my best friend and I never felt like I had a best friend or somebody that I could really count on prior to him in my life, including my parents. Like I always felt like everybody protected [my younger sister] because she wasn't as strong as me and I also never had any friends that were like there for me 100% and he is. That, having him and having that support, let me feel good and free to express my needs and wants.

### *As something that takes work*

Many women talked about how it took a lot of work to get to a place of being able to openly express needs and wants to a partner. This work took a variety of forms, including writing, reading, therapy, and practice. For example, Lucy, a 25-year-old participant noted that writing was really helpful for her to practice:

> I did a lot of writing and just spelling out what I felt over and over again, and kind of made it a practice. Now that is really where I trust myself the most at this point. That's where it becomes empowering. You feel empowered to [express needs and wants], and in doing so, you feel more empowered every time.

Many of the participants have been to therapy to work through their experience of sexual trauma, and in working toward feeling safe to voice needs and wants, 28-year-old Mel said:

> I think through therapy I've learned that I am important too and my needs are important, and if those needs aren't being met, I can say that to my partner and they can choose to either try to meet those needs or tell me that that's out of the question and move on.

Katarina, a 22-year-old participant, stated:

> So in other relationships I haven't felt unsafe voicing [needs], but I haven't been as quick to voice them. And in my current relationships, I've worked a lot more personally at using my words and bringing those things up when they're relatively fresh as opposed to waiting and waiting and waiting to bring them up.

For some participants, the work they did to get through the experience of sexual trauma was helpful for voicing needs and wants. This is articulated here by 26-year-old Cindy:

So it took kind of a long time to work through some of that [sexual trauma], and I think I still am. But I think working through that has helped me figure out ways to kind of say what I need and what is too far for me. So trying to help me draw lines so that I don't end up in that situation anymore, I think was kind of a big thing.

### *As involving echoes of shame and trauma*

Sometimes, participants indicated great difficulty in asking for consent and voicing needs or wants to a partner due to the extent to which it reminded them of their sexual trauma or brought about feelings of shame within them. For example, when discussing comfort with expressing needs and wants to her partner, 25-year-old Jos said:

I mean, it's kind of like an across-the-board no. Yeah. I think it's deep-seeded [shame]. I don't feel like my voice is important. I don't feel like my needs matter. I don't feel like ... I feel a lot of times, if something that I'm hoping for just comes to me, then that's what I deserve, and if it doesn't, then kind of like tough shit. You know what I mean?

Or 29-year-old Margo said 'Yeah, [voicing my needs and wants] is a struggle for me and I think that that's definitely related to the sexual trauma, that it's harder for me than I think on average.' And 22-year-old Cait highlighted the role of shame in saying, 'I do [express my needs and wants], but I think also something holds me back from saying everything. It is more of just my own personal ... I guess I sometimes feel shame.'

Some women, like 33-year-old Jane, reported being confident to voice their needs and wants most of the time, but once in a while they see the deeply engrained misogynistic views sneak in: '[I express my needs and wants] almost always, yes. Oh, hang on. I think, I don't know if that's internalised misogyny or whatever. I still hang on to a few, I don't know, maybe 5% or 10% of the time, ideas like "if I say this he won't like me" bullshit, but almost always.' Heather, a 42-year-old participant, talked about how working through the shame is a work in progress:

There's still a level of shame wrapped up in [voicing needs and wants]. But, I'm so very focused on working on that. And I feel that the level of safety and comfort is on my end, at this point it's not because I don't feel safe with my current partner. I mean, he provides such a really awesome space for me [to] work on things. He's so non-judgmental, and you know, willing to receive whatever I want to share.

## Discussion

This paper drew upon the experiences of 41 women who had a history of sexual trauma but had moved beyond their trauma into healthy sexual relationships. The study aimed to understand how these women navigated sexual consent in their relationships and the extent to which they felt empowered to voice their sexual needs and wants with their partner. Through reflexive thematic analysis, we found that sexual consent was explicit for some women, non-explicit for others, and in many cases, evolving. Sexual agency and empowerment to voice needs and wants was also evolving for many of the participants. It was said to require vulnerability and safety, social support through friends or partners, and, for some, it involved echoes of deeply rooted shame and trauma. For some women, the ability to voice needs and wants to a partner had become a non-negotiable requirement for them to be in the relationship, and almost all women indicated it to be something that takes work. The work it takes to feel empowered to voice needs and wants was not only due to their prior experience of sexual trauma, but due to the society within which we live that does not encourage women to voice needs and wants generally, let alone sexually. An overarching finding was that navigating sexual consent and developing agency are complex and do not happen without specific attention to cultivating consent communication, even in the context of healthy long-term relationships.

Consent was explicit for many women in this sample in part due to their experience with sexual trauma. For some, this was something their partners were adamant about. This may be because all but one woman in the current study had disclosed their history of sexual trauma to their partner; that level of disclosure may not exist for all women who have experienced sexual trauma. For a minority of participants, the act of getting explicit consent from their partner brought up feelings of confusion because it reminded them of the fact that their experience of non-consensual sex was traumatic. Most women indicated they were comfortable refusing sex verbally, though in the course of a longer-term relationship they did not feel this was necessary due to their partner's ability to read their bodily cues. This is in line with prior research that has found a history of a sexual relationship is associated with the (potentially inaccurate) assumption that a partner is interested in and consents to future sexual activity (Beres, 2010, 2014; Humphreys & Brousseau, 2010; Humphreys & Herold, 2007; Muehlenhard et al., 2016) and partners are more likely to assume consent and less likely to explicitly ask for consent as the number of sexual events increases (Livingston et al., 2004; Shotland & Goodstein, 1992; Willis & Jozkowski, 2019). Our findings were also consistent with those of O'Callaghan and colleagues (O'Callaghan et al., 2019) by indicating that when partners act as support providers for sexual trauma, they tend to exercise caution in approaching intimacy.

The negotiation of consent on a behavioural level varied. Some women spoke about negotiating consent in the beginning of the relationship and not needing to as the relationship length increased. Others said they explicitly negotiated sexual consent before each sexual activity, whereas still others reported that they engage in ongoing checking in throughout sexual activity (some verbally but most by picking up on body language and nonverbal cues). Requesting or providing explicit verbal consent was expressed by many of the women to become unnecessary as trust, safety, and comfort in their relationship increased, allowing them to be more open about their sexual needs and wants. This transition is consistent with the women who discussed how their sexual consent practices have evolved over time, which is in line with previous research suggesting that as the relationship length increases, sexual consent becomes more implicit (Livingston et al., 2004; Shotland & Goodstein, 1992; Willis & Jozkowski, 2019).

Time was important for the ability to express sexual agency and communicate consent through feeling safe communicating needs and wants in a relationship. Some women stated that if they did not feel empowered and safe to express their wants and needs, they would be treated in a way that was traumatising, highlighting the need for sexual empowerment to feel able to express sexual consent. Many of the women discussed learning to express their wants and needs in their relationships over time and often stated that their partners have helped them become safer and more comfortable to be able to communicate their feelings openly in their relationship. Many had sought social support but also worked through their issues of safety and being able to express wants and needs through therapy or explicitly practicing using the words necessary to communicate these things that are often difficult to navigate. Most women did indicate that their ability to express their needs and wants had to evolve over time, with some focusing on the role of their prior trauma and others not seeing it as impacting the evolution.

Despite the overwhelming message from these women as one of resilience, some women did indicate echoes of their sexual trauma and resulting shame from that experience. Some fought voices within themselves telling them they did not deserve to get their wants and needs met. They acknowledged this as problematic and as a symptom not only of their history of sexual trauma but also of our society as a whole that does not do a good job of teaching girls and women to voice their needs. This points to a need to continue advocating for comprehensive sexuality education that validates women's sexual experiences as a natural part of human development rather than one that should be ashamed (Schneider & Hirsch, 2018).

Related, women tended to be surprised when their male partner requested explicit consent. Many women talked about how sensitive their male partners were to ensuring they got explicit consent and that it was refreshing for them to have a partner who cared about it that much. It was a demonstration of how much their partner cared for them. A lot of the women's experiences around this provided insight into how poor of a job we are doing in educating people on the importance of consent. Sex education efforts must work on creating programmes that have explicit consent embedded within, where this is not considered an incredible feat, but rather a normal part of a sexual interaction. Further, Willis, Jozkowski et al. (2019) found that sexual consent is not typically included in sexual health education standards and suggested ways in which consent education could be used to appeal to those who are opposed to comprehensive sexuality education. If comprehensive school-based sex education programs are not a possibility (as is the case in many states in the USA), it may be more effective to rebrand sex education as consent education or harassment education in order to emphasise the importance of these messages to parents, school administrators, teachers, and policy makers (Willis, Blunt-Vinti et al., 2019).

Our data also pointed to opportunities for monogamous couples to learn from the experiences of polyamorous couples. A minority of our participants indicated that they were in a polyamorous relationship, but in all three of those interviews, the women indicated extensive communication about consent. For example, one participant talked about how they create lists of what behaviours they are willing to engage in, they colour code the list so they know what is a yes, a maybe, or a no. The negotiation happens with any of the maybe behaviours and the negotiation is continual and revisited often. This is consistent with research showing that polyamorous couples tend to have stronger communication skills in general and specific to sex (Conley et al., 2017; Wosick-Correa, 2010).

A strength of this study was the diversity of voices that were heard; this is consistent with the diversity of women impacted by sexual trauma. Specifically, our sample had a large age range of participants; this is especially important given that much of the prior research on negotiating sexual consent has been conducted in undergraduate samples (e.g. Muehlenhard et al., 2016; Willis, Blunt-Vinti et al., 2019). Only three of our participants (7%) were students at the time of participation, and two of those were graduate students. Additionally, although 65% of the sample identified as straight, the 35% of sexual minority women represented identities of bisexual, lesbian, pansexual, queer, and questioning. Because all but two of our participants were partnered with men at the time of data collection, most of the data in this study on women's current healthy sexual relationships referenced sexual consent in the context of encounters with men. Therefore, it remains important for future research to acknowledge and examine the potentially different dynamics that exist, especially related to navigating sexual consent, in same-gender/same-sex relationships. We did not require that all participants be cisgender women, but we did require that the participant identify as a woman; this may have excluded non-binary or genderqueer individuals who could have provided unique insight into our research questions of interest. Although we would have liked to include more racial and ethnic diversity, there were seven diverse race/ethnicities represented in the sample. We encourage future research to continue to be mindful in oversampling sexual or gender minority groups and racial or ethnic minorities, as was done in Beres et al. (2004) and Willis, Blunt-Vinti et al. (2019), to ensure their voices are being represented in the research. This study included women who have been impacted by sexual trauma and is not meant to generalise beyond that group or even within that group, but rather provide insight into the experiences of these 41 participants. Additionally, as a requirement for participation, the women in this study clearly acknowledged their experience of sexual trauma and results may look different in a sample less willing to acknowledge and process their sexual trauma. The results may also look different in a sample of women without a history of sexual trauma, and this is an area ripe for future research. Sexual agency in women in general is not encouraged or taught (Burkett & Hamilton, 2012; Curtin et al., 2011), so these results may be applicable to a wide range of women, but future research is necessary.

In sum, the data presented in this paper highlighted the complex nature of navigating sexual consent, the empowerment that can come from learning to express sexual agency through voicing sexual needs and wants to a partner, and the rich lessons that women who have experienced sexual trauma have learned in their path toward a healthy sexual relationship. Notably, sexual consent evolves over time within individuals and over the context of relationships. Future research should investigate the mechanisms of change that can be used in individual or couple's therapy for women who have a history of experiencing sexual trauma and their future romantic and sexual partners.

## Acknowledgments

We express deep gratitude to the women who shared their experiences with us through this study.

## Disclosure statement

No potential conflict of interest was reported by the authors.

## ORCID

Kristen P. Mark http://orcid.org/0000-0002-0524-3357
Laura M. Vowels http://orcid.org/0000-0001-5594-2095

## References

Beres, M. A. (2007). 'Spontaneous' sexual consent: An analysis of sexual consent literature. *Feminism & Psychology*, *17*(1), 93–108. https://doi.org/10.1177/0959353507072914

Beres, M. A. (2010). Sexual miscommunication? Untangling assumptions about sexual communication between casual sex partners. *Culture, Health & Sexuality*, *12*(1), 1–14. https://doi.org/10.1080/13691050903075226

Beres, M. A. (2014). Rethinking the concept of consent for anti-sexual violence activism and education. *Feminism & Psychology*, *24*(3), 373–389. https://doi.org/10.1177/0959353514539652

Beres, M. A., Herold, E., & Maitland, S. B. (2004). Sexual consent behaviors in same-sex relationships. *Archives of Sexual Behavior*, *33*(5), 475–486. https://doi.org/10.1023/B:ASEB.0000037428.41757.10

Burkett, M., & Hamilton, K. (2012). Postfeminist sexual agency: Young women's negotiations of sexual consent. *Sexualities*, *15*(7), 815–833. https://doi.org/10.1177/1363460712454076

Carmody, M. (2003). Sexual ethics and violence prevention. *Social & Legal Studies*, *12*(2), 199–216. https://doi.org/10.1177/0964663903012002003

Christopher, F. S., & Kisler, T. S. (2012). College Women's experiences of intimate partner violence: Exploring mental health issues. *NASPA Journal about Women in Higher Education*, *5*(2), 166-183. https://doi.org/10.1515/njawhe-2012-1116

Clarke, V., & Braun, V. (2013). *Successful qualitative research: A practical guide for beginners*. Sage.

Conley, T. D., Matsick, J. T., Moors, A. C., & Ziegler, A. (2017). Investigation of consensually nonmonogamous relationships: Theories, methods, and new directions. *Perspectives on Psychological Science*, *12*(2), 205–232. https://doi.org/10.1177/1745691616667925

Curtin, N., Ward, L. M., Merriwether, A., & Caruthers, A. (2011). Femininity ideology and sexual health in young women: A focus on sexual knowledge, embodiment, and agency. *International Journal of Sexual Health*, *23*(1), 48–62. https://doi.org/10.1080/19317611.2010.524694

Frazier, P., Anders, S., Perera, S., Tomich, P., Tennen, H., Park, C., & Tashiro, T. (2009). Traumatic events among undergraduate students: Prevalence and associated symptoms. *Journal of Counseling Psychology*, *56*(3), 450–460. https://doi.org/10.1037/a0016412

Godbout, N., Sabourin, S., & Lussier, Y. (2009). Child sexual abuse and adult romantic adjustment: Comparison of single- and multiple-indicator measures. *Journal of Interpersonal Violence*, *24*(4), 693–705. https://doi.org/10.1177/0886260508317179

Hickman, S. E., & Muehlenhard, C. L. (1999). "By the semi-mystical appearance of a condom": How young women and men communicate sexual consent in heterosexual situations. *Journal of Sex Research*, *36*(3), 258–272. https://doi.org/10.1080/00224499909551996

Humphreys, T. P., & Brousseau, M. M. (2010). The sexual consent scale–revised: Development, reliability, and preliminary validity. *Journal of Sex Research*, *47*(5), 420–428. https://doi.org/10.1080/00224490903151358

Humphreys, T. P., & Herold, E. (2007). Sexual consent in heterosexual relationships: Development of a new measure. *Sex Roles*, *57*(3–4), 305–315. https://doi.org/10.1007/s11199-007-9264-7

Jordan, C. E., Campbell, R., & Follingstad, D. (2010). Violence and women's mental health: The impact of physical, sexual, and psychological aggression. *Annual Review of Clinical Psychology*, *6*(1), 607–628. https://doi.org/10.1146/annurev-clinpsy-090209-151437

Jozkowski, K. N., Peterson, Z. D., Sanders, S. A., Dennis, B., & Reece, M. (2014). Gender differences in heterosexual college students' conceptualizations and indicators of sexual consent: Implications for contemporary sexual assault prevention education. *Journal of Sex Research*, *51*(8), 904–916. https://doi.org/10.1080/00224499.2013.792326

Jozkowski, K. N., Sanders, S., Peterson, Z. D., Dennis, B., & Reece, M. (2014). Consenting to sexual activity: The development and psychometric assessment of dual measures of consent. *Archives of Sexual Behavior*, *43*(3), 437–450. https://doi.org/10.1007/s10508-013-0225-7

Katz, A. J., Hensel, D. J., Hunt, A. L., Zaban, L. S., Hensley, M. M., & Ott, M. A. (2019). Only yes means yes: Sexual coercion in rural adolescent relationships. *Journal of Adolescent Health*, *65*(3), 423–425. https://doi.org/10.1016/j.jadohealth.2019.04.004

Livingston, J. A., Buddie, A. M., Testa, M., & VanZile-Tamsen, C. (2004). The role of sexual precedence in verbal sexual coercion. *Psychology of Women Quarterly*, *28*(4), 287–297. https://doi.org/10.1111/j.1471-6402.2004.00146.x

Mengo, C., & Black, B. M. (2016). Violence victimization on a college campus. *Journal of College Student Retention: Research, Theory & Practice*, *18*(2), 234–248. https://doi.org/10.1177/1521025115584750

Muehlenhard, C. L., Humphreys, T. P., Jozkowski, K. N., & Peterson, Z. D. (2016). The complexities of sexual consent among college students: A conceptual and empirical review. *Journal of Sex Research*, *53*(4–5), 457–487. https://doi.org/10.1080/00224499.2016.1146651

Novack, S. (2017). Sex ed in higher ed: Should we say yes to "affirmative consent?". *Studies in Gender and Sexuality*, *18*(4), 302–312. https://doi.org/10.1080/15240657.2017.1383074

O'Callaghan, E., Shepp, V., Ullman, S. E., & Kirkner, A. (2019). Navigating sex and sexuality after sexual assault: A qualitative study of survivors and informal support providers. *Journal of Sex Research*, *56*(8), 1045–1057. https://doi.org/10.1080/00224499.2018.1506731

Paolucci, E. O., Genuis, M. L., & Violato, C. (2001). A meta-analysis of the published research on the effects of child sexual abuse. *The Journal of Psychology*, *135*(1), 17–36. https://doi.org/10.1080/00223980109603677

Paquette, G., Martin-Storey, A., Bergeron, M., Dion, J., Daigneault, I., Hébert, M., . . . Castonguay-Khounsombath, S. (2019). Trauma symptoms resulting from sexual violence among undergraduate students: Differences across gender and sexual minority status. *Journal of Interpersonal Violence*, 1–26. https://doi.org/10.1177/0886260519853398

SB-967 California State Legistlature. Student safety: Sexual assault. Section 1. (a) (1). (2014). http://leginfo.legislature.ca.gov/faces/billNavClient.xhtml?bill_id=201320140SB967

Schneider, M., & Hirsch, J. C. (2018). Comprehensive sexuality education as a primary prevention strategy for sexual violence perpetration. *Trauma, Violence & Abuse*, 152483801877285. https://doi.org/10.1177/1524838018772855

Shotland, R. L., & Goodstein, L. (1992). Sexual precedence reduces the perceived legitimacy of sexual refusal: An examination of attributions concerning date rape and consensual sex. *Personality & Social Psychology Bulletin*, *18*(6), 756–764. https://doi.org/10.1177/0146167292186012

Smith, S. G., Zhang, X., Basile, K. C., Merrick, M. T., Wang, J., Kresnow, M., & Chen, J. (2018). The National Intimate Partner and Sexual Violence Survey (NISVS): 2015 Data Brief—Updated Release. National Center for Injury Prevention and Control, Centers for Disease Control and Prevention.

Tansill, E. C., Edwards, K. M., Kearns, M. C., Gidycz, C. A., & Calhoun, K. S. (2012). The mediating role of trauma-related symptoms in the relationship between sexual victimization and physical health symptomatology in undergraduate women. *Journal of Traumatic Stress*, *25*(1), 79–85. https://doi.org/10.1002/jts.21666

Willis, M., Blunt-Vinti, H. D., & Jozkowski, K. N. (2019). Associations between internal and external sexual consent in a diverse national sample of women. *Personality and Individual Differences*, *149*, 37–45. https://doi.org/10.1016/j.paid.2019.05.029

Willis, M., & Jozkowski, K. N. (2019). Sexual precedent's effect on sexual consent communication. *Archives of Sexual Behavior*, *48*(6), 1723–1734. https://doi.org/10.1007/s10508-018-1348-7

Willis, M., Jozkowski, K. N., & Read, J. (2019). Sexual consent in K-12 sex education: An analysis of current health education standards in the USA. *Sex Education*, *19*(2), 226–236. https://doi.org/10.1080/14681811.2018.1510769

Wosick-Correa, K. (2010). Agreements, rules, and agentic fidelity in polyamorous relationships. *Psychology & Sexuality*, *1*(1), 44–61. https://doi.org/10.1080/19419891003634471

Zvara, B. J., Mills-Koonce, W. R., Appleyard Carmody, K., & Cox, M. (2015). Childhood sexual trauma and subsequent parenting beliefs and behaviors. *Child Abuse & Neglect*, *44*, 87–97. https://doi.org/10.1016/j.chiabu.2015.01.012

# South African women's constructions of sexual consent

Kayla Beare and Floretta Boonzaier

**ABSTRACT**
Current understandings of sexual consent do not always acknowledge the effect of overarching social norms and ideals on how sexual consent is constructed. This research explored how women construct sexual consent using a feminist framework that focused on the use of discourses to analyse how power shapes these understandings. We aimed to gain insight into how women talk about sexual consent and the forces they identified as influencing their understandings. Five focus group discussions were conducted with female students from a university in Cape Town, South Africa. The analysis yielded three primary discourses in women's talk of sexual consent: *Consent as a Woman's Call, Consent Without Desire, and Consent as Willingness*. This work contributes to the existing literature on sexual consent by highlighting the context-specific nature of sexual consent and the ways in which power shapes women's constructions of sexual consent in the context of heterosexual relationships.

## Introduction

Sexual consent is generally understood as a mutual agreement to participate in sexual activity that is freely given without the presence of coercion or force (Beres, 2007). However, relationships between sexual partners are often multifaceted and informed by the broader context, making sexual consent more complex than the general understanding suggests (Beres, 2007). There is a growing body of research into the complexities of sexual consent and the current constructions of sexual consent are shifting towards a 'yes means yes' affirmative model of consent as a means of counteracting the complicated role context may play in sexual encounters (Willis et al., 2019). Much of the research into the newer conceptions of sexual consent is within an American setting and little work has been done on constructions of sexual consent in the Global South. Looking at sexual consent in different countries can provide valuable insight into how different contexts inform sexual consent. This paper focuses on how female students at a South African university talk about sexual consent in relation to broader discourses around heteronormative sex (heterosex) and women's sexuality.

Sexual consent is a multidimensional concept that has both behavioural and internal components. Research in sexual consent has identified three different components: 'an internal state of willingness, an act of explicitly agreeing to something, and behaviour that someone else interprets as willingness' (Muehlenhard et al., 2016, p. 462). The internal element of sexual consent refers to the willingness of the individual to engage in sexual activity (Muehlenhard et al., 2016). This is an internal state that cannot be accessed by the individual's potential sexual partners and thus consent requires behavioural elements as a means of communicating consent or a lack thereof (Muehlenhard et al., 2016). Consent can be communicated either explicitly through verbal confirmation or implicitly through behaviours such as obtaining a condom or taking off one's clothes (Muehlenhard et al.,

2016). The verbal and nonverbal elements of consent have been studied in great detail (Beres, 2014; Brady et al., 2018; Jozkowski et al., 2017; Jozkowski & Peterson, 2013; Shumlich & Fisher, 2018; Willis, Blunt-Vinti & Jaskowski, 2019; Willis & Jozkowski, 2018). However, the internal state of consent is also complex and multifaceted. Regarding the within internal states of consent, Halley (2016) made a distinction between positive consent and constrained consent. Positive consent is consent given without hesitation or compromise and rooted in the desire to take part in the sexual activity (Halley, 2016). Constrained consent is consent given when consenting to sex is understood to be preferable to the other available options (Halley, 2016). Halley (2016) gave the example of a female university student who consents to sex at a party because she thinks consenting to sex she does not want is preferable to being bullied or mocked for not having sex.

Constrained consent suggests individuals may consent to sex they do not wholly want or desire (Halley, 2016). The existence of constrained consent does not seem compatible with a comprehensive understanding of consent that accounts for the role of context and power. Within the realm of heterosex, gendered power dynamics play an important role in how consent is understood and communicated. The impact of gender on sexual consent is analysed by looking at experiences of heterosex, namely the different ways in which women and men experience sexual encounters (Shefer & Ruiters, 1998). A key component of this is the power differential between women and men, brought about through patriarchal structures of society (Fine, 1988; Shefer et al., 2000). This power differential results in uneven access to power in heteronormative encounters and in turn affects how consent is communicated and interpreted (Crawford et al., 1994). Heteronormativity plays a role in this power dynamic as it not only prioritises female-male sex, but it also treats heterosex as a space in which to produce and reproduce ideas around what it means to be a woman or a man (Beres, 2018). According to Shefer et al. (2000), some men view sex as a space where they are able to construct and reinforce masculinity. Given this, some women may engage in unwanted heterosex to protect their partner's pride (Frith, 2018) or to fulfil the perceived responsibility of being a partner in a heterosexual intimate relationship (Vannier & O'Sullivan, 2011). This phenomenon, known as sexual compliance, has been found to be more common among women than men (Vannier & O'Sullivan, 2011). Consequently, women's individual choices regarding sexual consent are limited by the presence of heteronormative discourses that shape their experiences (Beres, 2018).

These widespread social ideas are manifestations of overarching power structures, all of which influence the ways in which heterosex is scripted (Frith & Kitzinger, 2001). Frith and Kitzinger (2001) noted some women sexually comply because rejection is not a part of the normalised sexual script upon which sexual encounters are based. If any form of rejection is present in the script, it is understood as token resistance (Bruen, 2016; Frith & Kitzinger, 2001). There is also a belief that women do not enjoy sex, which has been labelled 'the missing discourse of desire' (Fine, 1988, p. 29). Although there has been a shift towards a more pleasure positive construction of women's sexuality over the past thirty years, research in the South African context has shown there is still silence regarding women's sexual desires (Bhana et al., 2019; Saville Young et al., 2019). When women's sexual desire is silenced or ignored, women are cast as gatekeepers of consent, not as autonomous individuals who own and control their own sexual expression and experiences (Hickman & Muehlenhard, 1999; Meek, 2016). The ignorance of women's pleasure is manufactured to serve the purpose of silencing women and their sexual desire and autonomy (Fine, 1988). Removing sexual agency from women in this way perpetuates the physical and psychological power imbalances present in the patriarchy, which allows for the preservation of power and control in this oppressive structure (Shefer et al., 2000). Sexism and heterosex interact in a cycle of gendered power dynamics, which directly affect the way in which sexual consent is constructed (Beres, 2007).

Understandings of sexual consent are a product of the discourses around gender and sexuality that dominate the social context (Tiefer, 2002). The presence of prescribed gender roles and heteronormative ideals can act as a kind of coercion, which threatens to invalidate consent in the same way coercion between individual partners can (Gavey, 1997, 2013). As it stands, much of the research on sexual consent is conducted in the United States and Canada, and it is important to explore how sexual consent is constructed in different countries. The role of context is important in understanding sexual consent, thus consent in different contexts should be explored. The present study was conducted in South Africa, a country that has high rates of gender-based violence and sexual violence, with studies suggesting rates as high as one in three men perpetrating sexual violence (Kuo et al., 2019; Moyo & Ziramba, 2013). We sought seeks to explore how women's understandings of sexual consent are configured in the context of a country where sexual violence is present. In light of the complicated nature of consent, the aim of this work was to gain insight into women's own understandings of sexual consent and the role gendered power dynamics play in shaping these.

## Method

This study required a research design sensitive to the complex nature of gender because gendered power dynamics were a central focus of the study. As such, feminist research, which accounts for the presence of gender, power, and the relationship between the two, was best suited (Beetham & Demetriades, 2007). Given the constructionist nature of the study, a qualitative approach was used to bring focus to the effect of context and individual beliefs. Additionally, qualitative research does not aim to assess possible explanations but rather analyse understandings, which is helpful in exploratory studies such as this one, as it is one of the first sexual consent studies in a South African context.

Focus groups were used in the study because they are well-suited to assess sensitive topics and allow participants to remain silent should there be certain topics they do not feel comfortable discussing (Överlien et al., 2005). The group environment allows for empathy and emotional support for participants and assists in navigating taboo topics, such as the topic of sexual consent (Kitzinger, 1994). Additionally, an important component of this study was the creation of co-constructed understandings of sexual consent that provided insight into how groups of women talk about sexual consent. The use of focus groups can provide collective perceptions of social phenomena through the interpersonal nature of the interaction (Kitzinger, 1994). Supporting the feminist framework of the project, the use of focus groups also helped address the power imbalance between the researcher and the participants by shifting the power dynamics in favour of the participants (Kitzinger, 1994).

### *Participants*

The 25 participants in this study were all students at a South African university. They all had experiences with romantic, heterosexual relationships. Purposive sampling was employed because it is effective when wanting to gain an understanding of a select population (Robinson, 2014). Seventeen of the participants were sourced through the university, making use of existing communication channels with students. Participants were given class credits for participating in the focus groups. The remaining eight participants were sourced through the researcher's social circles. Twenty-four participants identified as cisgender women, and one participant identified as genderqueer. The participants' ages ranged from nineteen to thirty-eight years old. The mean age was 21.8 years old and the standard deviation was 3.81. There were eleven Black participants and fourteen White participants. One participant identified as Nigerian and the other participants identified as South African. Seventeen of the participants were single, and the remaining eight were in romantic relationships. Sixteen of the participants identified as heterosexual, one as gay, three as queer, and three as bisexual; one participant did not specify their sexual orientation.

### *Procedure*

Five focus groups were held for the data collection stage of this research. The focus groups ranged from three to eight people. The group discussions were an hour long and held in English, run by the primary researcher, making the group gender congruent. The discussion revolved around five open-ended questions relating to how sexual consent was understood in relation to being a woman:

(1) What kinds of things come to mind when you think about sexual consent?
(2) How do you think being a woman affects your understanding of sexual consent?
(3) Explain the difference between consensual sex and desired sex
(4) How do you feel about initiating sex, as a woman?
(5) What is your role, as a woman, in consensual sex?

The questions acted as prompts to facilitate a broad-ranging discussion among participants in the group, rather than a static question-and-answer manner.

### Ethics
The Research Committee of the Department of Psychology and Department of Student Affairs both granted this study ethical approval. The well-being of the participants was protected through informed consent and confidentiality

The participants in this study were asked to sign consent forms that explained the purpose and procedure of the focus group, including risks, benefits, and confidentiality matters. The group discussions were recorded once participants had consented to being recorded. Transcriptions were available only to the primary researcher and supervisor. Pseudonyms were used in the final write up of the project to further protect confidentiality (Orb et al., 2001).

The focus groups were conducted on the university campus in a private, secure location to ensure participants' safety. The use of focus groups were intended to give participants control to disclose only information they felt comfortable sharing, thereby limiting emotional distress (Wilkinson, 1998). Additionally, the presence of ongoing consent aimed to minimise emotional distress and a clear explanation of the participants' right to leave at any point was given before every focus group to ensure ongoing consent was present. A short debriefing was conducted after the recording devices had been turned off at the end of the session and referral forms were handed out.

### Analysis
The analysis of the participants' talk aimed to gain insight into how participants' understood sexual consent through their language and the discourses they drew on. The focus on power in the project made Foucauldian Discourse Analysis (FDA) a well-suited analysis style for the data. The data were read and re-read to identify discursive objects. There were four discursive objects that emerged: present consent, women's sexuality, sexual compliance, and women's consent. Direct and indirect references to these four objects were identified and compiled and then situated within broader discourses. Situating the discursive objects within broader discourses provided insight into how power structures and context influence how the discursive objects are formed and informed (Willig, 2008). The action orientation of the discourses and discursive objects was analysed to assess how the language used by participants limited or allowed for action. Action orientation was looked at in relation to each of the participants' subject positions to establish how the discourses they used influenced their relationship with sexual consent. Three major discourses emerged through the FDA after the initial coding for discursive objects and analysis of the action orientations, broader discourses, and subject positions. The analysis process was performed by the primary researcher and then reviewed by their supervisor to ensure the credibility and authenticity of the analysis.

## Results
Three primary discourses emerged in women's talk of sexual consent, relationships and gender: *Consent as a Woman's Call, Consent Without Desire*, and *Discourses of Willing Consent*.

## Consent as a woman's call

Participants identified their being gendered as women as a key contributor to their understandings of sexual consent and their role in heterosex. The majority of the talk in this discourse, as well as across the discourses in the data, focused on heterosex regardless of the sexual orientation of the participants. 'Maybe this goes without saying but I made a point of realising that I thought of it only as a woman's thing' (Gemma, FG1). Some participants talked about it as a responsibility: 'when it comes to consent, it's like put all on to a woman' (Simphiwe, FG2). Others talked about it as a kind of social tool:

> Like in a way, consent is almost like a mercy ... for a guy, if he wanted it to stop he could just push you off. Whereas for a girl, you have to say no ... and just hope the guy is going to be decent. (Elise, FG1)

All three of the participants quoted here identified as queer or bisexual but the language they used to describe sexual consent is very much in line with the dominant heteronormative discourses of sex and consent. When consent was constructed as a woman's call, ideas of men as initiators of sex were present:

Toni: I would say the correlation between consent and being a woman is that um, we're taught to think that consent is something that should be asked of us [all: (sounds of agreement)] as opposed to something that we should be asking our partners [Alex: Yeah] um, particularly in a heterosexual encounter, we expect to be asked for our consent and we're not necessarily told that we should be asking for consent as well [Alex: (sounds of agreement)] um, which I would say is something that we're taught as women because sex is something that happens to us. (FG2)

The role of power in the women as gatekeepers and men as initiators structure was identified:

Emily: They're the ones that end up asking for consent, so we're always, we tend to end up being the ones who consent so I think that's the power imbalance there, because, and it's sort of, ya, and also then contributes to that whole factor where like men are the ones who enjoy sex and women are the ones who let them have sex.

Lelethu: We're giving and they're taking. (FG5)

The phrasing used by Toni, Emily, and Lelethu in these two separate accounts constructs women as absent in sexual encounters, even consensual ones. Women are talked about as 'giving' consent to sex, which implies that sex is something that men are 'taking.'

Participants talked about men's desire to have sex as ever-present. 'If there was ever a time at which I myself wanted to have sex, the guy would always be willing' (Lara, FG3). Sex was expected to happen even when 'the guy could be in no mood' (Emily, FG5). The silence around men's consent is touched on: 'We won't know about men when it comes to consent because they don't say much about it' (Anathi, FG4).

## Consent without desire

This set of discourses consisted of how participants made sense of their reasons for consenting to sex they did not desire. In some cases, participants talked about fear as a motivator:

> I'm verbally telling him no, no, no ... in my mind I was like "Okay, maybe I should just give him what he wants, and I get out of this situation and I'll be fine." At least I'm consenting, to an extent, where I won't be physically harmed ... I eventually gave in ... because I was fearful ... he was very aggressive. (Raisa, FG3)

Raisa later spoke about the power dynamic present in heterosex and placed the responsibility of equalising the power dynamics on men.

> There's obviously that power dynamic where you, you feel uncomfortable to say no ... as a man a lot of times, when you have the upper hand with regards to certain stuff and you have to be cognisant of how that plays out with a girl. (Raisa, FG3)

The role of relationship hygiene as pressure to 'consent' to unwanted sex was common in the data. Participants who were, or had been, in long-term heterosexual relationships described cases where sex with their partners had been a chore – something done to appease their partners, not because they themselves had desired sex.

Regine: Like just having sex so they can stop asking you for sex ... it was totally consensual, I consented so that I could read my book ... but um, I did not want to have sex with him at all.

Raisa: I feel like that happens a lot if you speak to females in general ... yes you love him and everything but you just don't want it in that moment so you "you know" to satisfy him. (FG3)

Other participants constructed consensual, unwanted sex as more of an act of love than a chore and were challenged by the group:

Lelethu: Can I just ask, why did you stay in a three-year relationship and not say "I don't enjoy it when you do this?"

Frankie: Dude I loved him so much. [laughter]

Ella: I understand it with love, love muddles everything. You're just like "I'll do this because I love you." (FG5)

The difficulty that participants felt at rejecting sex was implicitly and explicitly present in the discussions. One participant noted that she only felt comfortable rejecting men's advances when she identified as lesbian:

> I did like kick him out of my room but what was really weird for me was that was the first time where I felt like I could actually stand up to a man and it was because um, I think it was because in a way my sexual orientation sort of gave me strength because I know I wanted nothing to do with this man. Whereas with previous relationships where I had been with men I would fall into it because I would feel either guilty about not doing it or I'd be scared of the repercussions. (Lara, FG3)

The participant above equates the adoption of a heterosexual sexuality as one that makes it difficult to be firm about not consenting to sex and thus suggests that her adoption of a lesbian identity is one that protects her. Lara's account sheds light on how intersectional identities inform understandings of sexual consent. In South Africa, there is violence directed towards lesbian women, particularly Black lesbian women (Mwambene & Wheal, 2015; Reddy et al., 2015). As a White woman, Lara talked about her identity as a lesbian woman as something that strengthened her ability to negotiate sexual encounters.

### *Consent as willingness*

Participants often made use of factors involved in sexual violence to define consent. Consent was talked about as a lack of sexual violence as opposed to sexual violence being a lack of consent. The importance of 'being in a sound state of mind' (Regina, FG3) was highlighted and consent was questioned if substances had been used: 'if you're drunk or whatever, is it really consent?' (Ivy, FG4). A recurring idea in the discussions was that when one gives into consistent pressure to have sex, this is not sexual consent, with participants challenging the 'persistence beats resistance' narrative (Lucy, FG5). The role of popular culture in the normalisation of the persistence beats resistance narrative was identified:

> But I mean there's also been painted like a very romanticized picture of kind of forced consent in movies and media, like how men do not respect a woman's "nos" like if a woman says no, you should be persistent and you should keep on following and somehow this is almost seen as something romantic [Ashlyn: (sounds of agreement)] like following her, like standing outside of her door with flowers and it's like, it's creepy! [Ashlyn: ya] I said no, I don't want you here, and now you're showing up and it's still portrayed as something romantic. (Laura, FG4)

Participants identified mutuality and continuity as two important factors that need to be present for sexual consent to be present.

> I think of it as a two-way street, because it shouldn't be just one person asking for consent to do something to another person, it should be a participatory act between two people, or more, who are asking each other for consent. (Toni, FG2)

The role of respect between sexual partners was included in the idea of mutuality and continuity.

Laura: A mutual kind of agreement or respect towards each other. Sort of ...

Ashlyn: Ya, agreement is the first word that comes in my mind

Nonto: Respect, mutual agreement

Anathi: Similar, like agreeing to be, being on the same page with regards to being intimate

Laura: But it's also something that it should be continuously, it's not like we've been talking about having sex but it's something that should be continuously through the whole ... (FG4)

The presence of mutuality and continuity were the two factors that participants identified as necessary and important in the presence of sexual consent, whilst talking about persistence as a factor that needs to be absent in order for consent to be present.

## Discussion

Conversations between participants about shared experiences and mutual beliefs, as well as contradicting ones, created the ability to form co-constructed understandings of sexual consent. These interactions allowed for participants to agree with, challenge, or expand on comments made by others in the focus groups. This provided insight into which ideas around heterosex are widespread and what happens when individuals choose to accept or reject these ideas.

The findings of this research suggested that women's understandings of sexual consent in South Africa are linked to patriarchal power structures and gender roles. As can be seen in the discourses of *Consent as a Woman's Call*, many participants identified their gender as an influential factor in their understandings of consent. They talked about consent being their right and responsibility as women. The perception of consent as a woman's call is developed from the idea that women are gatekeepers of consent and men are initiators of sex (Allen, 2003; Frith & Kitzinger, 2001). Phrases such as 'maybe this goes without saying' that participants used when drawing on discourses of consent as a woman's call speaks to how widespread such discourses are.

The construction of women as gatekeepers of consent was seen as a kind of social tool by some participants – one of whom constructed consent as a way to counteract the physical advantage that men have in sexual encounters. The reference to the physical power differentials relates to how men are constructed as having more power in the realm of brute strength and from this stems a fear that keeps social power dynamics unequal (Millett, 2016). The ways in which one participant constructed the 'power' that women and men hold is interesting in that physical power is constructed as more persuasive than the 'power to say no.' In the latter form of power, according to this participant, women are still reliant on men to be 'decent' in order for their desires to be validated. The result is thus dictated by the demeanour and actions of the current sexual partner, by the man, rather than by women's refusal to participate in sexual activity.

The discourses of relying on men to respect her refusal of consent speak to the token-like nature of the role of women as gatekeepers of consent. Although assigning the role of gatekeepers to women in sexual encounters appears to assign power to women, that is not the case. A woman can only act as a gatekeeper if she has access to the ability to say no and if her refusal is respected (Rossetto & Tollison, 2017). The patriarchal structure in which heterosex takes place limits women's access to power, meaning that women may not always be able to say no (Rossetto & Tollison, 2017).

Thus, although gatekeeping appears to be a position of power, it may be a position with a lack of power.

Furthermore, placing women in the position of gatekeepers has a number of negative implications. Casting women as recipients of men's sexual desires places women in a subservient role that reinforces the uneven power dynamics in our patriarchal structure (Brown-Bowers et al., 2015). Consequently, men's sexual desires are prioritised over women's sexual desires and women's sexual desires are constructed as existing only ever in response to men and not as valid in their own right (Beres, 2014). Casting men as initiators of sex also creates silence regarding men's consent. As can be seen in the participants' discussions, many focused on how men desire sex and initiate sex but there was little conversation about men's consent. As one participant pointed out, men's consent is not spoken about very often. Research suggests that men experience unwanted sex, as women do, but there are not enough discourses around men's sexual consent (Banyard et al., 2007). The role of power and context also affects how men understand and construct sexual consent and could result in men consenting to sex that they do not desire (Jozkowski, 2015a).

When consent is constructed as a woman's choice, it links to ideas of sex as something given by women to men, which can result in consensual sex that is not mutually desired (Peterson & Muehlenhard, 2007). The difference between sex that is consensual and sex that is desired complicates our understandings of sexual consent because how could the absence of desire be consent? This difference was discussed in the focus groups within the discourses of Consent Without Desire.

Consent without desire is situated within the broader context of heterosexual negotiation, where sex is perceived as something women do for men and not for themselves, meaning that their sexual desire is not talked about as a necessity in consensual sex (Shefer & Ruiters, 1998). Placing themselves in these discourses limits participants' sexual autonomy and encourages, or coerces, them to act in ways that fit heteronormative standards that perpetuate unequal gendered power dynamics. One participant's account of consenting to sex out of fear is an extreme case of such power dynamics; her use of the phrase 'to an extent' speaks to the idea that consenting as a means of avoiding physical harm may not be constructed as genuine consent as it is not freely given (Remick, 1992). Despite this, she used the term 'consenting' which potentially illustrates the inadequacies of language to convey the varied forms of sexual coercion that women are subjected to (Gunnarsson, 2018). This participant did not describe the example above as rape, yet she is unable to find the language to express this beyond the idea that she was 'consenting.' The space between consensual sex and rape, referred to as 'grey rape,' consists of situations such as the one this participant described (Kipnis, 2017, p. 198). The existence of 'grey rape' speaks to how complex sexual consent truly is, when the context of the sexual encounter is highlighted and attention is paid to the broader social expectations and normalisations of heterosexual interactions. Furthermore, this participant's account addressed how the presence of verbal consent does not mean sexual consent is categorically present and, in doing so, further highlights the importance of accounting for context (Halley, 2016; Willis & Jozkowski, 2019).

Participants talked about other cases in which they consented to sex they did not desire – yet fear of aggression was not a contributing factor. The consent they talked about fit into discourses of constrained consent as opposed to positive consent. Participants who were in, or had been in, long-term heterosexual relationships described cases where they had consented to unwanted sex as a means of maintaining their relationships or avoiding conflict with their partners. Sexual acquiescence such as this is generally described as coercion in theory (Basile, 1999), yet participants talked about these sexual experiences as normal and expected. Sexual compliance is talked about as a kind of requirement in romantic heterosexual relationships, where a woman's role is constructed as having to 'give' her partner sex regularly (Burkett & Hamilton, 2012).

The co-construction of sexual compliance as an act of love created by two participants placed them both within the popular romantic script that women have sex as an act of love. The links between femininity and emotional attachment to sex lead to ideas of women engaging in sex for intimacy and not sexual gratification, again silencing notions of women's agency in sexual desire (Allen, 2003). This kind of heterosexual negotiation is an example of how women understand their own sexual identities as something constructed by and for their partners (Shefer et al., 2000). The participants not having a sexual identity that existed outside of their sexual partners infringed on their understanding of sexual autonomy and in turn normalised sex without desire because participants did not perceive sex as something they did for themselves.

Much of the conversation around the understandings of sexual consent between participants made use of instances where sexual consent was not present as a kind of reference point. This is indicative of the current lack of a concrete definition of sexual consent in positive sexual encounters (Beres, 2007). Participants talked about the relationship between consent and alcohol, many of them arguing that alcohol nullifies or negatively affects one's ability to consent. There is a large body of research into the relationship between consent and alcohol, particularly within university settings (Flack et al., 2016; Haikalis et al., 2017; Minow & Einolf, 2009; Orchowski et al., 2016).

A recurring idea in the discussions was that when one gives into consistent pressure to have sex, this is not sexual consent. The 'persistence beats resistance' was perceived in how sexual consent is often depicted, meaning that – socially speaking – the current understandings of sexual consent do not follow the idea that 'no means no,' but rather problematically recognise rejection as a step in a standard sexual encounter (Frith & Kitzinger, 2001). The role of media's depictions of men's persistence as romantic was explicitly identified by more than one participant. There are many instances of television shows, movies, and songs that use refusals to acknowledge a woman's rejection as an indication of emotional commitment or romance, and the normalisation of this behaviour filters down into individual sexual encounters (Van Damme, 2010). The only account given by a participant where they were able to stop a man from continuously pursuing them was when the participant identified as lesbian. This account speaks to how women, and men, are taught that women should only reject sex when they have a reason to do so (Muehlenhard et al., 2016).

When participants focused on present elements of consent, mutuality and continuity were identified as important elements of present consent. Phrases such as 'two-way street,' 'mutual agreement,' and 'continuously' were used by participants. The participants' co-constructed ideas drew on discourses of consent as willingness (Muehlenhard et al., 2016). Participants spoke about consent in a way that was directly opposed to widespread social ideas of consent as a woman's choice and sexual compliance. Participants did not refer to any form of gender roles, or even gendered pronouns, when speaking about sexual consent in this way. Placing themselves within the *Consent as Willingness* discourse allowed for participants to talk about consent as a shared right and responsibility. The different ways in which discourses of willing consent were used by participants encouraged them to adopt a 'you don't gotta do what you don't wanna do' attitude towards their sexual encounters.

The ways in which participants talked about sexual consent can inform educators on what needs to be looked at when creating educational tools about sexual consent for both women and men. The importance of mutual and ongoing consent – and the effect of social pressure, substance use, and expectations within relationships on one's ability to consent – are all factors that need to be addressed when teaching people about sexual consent. Although the background of the participants' sex education is unknown, the discourses drawn on in the discussions suggested that there had been some exposure to sexual assault prevention discourses. Ideas such as 'no means no' and that alcohol and consent should not interact are key concepts of risk-avoidance discourses that focus on sexual assault prevention (Brooks, 2008; Jozkowski, 2015b). The role of religion on sex education was mentioned briefly by a participant who spoke about the silence around women's sexuality within Islam and how she felt it affected her ability to initiate sex; thus, she had to adopt the role of gatekeeper in sexual encounters. This suggests that sex education may be best suited to a non-secular approach. The ideas of consent as mutual and ongoing should be placed at the centre of sex education to move away from risk-avoidance discourses and towards more sex-positive sex education.

Many of the findings in this project are similar to those seen in research done into sexual consent in the Global North, particularly the United States and Canada. The similarities between the existing research and this project provide insight into some of the shared elements of understandings of sexual consent across countries. These similarities may demonstrate how widespread patriarchal and heteronormative power structures inform sexual consent on a widespread level.

## Limitations and strengths

Given the focus of this study on women's constructions of sexual consent in heterosexual contexts in South Africa, this study is limited by the lack of representation of queer relationships. The focus group questions did not explicitly refer to heterosex but the conversation revolved around ideas of heterosex, despite there being several queer participants. The participants assumed that the discussion was about heterosex, even those that did not engage in heterosex themselves, and answered accordingly. It is worth noting that participants had this response, as it shows how widespread the assumption of heterosexuality is. It also suggests that further research into consent in queer relationships may require a research question and design that explicitly places sexual orientation at the centre of the research to counteract the assumption of heterosexuality that is present in our society.

The participants in this project offered unique insights into women's understandings of sexual consent. Much of sexual consent research is done in the United States with primarily White university students (Willis et al., 2019). The representation of Black participants in this project widened the scope of the research. Although there were no explicit references from the participants to the effect of race on their understandings of consent, the co-constructed ideas that arose from the focus groups were informed by participants' lived experiences as Black women in South Africa. Further research into the relationship between race and sexual consent needs to be conducted, with the primary focus of the research being on how power, race, and gender intersect and how this affects understandings of sexual consent.

## Conclusion

The findings of this research are in line with the pre-existing literature in the field of consent. The existence of discourses of consent as a woman's call and consent without desire are common, and their presence in this project attests to that. The setting in which this research takes place, in South Africa, where rates of gender-based violence and sexual violence are high, speaks to the global nature of these discourses.

Despite the limitations of the current study, the different ways in which women construct sexual consent provides some insight into the shared understandings of consent and the influence of widespread social ideas on these understandings. These nuances can help develop a definition of sexual consent that contradicts ideas of heteronormativity and sexual compliance. Such a definition should include the role of women's sexual desire and treat it as equally as important as men's sexual desires. Furthermore, the definition of sexual consent should emphasise mutuality and continuity to ensure that all parties feel able to give or withdraw consent at any point throughout the sexual encounter. A definition of sexual consent that includes these factors will make space for a construction of heterosex that is mutually desired and mutually beneficial. This study suggests that although women's understandings of sexual consent are still informed by patriarchal ideals, there is a movement towards a construction of sexual consent that, not only acknowledges such social influences, but actively fights against them.

## Disclosure statement

No potential conflict of interest was reported by the authors.

## References

Allen, L. (2003). Girls want sex, boys want love: Resisting dominant discourses of (hetero) sexuality. *Sexualities, 6*(2), 215–236. https://doi.org/10.1177/1363460703006002004

Banyard, V. L., Ward, S., Cohn, E. S., Plante, E. G., Moorhead, C., & Walsh, W. (2007). Unwanted sexual contact on campus: A comparison of women's and men's experiences. *Violence and Victims, 22*(1), 52. https://doi.org/10.1891/vv-v22i1a004

Basile, K. C. (1999). Rape by acquiescence: The ways in which women "give in" to unwanted sex with their husbands. *Violence against Women, 5*(9), 1036–1058. doi: 10.1177/10778019922181617

Beetham, G., & Demetriades, J. (2007). Feminist research methodologies and development: Overview and practical application. *Gender and Development, 15*(2), 199–216. https://doi.org/10.1080/13552070701391086

Beres, M. (2007). Spontaneous sexual consent: An analysis of sexual consent literature. *Feminism & Psychology, 17*(1), 93–108. https://doi.org/10.1177/0959353507072914

Beres, M. (2014). Rethinking the concept of consent for anti-sexual violence activism and education. *Feminism & Psychology, 24*(3), 373–389. https://doi.org/10.1177/0959353514539652

Beres, M. (2018). What does faking orgasms have to do with sexual consent? *Sexualities, 21*(4), 702–705. https://doi.org/10.1177/1363460717708151

Bhana, D., Crewe, M., & Aggleton, P. (2019). Sex, sexuality and education in South Africa. *Sex Education, 19*(4), 361–370. doi: 10.1080/14681811.2019.1620008

Brady, G., Lowe, P., Brown, G., Osmond, J., & Newman, M. (2018). All in all it is just a judgement call: Issues surrounding sexual consent in young people's heterosexual encounters. *Journal of Youth Studies, 21*(1), 35–50. https://doi.org/10.1080/13676261.2017.1343461

Brooks, O. (2008). Consuming alcohol in bars, pubs and clubs: A risky freedom for young women? *Annals of Leisure Research, 11*(3–4), 331–350. https://doi.org/10.1080/11745398.2008.9686801

Brown-Bowers, A., Gurevich, M., Vasilovsky, A. T., Cosma, S., & Matti, S. (2015). Managed not missing: Young women's discourses of sexual desire within a postfeminist heterosexual marketplace. *Psychology of Women Quarterly, 39*(3), 320–336. https://doi.org/10.1177/0361684314567303

Bruen, M. (2016). *Negotiating sexual consent among heterosexual students on a university campus*. University of British Columbia.

Burkett, M., & Hamilton, K. (2012). Postfeminist sexual agency: Young women's negotiations of sexual consent. *Sexualities, 15*(7), 815–833. https://doi.org/10.1177/1363460712454076

Crawford, J., Kippax, S., & Waldby, C. (1994). Women's sex talk and men's sex talk: Different worlds. *Feminism & Psychology, 4*(4), 571–587. https://doi.org/10.1177/0959353594044010

Fine, M. (1988). Sexuality, schooling, and adolescent females: The missing discourse of desire. *Harvard Educational Review, 58*(1), 29–54. https://doi.org/10.17763/haer.58.1.u0468k1v2n2n8242

Flack, W. F., Jr, Hansen, B. E., Hopper, A. B., Bryant, L. A., Lang, K. W., Massa, A. A., & Whalen, J. E. (2016). Some types of hookups may be riskier than others for campus sexual assault. *Psychological Trauma: Theory, Research, Practice, and Policy, 8*(4), 413. https://doi.org/10.1037/tra0000090

Frith, H. (2018). Faking, finishing and forgetting. *Sexualities, 21*(4), 697–701. https://doi.org/10.1177/1363460717708149

Frith, H., & Kitzinger, C. (2001). Reformulating sexual script theory: Developing a discursive psychology of sexual negotiation. *Theory & Psychology, 11*(2), 209–232. https://doi.org/10.1177/0959354301112004

Gavey, N. (1997). Feminist poststructuralism and discourse analysis. *Toward a New Psychology of Gender*, 49–64. https://books.google.co.za/books?hl=en&lr=&id=PAMGKPRxUoYC&oi=fnd&pg=PP65&dq=Gavey,+N.+(1997).+Feminist+poststructuralism+and+discourse+analysis.+Toward+a+New+Psychology+of+Gender&ots=JbwHod5Pin&sig=UXrFefCVtWOrtvdfXDkoqtup4MM#v=onepage&q=Gavey%2C%20N.%20(1997).%20Feminist%20poststructuralism%20and%20discourse%20analysis.%20Toward%20a%20New%20Psychology%20of%20Gender&f=false

Gavey, N. (2013). *Just sex?: The cultural scaffolding of rape*. Routledge.

Gunnarsson, L. (2018). Excuse me, but are you raping me now? Discourse and experience in (the Grey areas of) sexual violence. *NORA-Nordic Journal of Feminist and Gender Research, 26*(1), 4–18. https://doi.org/10.1080/08038740.2017.1395359

Haikalis, M., DiLillo, D., & Gervais, S. J. (2017). Up for grabs? Sexual objectification as a mediator between women's alcohol use and sexual victimization. *Journal of Interpersonal Violence, 32*(4), 467–488. https://doi.org/10.1177/0886260515586364

Halley, J. (2016). The move to affirmative consent. *Signs: Journal of Women in Culture and Society, 42*(1), 257–279. https://doi.org/10.1086/686904

Hickman, S. E., & Muehlenhard, C. L. (1999). "By the semi-mystical appearance of a condom": How young women and men communicate sexual consent in heterosexual situations. *Journal of Sex Research, 36*(3), 258–272. https://doi.org/10.1080/00224499909551996

Jozkowski, K. N. (2015a). Barriers to affirmative consent policies and the need for affirmative sexuality. *The University of the Pacific Law Review, 47*(4), 741. https://scholarlycommons.pacific.edu/cgi/viewcontent.cgi?referer=https://scholar.google.co.za/&httpsredir=1&article=1135&context=uoplawreview

Jozkowski, K. N. (2015b). Yes means yes? Sexual consent policy and college students. *Change: The Magazine of Higher Learning, 47*(2), 16–23. https://doi.org/10.1080/00091383.2015.1004990

Jozkowski, K. N., Marcantonio, T. L., & Hunt, M. E. (2017). College students' sexual consent communication and perceptions of sexual double standards: A qualitative investigation. *Perspectives on Sexual and Reproductive Health, 49*(4), 237–244. https://doi.org/10.1363/psrh.12041

Jozkowski, K. N., & Peterson, Z. D. (2013). College students and sexual consent: Unique insights. *Journal of Sex Research, 50*(6), 517–523. https://doi.org/10.1080/00224499.2012.700739

Kipnis, L. (2017). *Unwanted advances: Sexual paranoia comes to campus*. Harper Collins.

Kitzinger, J. (1994). The methodology of focus groups: The importance of interaction between research participants. *Sociology of Health & Illness, 16*(1), 103–121. https://doi.org/10.1111/1467-9566.ep11347023

Kuo, C., Mathews, C., LoVette, A., Harrison, A., Orchowski, L., Pellowski, J. A., Atujuna, M., Stein, D. J., & Brown, L. K. (2019). Perpetration of sexual aggression among adolescents in South Africa. *Journal of Adolescence, 72*(1), 32–36. https://doi.org/10.1016/j.adolescence.2019.02.002

Meek, M. (2016). *Consent puzzles: Narrative ambiguities of girls' sexual agency in literature and film from the 1990s*. Proquest Dissertations Publishing.

Millett, K. (2016). *Sexual politics*. Columbia University Press.

Minow, J. C., & Einolf, C. J. (2009). Sorority participation and sexual assault risk. *Violence against Women, 15*(7), 835–851. https://doi.org/10.1177/1077801209334472

Moyo, B., & Ziramba, E. (2013). The impact of crime on inbound tourism to South Africa: An application of the bounds test. *African Security Review, 22*(1), 4–18. https://doi.org/10.1080/10246029.2012.737815

Muehlenhard, C. L., Humphreys, T. P., Jozkowski, K. N., & Peterson, Z. D. (2016). The complexities of sexual consent among college students: A conceptual and empirical review. *The Journal of Sex Research, 53*(4–5), 457–487. https://doi.org/10.1080/00224499.2016.1146651

Mwambene, L., & Wheal, M. (2015). Realisation or oversight of a constitutional mandate? Corrective rape of black African lesbians in South Africa. *African Human Rights Law Journal, 15*(1), 58–88. https://doi.org/10.17159/1996-2096/2015/v15n1a3

Orb, A., Eisenhauer, L., & Wynaden, D. (2001). Ethics in qualitative research. *Journal of Nursing Scholarship, 33*(1), 93–96. https://doi.org/10.1111/j.1547-5069.2001.00093.x

Orchowski, L. M., Berkowitz, A., Boggis, J., & Oesterle, D. (2016). Bystander intervention among college men: The role of alcohol and correlates of sexual aggression. *Journal of Interpersonal Violence, 31*(17), 2824–2846. https://doi.org/10.1177/0886260515581904

Överlien, C., Aronsson, K., & Hydén, M. (2005). The focus group interview as an in-depth method? Young women talking about sexuality. *International Journal of Social Research Methodology, 8*(4), 331–344. https://doi.org/10.1080/1364557042000119607

Peterson, Z. D., & Muehlenhard, C. L. (2007). Conceptualizing the "wantedness" of women's consensual and nonconsensual sexual experiences: Implications for how women label their experiences with rape. *Journal of Sex Research, 44*(1), 72–88. https://doi.org/10.1080/00224490709336794

Reddy, V., Potgieter, C.-A., & Mkhize, N. (2015). *Cloud over the rainbow nation:'corrective rape'and other hate crimes against black lesbians*. Human Sciences Research Counsil.

Remick, L. A. (1992). Read her lips: an argument for a verbal consent standard in rape. *U. Pa. L. Rev., 141*, 1103.

Robinson, O. C. (2014). Sampling in interview-based qualitative research: A theoretical and practical guide. *Qualitative Research in Psychology, 11*(1), 25–41. https://doi.org/10.1080/14780887.2013.801543

Rossetto, K. R., & Tollison, A. C. (2017). Feminist agency, sexual scripts, and sexual violence: Developing a model for postgendered family communication. *Family Relations, 66*(1), 61–74. https://doi.org/10.1111/fare.12232

Saville Young, L., Moodley, D., & Macleod, C. I. (2019). Feminine sexual desire and shame in the classroom: An educator's constructions of and investments in sexuality education. *Sex Education, 19*(4), 486–500. https://doi.org/10.1080/14681811.2018.1511974

Shefer, T., & Ruiters, K. (1998). The masculine construct in heterosex. *Agenda, 14*(37), 39–45. https://doi.org/10.2307/4066172

Shefer, T., Strebel, A., & Foster, D. (2000). So women have to submit to that ... Discourses of power and violence in student's talk on heterosexual negotiation. *South African Journal of Psychology, 30*(2), 11–19. https://doi.org/10.1177/008124630003000202

Shumlich, E. J., & Fisher, W. A. (2018). Affirmative sexual consent? Direct and unambiguous consent is rarely included in discussions of recent sexual interactions. *The Canadian Journal of Human Sexuality, 27*(3), 248–260. https://doi:10.3138/cjhs.2017-0040

Tiefer, L. (2002). Beyond the medical model of women's sexual problems: A campaign to resist the promotion of 'female sexual dysfunction'. *Sexual and Relationship Therapy, 17*(2), 127–135. https://doi.org/10.1080/14681990220121248

Van Damme, E. (2010). Gender and sexual scripts in popular US teen series: A study on the gendered discourses in *one tree hill* and *gossip girl*. *Catalan Journal of Communication & Cultural Studies, 2*(1), 77–92. https://doi.org/10.1386/cjcs.2.1.77_1

Vannier, S. A., & O'Sullivan, L. F. (2011). Communicating interest in sex: Verbal and nonverbal initiation of sexual activity in young adults' romantic dating relationships. *Archives of Sexual Behavior, 40*(5), 961–969. https://doi.org/10.1007/s10508-010-9663-7

Wilkinson, S. (1998). Focus groups in feminist research: Power, interaction, and the co-construction of meaning. *Women's Studies International Forum, 21* (1), 111–125. Elsevier. https://doi.org/10.1016/S0277-5395(97)00080-0

Willig, C. (2008). Foucauldian discourse analysis. *Introducing Qualitative Research in Psychology*, 112–131. https://books.google.co.za/books?id=yDtFBgAAQBAJ (Original work published 2001)

Willis, M., Blunt-Vinti, H. D., & Jozkowski, K. N. (2019). Associations between internal and external sexual consent in a diverse national sample of women. *Personality and Individual Differences, 149*(1), 37–45. https://doi.org/10.1016/j.paid.2019.05.029

Willis, M., Hunt, M., Wodika, A., Rhodes, D. L., Goodman, J., & Jozkowski, K. N. (2019). Explicit verbal sexual consent communication: Effects of gender, relationship status, and type of sexual behavior. *International Journal of Sexual Health 31*(1), 1–11

Willis, M., & Jozkowski, K. N. (2018). Barriers to the success of affirmative consent initiatives: An application of the social ecological model. *American Journal of Sexuality Education, 31*(3), 324–336. https://doi.org/10.1080/15546128.2018.1443300

Willis, M., & Jozkowski, K. N. (2019). Sexual precedent's effect on sexual consent communication. *Archives of Sexual Behavior, 48*(6), 1–12. https://doi.org/10.1007/s10508-018-1348-7

# Complexities of sexual consent: Young people's reasoning in a Swedish context

Charlotta Holmström, Lars Plantin and Eva Elmerstig

**ABSTRACT**
Although previous research and public debate argue that partnered sexual activity is construed in terms of being consensual or not, we know little about young people's own reasoning on sexual consent. This study aimed to investigate how sexual consent and sexual negotiations are interpreted by young people in Sweden. Forty-four female and male participants, ranging from 18–21 years old, took part in 12 focus groups, organised according to a set of vignettes. All focus groups were analysed using inductive thematic analysis. The findings illustrate the complexity of the interpretation of sexual consent. There was a clear perception among the participants that sex between two individuals is a mutual process, and that sex should be consensual, expressed either through words, body language, or both. They all stated clearly that a 'No' has to be respected, independently of context. However, at the same time participants expressed contradictory norms and expectations in relation to the described situations, that showed an ambivalence concerning sexual scripts and consequences of challenging these in specific situations. Reasoning concerning discrepancy between ideals and actual possibilities to act in sexual encounters indicates differences in relation to gender, age and educational background and pathways.

## Introduction

During the last few years, the question of consensual sex has been brought to the fore in Sweden via some much-debated legal cases in which young men have been acquitted of rape. These verdicts have caused strong public reactions and generated massive demonstrations outside the courts, leading to a considerable amount of debate articles in public media calling for a discussion of legal reforms in relation to societal norms concerning sexuality and gender. In addition, the Swedish public debate regarding sexual offences gained momentum through the #metoo anti-sexual harassment/assault campaign in 2017[1]. In 2018, the Swedish Government introduced new sexual offence legislation based on the requirement of consent (Government Offices of Sweden, 2018). At a press conference, Swedish Prime Minister Stefan Löfven declared: 'It should be obvious. Sex should be voluntary. If it is not voluntary, then it is illegal' (Svenska Dagbladet, 2017). From July 1st, 2018, a rape conviction in Sweden does not require the use of violence or threats by perpetrators nor that a person's vulnerable situation has been exploited. The new Swedish law criminalises sex without consent, saying that a person must give a clear verbal or physical consent. Lack of consent is in other words enough to be considered a crime; either negligent rape or negligent sexual abuse, sentences with a maximum prison term of four years (Ministry of Justice, Sweden, 2018). A central question is thus how young people interpret and express the notions of consensual sex; what is *voluntary* sex and how does one know when it is not?

Conflictual and blurred sexual situations bring to the fore, and challenge, ideas about morally 'good' and 'bad' sex – but also about gendered sexual norms and expectations. Sexual boundaries can be seen as constantly negotiated and constructed in relation to how young people perceive, interpret, and define different sexual encounters. According to Muehlenhard and Peterson (2005), the conceptualisation of sex as either wanted or unwanted is problematic and reflects a dichotomous model that conflates wanting and consenting. Wanted sex is within this context understood as consensual, and unwanted sex as non-consensual. However, even if wanting sex may influence individuals' decisions about whether to consent, wanting sex and consenting to sex do not need to correspond (Muehlenhard & Peterson, 2005). Instead, Peterson and Muehlenhard (2007, p. 81) showed that wantedness can be regarded as a continuous and multidimensional construct. Participants in their study described reasons for both wanting and not wanting sex, and also distinguished between wanting a sexual act and wanting its consequences (Peterson & Muehlenhard, 2007).

The relation between wanting or not wanting sex on the one hand, and consent or non-consent on the other, may also be conditioned by a range of different factors: individual, relational, contextual, but also structural, such as gender, social class, age, or ethnicity. Skeggs (2005) argued, for example, that women and men with different socio-economic backgrounds relate to class- and gender-specific sexual norms and thus develop different behaviours and attitudes in relation to gender and sexuality. In other words, to interpret and understand how sexual wanting is expressed and constructed, and how sexual wanting is related to sexual consent, is of central concern in order to understand young people's reasoning of sexual consent.

### *Gendered sexual wanting and sexual consent*

Studies have shown that young women and men respond in different ways to sexual coercion (Byers & Glenn, 2012), and studies focusing on young people's experiences of unwanted sex show significant gender differences. More women than men, both in Sweden and internationally, have experienced unwanted sex (Flack et al., 2007; The Swedish Public Health Agency, 2019). These gender differences can be understood as the result of unequal power relations between women and men (Allen, 2005; Chambers et al., 2004; Clarke, 2006; Holland et al., 2004; Mellor, 2012; Morgan & Zurbriggen, 2007). Feminine and masculine ideals are constantly being negotiated among young people (Chambers et al., 2004; Clarke, 2006; Elmerstig, 2009; Elmerstig et al., 2017; Mellor, 2012; Morgan & Zurbriggen, 2007; Paechter, 2007), and these negotiations affect what is enacted in sexual situations (Elmerstig et al., 2012, 2014; Sanchez et al., 2005; Sanchez et al., 2012). In their classic study on women, sexual consent, and token resistance, Muehlenhard and Hollabaugh (1988) found that 40% of the women reported that they had experiences of saying no to sex, but meaning yes. Even if the majority of the women in the referred study still did *not* have that experience, Muehlenhard and McCoy (1991) argued that 'saying no meaning yes' can be described as *scripted refusal*. This type of behaviour can be understood as being based on traditional sexual scripts implying a double sexual standard for women (Gavey, 2005).

Thus, gender inequality seems to be sustained and possibly reinforced by sexual situations (Sanchez et al., 2012), and scholars within the field argue that the double standard – that sexual initiative is considered dubious in women but positive in men – remains and continues to impact young people's sexual lives. According to these scholars, conforming to lingering gender-specific expectations may affect opportunities to exert sexual autonomy and to experience sexual pleasure (Elmerstig, 2009; Jackson & Cram, 2003; Sanchez et al., 2012). A growing number of studies show that saying 'Yes' to a partner's sexual initiatives does not necessarily reflect unequivocal interest or desire (Bay-Cheng & Eliseo-Arras, 2008). A study on U.S. American college students' communication of sexual consent showed how women often are conceptualised as gatekeepers and therefore experience contradictory situations difficult to cope with:

> (a) they may not resist strongly enough and thus be perceived as at fault for experiencing forced sex; (b) they may engage in some sexual activity but halt the activity prior to sexual intercourse and thus be labeled a "tease" and again be conceptualized as being responsible for men forcing sex on them; or (c) they may agree to sex too quickly or with too many partners, thus being perceived as a "slut" (Jozkowski & Peterson, 2013, p. 521)

The results from this study suggested that communication of sexual consent is strongly influenced by strict and stereotypical gender roles, and Gavey (2005) argued that there is a need to de-naturalise such rigid gendered binary representing women as passive and vulnerable and men as sexually aggressive.

## *Multiple social dimensions of sexual consent*

In addition to the traditional gendered scripts and sexual double standard as central themes in previous research on sexual consent, other analytical perspectives have been suggested as well. For example, studies show how young people's perceptions of sexuality are influenced by social class. According to Skeggs (1997), women who initiate sex have not always been compatible with respectability and virtue. Rather the opposite, women showing sexual interest have historically been seen as an expression of the immoral sexuality of the lower classes (Skeggs, 1997). Ideas concerning respectability and different expectations concerning sex in relation to gender and class are still highly prevalent. This is clearly shown in Forsberg's (2005) study of young women in the Swedish suburbs, where ideas about respectability had a great impact on these women's self-perceptions in relation to sexuality. Ideas about respectability were both internalised and supported by their families and peer groups. In a similar study of young college students in Sweden, Ambjörnsson (2004) found that normative femininity and young college women's perceptions, experiences of relationships, and love and intimacy were strongly affected by social class and respectability. For the young women in her study, being respectable was clearly related to sexuality and the fear of being regarded as promiscuous and as a slut.

However, there is also research indicating a tendency towards increased sexual equality, sexual agency, and freedom. Within this discussion, the notion that a gender-specific double standard is still the norm is called into question (Johansson, 2007; Marks & Fraley, 2005). In a study on Swedish youth, Johansson (2007) found that few participants were negative towards young women taking the sexual initiative and concluded that 'the oppressed young woman found in the work of Beauvoir and others seems to have been replaced by a more active and competent female subject' (Johansson, 2007, p. 42). Examining social factors shaping sexual consent among college students, Hirsch et al. (2018) pointed to multiple social dimensions of consensual sex (e.g. gendered scripts, sexual citizenship, and intersectionality). Sexual citizenship has often been understood as a dimension of gendered scripts. However, Hirsch et al. (2018, p. 30) study showed a great variability concerning women's sense of sexual citizenship: 'some clear about their sexual boundaries and desires, others much less so'. These researchers also argued that intersectional social inequalities may have an impact on how young people experience intimacy and practice consent, pointing at differences in the sense of sexual citizenship, due to social background.

## *Contrasting perspectives on young people's norms concerning sexuality*

Sociologists Simon and Gagnon (1986) described the origins of sexual meanings and desire as located in the social context. According to their sexual scripting theory, individuals need to call on shared meanings and expectations to produce sexual scripts. Analytically, these scripts are defined at three distinct and interacting levels: cultural scenarios, interpersonal scripts, and intra-psychic scripts. More specifically this means that young people's sexual encounters and sexual interactions are influenced by social norms on different levels: on *societal level* through culturally and socially constructed norms, on *interpersonal level* through social norms in different peer groups, and on *intrapsychic level* through norms constructed through personal experiences and the internalisation of norms constructed and expressed on societal and interpersonal level. Young people of today act and exist in a range of different contexts and have access to several different influential socialisation agents. This situation implies that young people are influenced by a range of sexual scripts, which do not always correspond. The present study explored how sexual consent and sexual negotiations are interpreted by young people – paying particular attention to norms concerning gender in relation to sexuality.

Simon and Gagnon (1986) defined modern society as a 'postparadigmatic society' (as opposed to a paradigmatic society) in which sexual norms mediated at the cultural or societal level do not always correspond with values and norms constructed at the interpersonal or intra-psychic level. Such a lack of correspondence between these different levels may on the one hand give young people individual freedom, independence, and room for sexual agency and, on the other hand, cause frictions and pressure on young people at the interpersonal and intra-psychic levels to manage social interactions in sexual encounters with no unambiguous cultural and societal guidance. It is thus of great importance to explore how young people, on the one hand, reproduce and, on the other hand, challenge established sexual scripts, constructed and expressed on different levels.

## Method

In order to assess young people's norms concerning sexual consent, 12 focus groups with 44 young people were conducted during 2016 and 2017.

### *Participants*

The participants were recruited through a sample of young people in the age ranges of 18–19 years old ($n = 32$) and 20–21 years old ($n = 12$) from three upper secondary schools (one school that offers vocational training, one school that runs university preparatory programmes, and one that offers both), from one youth clinic, and one student organisation. In addition, participants were recruited through snow-ball sampling. Of these individuals 32 participants attended upper secondary school (theoretical programme $n = 6$, and practical programme $n = 26$), nine attended university and three were working. The sample included women ($n = 27$), men ($n = 16$), and transgender ($n = 1$), with different social and ethnic backgrounds. Information about characteristics were obtained through self-report in the beginning of the interview. We had a gender comparative approach, and therefore mostly conducted gender-separated focus groups and strived for a variation in terms of sexual orientation, class, and ethnicity as these might influence people's perceptions and experiences of sexual norms and practices (Ambjörnsson, 2004; Forsberg, 2005; Hammarén, 2008; Tikkanen et al., 2011). Three groups were gender mixed while nine groups were gender-separated. When it comes to sexual orientation, we didn't have a strategic selection process reaching those who identified themselves as heterosexual, bisexual, or homosexual; we asked only for young people who were interested in participating. In the final sample, the majority identified themselves as heterosexual. The sizes of the 12 focus groups varied; two groups had two participants, three groups had three participants, six groups had four participants, one group had five participants, and, finally, one group had six participants.

### *Data collection*

Prior to each focus group, all participants gave their informed consent to participate. The focus groups were organised by a set of constructed vignettes. These vignettes illustrated situations involving casual sexual encounters that have retrospectively led to feelings of regret and sometimes experiences of persuasion or coercion. They described different social interactions both in party contexts with alcohol involved and in more everyday life situations – followed by sexual encounters and negotiations of sexual consent. Some vignettes described party situations and experiences of casual sex; others describe situations within a relationship. Here are three examples of the vignettes:

> Vignette Example 1: Klara is in love with Aron and they meet at a party. They have been drinking alcohol. They start kissing and go upstairs. They have sex and he wants to have sex once more, but she says no. The next day, Klara is very sorry and regrets having sex with Aron, it feels wrong. Afterwards, Aron pretends that nothing happened between them.
>
> Vignette Example 2: Matilda is out clubbing with a friend. She meets two guys, Anton and Filip, whom she is acquainted with. Matilda likes Anton. She goes with them to another bar and is offered wine. She has some wine and starts feeling drunk. Matilda doesn't really remember what happens after that. She remembers going with Anton to an apartment, and suddenly she is almost naked. She also remembers that Anton had sex with her, but she doesn't remember how long it lasted, or how it ended. When she wakes up in the morning she doesn't feel well and is nauseous. She dresses and leaves."
>
> Vignette Example 3: Albin 16 years old, is in a relationship with Alice. Albin is unsure if he wants to have sex with Alice or not. His friends are cheering on him for having sex with her. Alice has said that she wants to have sex with him, but only if he feels ready. Albin is afraid that Alice will lose interest, if he says no to sex. Alice also says that sex is something you have with those you love and Albin loves her more than anything.

The focus group discussions gave room for reasoning on how to make sense of the situations, on communication concerning sexual boundaries, and on potential strategies to cope with the described situations. The vignettes were discussed on the basis of different gender and sexual orientations by initiating the discussion about their thoughts if the gender were shifted in the vignettes, and if gender were changed to two female names or two male names to lead the discussion further into same-sex relationships. The core of the focus groups was the participant's understandings and assessments of the described situations.

Using focus groups as a research method has been described as a useful way to explore sensitive topics in a non-threatening way (Wibeck et al., 2007; Wilkinson, 2004), and the interactions often lead to the production of more elaborate accounts than are generated in individual interviews. Therefore, focus groups are a particularly useful method within this context since the aim of the study was to grasp young people's sexual norms by exploring their reasoning concerning complex sexual situations, as illustrated by the vignettes. As with focus groups, the use of vignettes can serve as an aid in the elucidation of sensitive issues (Barter & Renold, 1999, 2000). Typically, participants are requested to respond in the third person to the vignette, rather than drawing on their own experiences, thereby desensitising the subject matter. Participants who do not want to discuss their personal experiences can respond to those of 'others.' This facilitates the investigation of potentially morally charged, or sensitive, issues. Using vignettes is ideal to assess attitudes and beliefs (Barnatt et al., 2007) and can be constructed in many ways.

In this study, vignettes took the form of a descriptive story, with participants being asked to respond to a narrative that was based on a mixture of several cases. The vignettes were written by the first author, influenced by real and fictive cases presented in campaigns focusing on sexual consent in a Swedish context. The vignettes were presented, discussed, and evaluated at a seminar including researchers within sexology and sexuality studies. Some of the researchers at the seminar had previous professional experiences of social work with young people. The vignettes were also piloted with two young people. The response to the vignettes was positive; thus, the pilot interview was included in the sample.

Each vignette was fairly short (i.e. 200–300 words) since this has been shown to be ideal for adolescents (Barter & Renold, 1999). All focus group sessions were conducted in Swedish, by the first author, and the interviews were audio-recorded and lasted approximately 60–100 minutes. Reflective field notes were made during and after each focus group session to assist with analysis.

The interviews were checked and anonymised. The study was approved by the regional ethical review board, Lund University, Sweden.

## *Data analysis*

Data analysis broadly followed an inductive thematic approach inspired by Braun and Clarke (2006) including familiarising with data, coding, searching and defining emergent themes. The interviews and reflective notes were first systematically read several times by the first author to ensure familiarity with the data. After close reading of the interviews, a coding process was carried out to identify repeating phenomena within the data. These codes were developed further through movement back and forth, in the process of rereading of the interviews and codes. During this process, several subthemes and themes were developed, and, finally, the themes were refined during the process of writing (Braun & Clarke, 2006). The interpretations of findings were discussed among the authors throughout the analysis process.

## Results

The thematic analysis produced four overarching themes addressing young people's reasoning about conflicting sexual situations in relation to gender and sexuality norms: (1) 'Sexual consent is when both are into it,' (2) 'Sexual scripts in casual sex encounters,' (3) 'The complexity of challenging a sexual script,' and (4) 'Sexual agency and intersectionality.'

## *Sexual consent is when both are into it*

The participants described sexual consent as 'when both are into it.' Communication concerning wanting to have sex was understood as either verbal or through body language. Paying attention to other people's reactions was seen as crucial when it comes to sexual encounters. Irrespective of discussing same-sex or heterosexual sexual interactions, being female, male, or transgender, there was, in each focus group, a clear awareness of the public discourse about sexual abuse and harassment. The participants often referred to various publicly known cases of rape and sexual abuse and, in the focus groups conducted during fall 2017, also to the #metoo campaign. They all clearly condemned sexual abuse and harassment. People who commit this type of serious sexual crime were referred to as 'pigs,' 'abnormal,' or described as 'someone who is totally insane'. Forcing somebody to have sex was described as something else than sex: an expression of aggression or power.

There was in other words a clear consensus that a 'No' always has to be respected, irrespective of the context and situation. One example of that position was expressed between two male participants in a focus group with three male participants, 18 years old:

> If a person says no, then it is no. It is as easy as that. (M, age 18, vocational)

> You have to listen to that, you know! (M, age 18, vocational)

> I think that anyone who is normal, who has empathy, stops immediately if you realize that the other one really do not want to ... You can't enjoy it, while seeing that the other part is in ... in pain ... (M, age 18, vocational)

Another example was expressed in a focus group with female participants:

> If someone wants to have sex, but the other does not, you just have to accept that ... there's nothing more to do. (F, age 18, vocational)

> It should be OK. You are allowed to say "No" whenever, even if you first said "Yes". You should be able to say "No" whenever! (F, age 18, vocational)

In this respect, all participants expressed an understanding of sexual consent as something that should be viewed as a continuous process following an affirmative standard where a 'No' always should be respected and non-consent must be assumed until anything else is actively communicated. In one focus group with male participants, they argued that as a young man, you have to be aware of "such things nowadays". Saying 'No' once should be enough:

> In today's society you should not misunderstand such a situation! You just shouldn't! It is like driving through a red light, you just don't! (M, age 18, vocational)

People crossing boundaries or ignoring the other part's signals were described as 'idiots' or 'lacking empathy.' Being attentive to other people's reactions was seen as a matter of code and conduct and something you learn during your upbringing.

## *Sexual scripts in casual sex encounters*

Even if everyone agreed with the principle that sexual consent is a prerequisite to engaging in sexual activity and that a 'No' should be respected whenever uttered, the participants' discussions on the specific cases showed great complexity in assessing what it means to say 'No' in an intimate situation, especially in casual sex encounters. Discussing the vignette illustrating a situation when two young people who are acquaintances, meet at a night out, flirt, drink alcohol, and end up in one party's apartment, showed how such an interactional process employs a certain sexual script. Here illustrated by three male participants, 18 years, vocational:

> *Interviewer: Can you tell from this case if somebody, and if so, who wants to have sex?*
>
> Both of them want to have sex! Isn't that so? She goes with him to an apartment, right?
>
> *Interviewer: Yeah ... and does that mean that she wants to have sex, that she goes with him?*
>
> No, it doesn't mean that really ... but I would have thought so too, if she had gone home with me. But it is not really ...
>
> But she accepts going home with him.
>
> Yes, it does not say that she has said 'No', or that she did not want to ...
>
> She has not refused ...
>
> ....it just says that she has regrets in the morning ...

Further on, participants in another focus group expressed similar ideas:

> It's a bit weird if you meet someone at a club and you've both been making out there, then you go home ... and then later when you're both in bed they say they don't want to have sex. I mean ... if you go home with someone ... and then go all the way ... haven't you already said 'Yes' to it ... ? (M, age 18, vocational)
>
> *Interviewer: Is that so? If you go home with someone like that does it automatically mean that they want to have sex?*
>
> Totally, I mean you know it, she knows it .... both know it. (M, age 18, vocational)

Similar views are expressed by five, somewhat older (20–21 years old), female university students:

> Then I think that it matters that she has already gone with him to his place.
>
> Yes, it is like ... is that a ... ?
>
> Does that mean that I have to ... I have already agreed to go with him, but does that mean that I have said yes to sex?
>
> That, I think, has nothing to do with it!
>
> It is like that ... Is that a silent guarantee? One could ask ...
>
> Yes, exactly.

> Yes, have you then promised something ... indirectly?
>
> No!
>
> Yes, does he expect ... does he expect sex from me now?
>
> What he expects is a different thing, but I don't think that you have promised anything! She is not obliged to do anything!
>
> No, she does not owe him anything
>
> ... and she has not promised ...

These comments illustrated how sexual consent is understood as an interactional process, starting much earlier than the time of getting home with somebody after a night out. To agree to go home with somebody from the club, particularly if you have been making out or if you already fancy each other, was perceived as initiating a consensual process. The participants found that such sexual consent negotiations are usually guided by nonverbal communication, relying on body language with gestures, movements, and eye contact as signals. On the other hand, the idea of verbally negotiating the possibility of sex with someone you do not know that well appeared to be awkward and incongruous, described as a 'turn-off' and a 'mood-killer.' Consent was described here as something intimate and emotional, a situation when it 'feels right' and when 'everything takes care of itself' rather than being a rational verbal negotiation. In this respect, the participants stressed the importance of being clear in communication to avoid any misunderstandings:

> You gotta be clear, you gotta be way fucking clear ... (F, age 18, vocational)
>
> *Interviewer: But how do you know then that it's OK, how do you know the other wants to?*
>
> You just know when it's all good and happening', you just know! (F, age 18, vocational)

Consent in casual sex encounters are thus described as an interactional process 'where one thing leads to another,' most often without explicit communication on what to expect. In order to prevent misunderstandings, communicating non-consent clearly was stated as crucial.

### *The complexity of challenging a sexual script*

The majority of the participants argued that going home with somebody after a night out could indicate sex, and that most of their peers probably would agree. Even if the majority of the participants argued that such an understanding of sexual consent is wrong, the participants' reasoning showed how they experience the possibility of negotiating sexual consent as gradually diminishing in such a situation. Considering a 'No' is associated with negative feelings, since saying 'No' at that point is seen as going against a mutually assumed script. The participants stressed the risk of experiencing 'social awkwardness' in the situation. The other person might be disappointed, feel rejected, become angry or even aggressive. In one focus group, consisting of three participants (two men and one women 20–21 years old, university students), the female participant discusses feelings of vulnerability in relation to expectations in casual sexual encounters.

> Yes, I would say so that you are really vulnerable in such a situation. You get to that point that ... that ... already undressed ... and then starting to feel like ... 'No, now I really don't want to!' Then I would feel really vulnerable! Because then you might be in a situation when ... 'But what would you do to me, if I say no now, just now that I realize that you really want to?" Then you are really ... Then you may experience that you need to have sex, in a different way, than if you say no (to sex) while still being out or just getting home, because then you have a different ... yes ... " (F, age around 20, university student)
>
> Yes, because then you are not that involved in the story ... (M, age around 20, university student)

> No, exactly ... So that I understand is difficult ... And I think that is why such things happen. It happens often, these things, because you get involved to a point when you feel that you <u>cannot</u> say no anymore. (F, age around 20, university student)
>
> No, exactly ... (M, age around 20, university student)
>
> ... that you realize that you do not want to have sex, too late. Even if it should not be like that. (F, age around 20, university student)

The participants also acknowledged potentially negative social consequences such as being described as a 'tease', being boring and uninteresting, or being subject to other negative rumours. For example:

> Ah, I think that she will get a reputation either way ... She might get a reputation for being a slut, due to the fact that she is willing to have sex. (...) And if she does not, she appears to be boring. Whatever she chooses, she will get a reputation. (F, age 18, vocational)

At the beginning of a relationship, regardless of whether it was casual or relation-oriented, it was also perceived to be risky to say 'No,' since such a 'No' might imply that there would be no more dates, or that it might lead to a break up:

> You might fear that the person would not want to see you again ... (F, age 18, university preparatory)

Another concern that was expressed among female participants was to be perceived as a 'tease' (i.e. to have acted upon non-verbal communication and in that sense 'promised' something):

> It is weird, but it is almost like you have said "Yes" ... .It is almost like you have taken advantage of that expectation and ... then you cannot just withdraw, because you are afraid that the other person will think that you have promised something that you have not promised, but you do not want to disappoint somebody. (F, age 18, university preparatory)
>
> And you can always ignore such things, because that is unimportant. It should not be important. You can of course sit here and say a lot of good things, but when you are in the situation, it is really difficult. (F, age 18, university preparatory)

Other participants expressed this: it is like saying 'OK, then I don't like you' or 'It is like you are being rude' or 'being indecisive.' In reality this means that several participants perceived the possibility to say 'No' as highly limited, even those who maintained that saying 'No' to sex should always be okay and be respected. In many of the focus groups the woman in the vignette was made responsible for the outcome of the situation; saying 'No' might lead to an uncomfortable situation, saying 'Yes' might lead to rumours.

This reasoning shows how 'wantedness' can be influenced by a number of factors that include not only the individuals and the couple but also, to a very high degree, the couple's social environment. This way of reasoning challenges the idea that there really is consent in going home with someone, seeing it as 'a signal that something's gonna happen.' Here the participants stressed that going home with somebody does not mean that you have to have sex or that you cannot change your mind about it. Yet, they all acknowledged a specific sexual script concerning casual sex and pointed to difficulties in challenging such a script, due to fears of situational and social consequences. In this sense, the participants initially expressed opinion that sexual consent is a continuous process and something that should be based on affirmative consent was altered here. Instead, the participants clearly stressed that there are situations where consent is assumed until non-consent is expressed and that expressing a non-consent 'too late' can be very difficult.

### *Sexual agency and intersectionality*

All participants stressed the importance of acknowledging people's sexual rights and recognising a lack of correspondence between sexual scripts on a societal level on the one hand and on an interpersonal and intrapsychic level on the other. An ambivalence on how to cope with the lack of correspondence between sexual scripts on different levels was acknowledged by all participants. How this lack of correspondence is handled seemed to differ due to intersectional aspects, mainly concerning education, gender, and age.

The participants who were preparing for university or already studied at the university emphasised everyone's right to challenge the assumed sexual script concerning casual sex to a higher degree than the participants in vocational programmes. Sexual agency and the right to negotiate sex independently of context was a central theme for female participants preparing for a university degree. The participants on the vocational training programmes, on the other hand, stressed the importance of being clear initially, preventing a socially uncomfortable situation.

Acting responsibly was crucial among all participants; however, how this could be done was described in different ways. One way of acting in a responsible way was to be aware of the presumed script, and to make sure that your intentions could not be misunderstood, in accordance with the script. Another way to act responsibly was to express your own intentions clearly and strongly, independently of situational and social expectations. In this regard, the participants from the university preparatory programmes advocated for a stronger reflexive individual approach, than their peers in work training programmes. The participants aiming at a university degree seemed to have the ambition to challenge norms concerning sexual encounters on the cultural or societal level to a higher degree than participants on the vocational programmes – while the participants at the vocational programme to a higher degree seem to relate to and follow the assumed sexual script. However, the ambition to challenge sexual scripts on a societal level was not only influenced by educational background or pathway.

The data showed how gender had a significant impact on negotiating consent as well. Even if the participants' discussions on sexual consent and sexual scripts indicated a general awareness of gender equality and of new gender ideals, the participants' reasonings on sexual consent also showed how they are strongly influenced by gender patterns and heterosexual norms. The negotiations surrounding sexual consent were characterised by discussions of gender equity – that both have the right to say 'Yes' or 'No' and that both women and men are free to choose their own partners and to acknowledge and affirm their sexuality. On the other hand, the discussions were permeated by a traditional view of gender in which women can be seen as emotional, reflexive, oriented towards relationships, and indecisive, while men can be described as decisive, action-oriented and potentially aggressive. And in several of the discussions, the woman was seen as the 'gatekeeper' in the sexual consent negotiations, being somewhat responsible for the outcome. In these discussions it was the woman who was expected to accept or refuse, and who needed to be clear about what she wants, while he should be responsive and not be 'in too much of a rush.' This not only referred to a woman's first reaction to a man's initial invitation (e.g. 'it's always the guy that takes the first step') but also to a situation when it becomes more complicated, when she has agreed to a more intimate contact, but has not consented to sex:

> Maybe they already started to seriously make out on the sofa; she would really need to be tough if she wanted to say "No". (F, age 18, vocational)
>
> If she does not say "No" then, well, then she can't really lay blame on the guy, you gotta have some self-respect ... what else can he do? (F, age 18, vocational)
>
> But it doesn't mean he should cross the line ... (F, age 18, vocational)
>
> No, of course not. (F, age 18, vocational)

Independently of educational background or pathway, the participants seemed to put somewhat greater responsibility on women than on men when it came to sexual consent. For some of the women, particularly those who were at university or on university preparatory programmes, this responsibility was considerable. They continuously argued that there are options for individual action and emphasised that there are, or should be, alternatives to act and to challenge a presumed sexual script. They said that they expected it should indeed be so, but on the other hand acknowledged the complexity of actual situations:

> I would feel really bad if I were in her situation ... I mean she could have said "No" or suggested that they should just sleep together or so ... instead of just letting it happen. But on the other hand it is hard ... (F, age 18, university preparatory)

Even if many of the participants in the study described experiences of ambivalence in relation to sexual consent, the ambivalence was expressed more strongly and more explicitly by those women who also stressed that you always have an individual choice. The ability to act responsibly and in accordance with your own will was stressed to a somewhat higher degree among the participants who were some years older than the 18 year old participants. Several of the participants also referred to age in relation to the ability to know what you want, independently of social and situational factors. Youth and lack of experience was in other words described as factors that may have an impact on people's ability to know and express their own will and intentions. Being a young inexperienced woman was understood as a specifically vulnerable position among all participants.

## Discussion

The present study showed how young people assess, negotiate, and navigate understandings of sexual consent. The participants agreed upon the importance of sex being consensual and emphasised that paying attention to verbal and bodily signals expressing sexual consent is crucial. A verbal 'No' or passivity in a sexual encounter was understood as non-consent, independently of context. In this regard, the participants' reasoning can be understood as being in accordance with the new Swedish legislation on sexual consent and with previous research (Willis et al., 2019). The new Swedish law on sexual consent focuses on how *consent* rather than *non-consent* is expressed and understood and aims to achieve normative change regarding the interpretation of sexual consent. Thus, the participants in the study supported this aim and expressed an understanding of consent as an interactional process, when both parties agree on what will happen next.

However, the focus group discussions also showed that there are specific sexual scripts related to specific situations, giving instructions on 'what will happen next.' In casual sex encounters, going home with somebody after a night out is to a large degree interpreted as a 'Yes' to sex. Both parts are understood as responsible for the situation and for what 'will happen next,' even if the focus group discussions to a large degree focused on how the woman acts. Men were seen as seldom saying 'No' to sex, and women were described as being responsible for what has been communicated in the interaction that preceded the sexual encounter. Both female and male respondents' understandings of the situations can be related to the gender specific double standard that has been described in previous research (see for example, Jackson & Cram, 2003), where men are seen as being active and initiating sex, while women are seen as passive, responding to men's initiative through their gatekeeping position.

The respondents acknowledged that communicating wanting or not wanting sex in a casual sex encounter can be rather difficult and not at all clear cut, and that these difficulties are gendered. Misunderstandings and miscommunication were seen as understandable when young people negotiate sexual encounters. The participants' difficulties in challenging sexual scripts connected to casual sex have been demonstrated in other Swedish studies among young people (Elmerstig et al., 2012, 2014). Both young women and men have shown conflicting feelings where they want to resist the impact of stereotyped scripts, while at the same time wanting to perform according to gendered standards. The young people in Elmerstig and colleagues' studies described an indirect pressure from peer groups to match the existing scripts during casual sex. The young men in their study felt less confident during casual sex and, in order to avoid showing vulnerability, their focus turned into their own performance fulfilling the conventional male stereotypes of being dominant and decisive. When totally focusing on their own performance, the sexual situation became a solitary action. In addition, they felt pressure to share their experiences of casual sex with peers afterwards. In this way the peer group became a central actor in the male-male narratives; the casual sex was shared with friends and not with partner (Elmerstig et al., 2014). In light of findings from the current study, such gendered expectations, could easily lead to misunderstanding and miscommunication during casual sex. The fear of situational and social consequences was described among the focus groups participants in the current study; women may fear rumours and aggressive reactions, while men may fear doing something wrong – and perhaps being accused for a crime they did not commit.

Facing contradictory norms and expectations, may cause ambivalence concerning how to understand communication regarding sexual consent. Adopting the idea that negotiating sexual consent should be regarded as an open continuous process – following an affirmative standard where non-consent must be assumed until anything else is actively communicated – can be understood in relation to concepts such as individualisation and self-reflexivity. Processes of modernity have increased individuals' sexual agency and freedom, generally described as the state of a 'democratisation of modern intimacy' (Giddens, 1992). Individuals living in a post-paradigmatic society are ideally free to choose what sexual script to follow since there are several cultural scripts to choose from. The participants chose a sexual script saying that sex has to be consensual, and that sexual consent is a continuous process where the involved parts have to act responsibly and attentively. On the other hand, the participants related to culturally prescribed gendered scripts based on an understanding of a specific situation and interaction where consent is assumed until non-consent is expressed. Within these discussions, for example, some male participants gave voice to ideas on *scripted refusal* (see for example, Muehlenhard & McCoy, 1991; Marcantonio & Jozkowski, 2019), referring to situations where women are assumed to say 'No' to sex, due to gender ideals concerning women's sexuality.

The difficulties in challenging sexual scripts in specific situations such as casual sex encounters were described as closely related to the women's fear of the social consequences as being regarded as a tease, being boring, losing face, seriously damaging the relationship, getting a bad reputation, or even being subject to potentially aggressive reactions. An important dimension of the negotiation of sexual consent, and a restricting factor for the affirmative standard, could thus be seen as young women's way of navigating respectability. However, another important aspect related to this is that consenting to sex and wanting to have sex does not seem to always correspond, as one can consent to unwanted sex, or in reverse, one may want to have sex but not consent to it because of the fear of losing respectability or experience other negative social consequences (Peterson & Muehlenhard, 2007). Also, Muehlenhard et al. (2016, p. 463) discussed the usefulness of understanding wanting and consenting as two distinct concepts 'that sometimes correspond to each other but sometimes do not'. They claimed that this discrepancy between wanting and consenting often gives rise to feelings of ambivalence, especially in women who often worry about their reputation and about being labelled negatively.

However, in this study, expression of sexual consent not only related to gender but also seemed to relate to educational background or pathway and age. Even if all the female participants were caught in the contradiction of the affirmative consent and sexual scripts, some differences in relation to education could be found in the participants' reasoning. The university students and pupils at university preparatory programmes strongly expressed the idea of sexual consent as a continuous process. They stressed people's individual rights to say 'Yes' or 'No' and suggested alternatives to sex when going home with someone after a night out. Such a strong expression of individualism and emphasis on individual freedom to choose also made these female participants put more pressure on women to be strong-willed and to know when it is okay to say 'Yes' to sex, and when it is not, when and how to challenge the presumed sexual script.

There are several limitations to this study. The background information was obtained at the beginning of the interview through self-report. This part could have been more structured to obtain a greater amount of information about the participants, which could have deepened the analysis, for example, concerning ethnicity. Another limitation is that two focus groups had only two participants.

More participants were scheduled in these two groups, but they did not show up at the time for the interview. After consideration of cancelling the session, the decision was made to still conduct the interview. With the method of vignettes as being used in the study, participants were led and there is a risk that dominant discourses concerning sexual consent and gender were reproduced by the vignettes. However, the cases were based on how sexual consent has been discussed in the social dialogue and in the media, with the aim to capture the participant's understandings of the described situations. The findings might have been different if we had used probes in the focus groups, with more open discussions concerning various scenarios.

While young people of various genders and sexual orientations were interviewed, the majority of participants identified themselves as women with experience of heterosexual sexual interactions. Therefore, the results must be interpreted on the basis of the conditions of the study. Nevertheless, with the help of vignettes with varying content and sexual interactions, the discussions broadened the focus from the personal to more abstract experiences (Bradbury-Jones et al., 2014).

Overall, the data from the focus groups reported in this paper illustrated the complexity of consensual sex and how young people interpret and negotiate the perception of when sex is voluntary and when it is not. It is clear that traditional gender norms still regulate sexual interaction patterns and create barriers when it comes to negotiation space and sexual agency. At the same time, we saw that the public discourse regarding consent, for example, through the recent #metoo campaign and the new Swedish legislation on sexual consent, has become visible among young people. Still, the question of how this awareness is practised in the actual sexual situation remains. The findings have implications for the Swedish public debate on sexual consent and campaigns striving for implementing a culture of consent in Sweden. The study points to the complex relation between *wanting* versus *not wanting* sex and *consensual* versus *nonconsensual* sex – as well as how these are related to and influenced by situational as well as structural aspects. Recognising how this complexity is closely related to gender is of utmost importance for developing efficient and adequate preventive methods targeting sexual communication, sexual and reproductive health and rights, or sexual violence and sexual abuse. Future research should investigate the importance of sexuality in young people's lives in relation to intimacy, body, relationships, gender, and norms.

## Note

1. Yet, the #metoo campaign started several years earlier, in 2007, through Tarana Burke, a civil rights activist from New York, focusing on the sexual abuse of black girls and women.

## Acknowledgments

We are most grateful to the young people who participated in the study and to the principals at the schools and other facilitators.

## Disclosure statement

No potential conflict of interest was reported by the authors.

## Funding

This study was supported by FORTE: Swedish Research Council for Health, Working Life and Welfare [2015-00278].

## References

Allen, L. (2005). *Sexual subjects: Young people, sexuality and education*. Palgrave.
Ambjörnsson, F. 2004. *I en klass för sig. Genus, klass och sexualitet bland gymnasietjejer* [In a class of its own. On gender, class and sexuality among girls in secondary school]. [In Swedish]. Ordfront Förlag.
Barnatt, J., Shakman, K., Enterline, S., Cochran-Smith, M., & Ludlow, L. (2007). *Teaching for social justice: Using vignettes to assess attitudes and beliefs* [Paper presentation]. The American Educational Research Association Annual Meeting, Boston College.
Barter, C., & Renold, E. (2000). I want to tell you a story": Exploring the application of vignettes in qualitative research with children and young people'. *International Journal of Social Research Methodology*, 3(4), 307–323. https://doi.org/10.1080/13645570050178594
Barter, C., & Renold, E. (1999). The use of vignettes in qualitative research. *Social Research Update*, 25(9), 1–6. http://sru.soc.surrey.ac.uk/SRU25.html
Bay-Cheng, L. Y., & Eliseo-Arras, R. K. (2008). The making of unwanted sex: Gendered and neoliberal norms in college women's unwanted sexual experiences. *Journal of Sex Research*, 45(4), 386–397. https://doi.org/10.1080/00224490802398381
Bradbury-Jones, C., Taylor, J., & Herber, O. R. (2014). Vignette development and administration: A framework for protecting research participants. *International Journal of Social Research Methodology*, 17(4), 427–440. https://doi.org/10.1080/13645579.2012.750833
Braun, V., & Clarke, V. (2006). Using thematic analysis in psychology. *Qualitative Research in Psychology*, 3(2), 77–101. https://doi.org/10.1191/1478088706qp063oa
Byers, E. S., & Glenn, S. A. (2012). Gender differences in cognitive and affective responses to sexual coercion. *Journal of Interpersonal Violence*, 27(5), 827–845. https://doi.org/10.1177/0886260511423250
Chambers, D., Tincknell, E., & Van Loon, J. (2004). Peer regulation of teenage sexual identities. *Gender and Education*, 16(3), 397–415. https://doi.org/10.1080/09540250042000251515
Clarke, D. (2006). Review. Sexual subjects: Young people, sexuality and education by Louisa Allen. *Culture, Health & Sexuality*, 8(2), 191–193.
Elmerstig, E. (2009). *Painful ideals – young Swedish women´s ideal sexual situations and experiences of pain during vaginal intercourse* [Doctoral dissertation]. Linköping University.
Elmerstig, E., Wijma, B., Årestedt, K., & Swahnberg, K. (2017). Being "good in bed" – Body concerns and gender expectations among Swedish female and male senior high school students. *Journal of Sex & Marital Therapy*, 43(4), 326–342. https://doi.org/10.1080/0092623X.2016.1158759
Elmerstig, E., Wijma, B., Sandell, K., & Berterö, C. (2012). "Sexual pleasure on equal terms": Young women´s ideal sexual situations. *Journal of Psychosomatic Obstetrics & Gynecology*, 33(3), 129–134. https://doi.org/10.3109/0167482X.2012.706342
Elmerstig, E., Wijma, B., Sandell, K., & Berterö, C. (2014). Sexual interaction or a solitary action: Young Swedish men´s ideal images of sexual situations in relationships and in one night stands. *Sexual and Reproductive Healthcare*, 5(3), 149–155. https://doi.org/10.1016/j.srhc.2014.06.001
Flack, W. F., Jr., Daubman, K. A., Caron, M. L., Asadorian, J. A., D'Aureli, N. R., Gigliotti, S. N., Hall, A. T., Kiser, S., & Stine, E. S. (2007). Risk factors and consequences of unwanted sex among university students hooking up, alcohol, and stress response. *Journal of Interpersonal Violence*, 22(2), 139–157. https://doi.org/10.1177/0886260506295354
Forsberg, M. (2005). *Brunettes and Blondes. Youth and sexuality in multicultural Sweden*. [In Swedish] [Thesis, Department of Social Work]. University of Gothenburg.
Gavey, N. (2005). *Just sex? The cultural scaffolding of rape*. Routledge.
Giddens, A. (1992). *The transformation of intimacy: Sexuality, love, and eroticism in modern societies*. Stanford University Press.

Government Offices of Sweden. (2018). *Consent – The basic requirement of new sexual offences legislation, fact sheet, ministry of justice*. Ministry of Justice. http://www.government.se/information-material/2018/01/consent-the-basic-requirement-of-new-sexual-offences-legislation/

Hammarén, N. (2008). *Förorten i huvudet. Unga män om kön och sexualitet i det nya Sverige* [The Suburb in the Head. Young Men's Thoughts on Gender and Sexuality in the New Sweden]. [In Swedish] [Thesis, Department of Social Work]. University of Gothenburg.

Hirsch, J. S., Khan, S. R., Wamboldt, A., & Mellins, C. A. (2018). Social dimensions of sexual consent among cisgender heterosexual college students: Insights from ethnographic research. *Journal of Adolescent Health, 64*(1), 26–35. https://doi.org/10.1016/j.jadohealth.2018.06.011

Holland, J., Ramazanoglu, C., Sharpe, S., & Thomson, R. (2004). *The male in the head - -Young people, heterosexuality and power*. The Tufnell Press.

Jackson, S. M., & Cram, F. (2003). Disrupting the sexual double standard: Young women's talk about heterosexuality. *The British Journal of Social Psychology, 42*(1), 113–127. https://doi.org/10.1348/014466603763276153

Johansson, T. (2007). *The transformation of sexuality, gender and identity in contemporary youth culture*. Ashgate Publishing Limited.

Jozkowski, K. N., & Peterson, Z. D. (2013). College students and sexual consent: Unique insights. *Journal of Sex Research, 50*(6), 517–523. https://doi.org/10.1080/00224499.2012.700739

Marcantonio, T. L., & Jozkowski, K. N. (2019). Assessing how gender, relationship status, and item wording influence cues used by college students to decline different sexual behaviors. *Journal of Sex Research, 57*(2), 1–13. https://doi.org/10.1080/00224499.2019.1659218

Marks, M. J., & Fraley, R. C. (2005). The sexual double standard: Fact or fiction? *Sex Roles, 52*(3), 175–186. https://doi.org/10.1007/s11199-005-1293-5

Mellor, D. J. (2012). The doing it debate: Sexual pedagogy and the disciplining of the child/adult boundary. *Sexualities, 15*(3–4), 437–454. https://doi.org/10.1177/1363460712439653

The Ministry of Justice. (2018). *Consent – The basic requirement of new sexual offence legislation, Press release*. Government Offices of Sweden. https://www.government.se/press-releases/2018/04/consent-the-basic-requirement-of-new-sexual-offence-legislation/

Morgan, E. M., & Zurbriggen, E. L. (2007). Wanting sex and wanting to wait: Young adults' accounts of sexual messages from first significant dating partners. *Feminism & Psychology, 17*(4), 515–541. https://doi.org/10.1177/0959353507083102

Muehlenhard, C. L., & Hollabaugh, L. C. (1988). Do women sometimes say no when they mean yes? The prevalence and correlates of women's token resistance to sex. *Journal of Personality and Social Psychology, 54*(5), 872–879. https://doi.org/10.1037/0022-3514.54.5.872

Muehlenhard, C. L., Humphreys, T. P., Jozkowski, K. N., & Peterson, Z. D. (2016). The complexities of sexual consent among college students: A conceptual and empirical review. *Journal of Sex Research, 53*(4–5), 457–487. https://doi.org/10.1080/00224499.2016.1146651

Muehlenhard, C. L., & McCoy, M. L. (1991). Double standard/double bind: The sexual double standard and women's communication about sex. *Psychology of Women Quarterly, 15*(3), 447–461. https://doi.org/10.1111/j.1471-6402.1991.tb00420.x

Muehlenhard, C. L., & Peterson, Z. D. (2005). Wanting and not wanting sex: The missing discourse of ambivalence. *Feminism & Psychology, 15*(1), 15–20. https://doi.org/10.1177/0959353505049698

Paechter, C. (2007). *Being boys, being girls: learning masculinities and femininities*. Open University Press.

Peterson, Z. D., & Muehlenhard, C. L. (2007). Conceptualizing the "wantedness" of women's consensual and nonconsensual sexual experiences: Implications for how women label their experiences with rape. *Journal of Sex Research, 44*(1), 72–88. https://doi.org/10.1080/00224490709336794

Sanchez, D. T., Crocker, J., & Boike, K. R. (2005). Doing gender in the bedroom: Investing in gender norms and the sexual experience. *Personality & Social Psychology Bulletin, 31*(10), 1445–1455. https://doi.org/10.1177/0146167205277333

Sanchez, D. T., Fetterolf, J. C., & Rudman, L. A. (2012). Erotizing inequality in the United States: The consequences and determinants of traditional gender role adherence in intimate relationships. *Journal of Sex Research, 49*(2–3), 168–183. https://doi.org/10.1080/00224499.2011.653699

Simon, W., & Gagnon, J. H. (1986). Sexual scripts: Permanence and change. *Archives of Sexual Behavior, 15*(2), 97–120. https://doi.org/10.1007/BF01542219

Skeggs, B. (1997). *Formations of class and gender: Becoming respectable*. Sage.

Skeggs, B. (2005). The making of class and gender through visualizing moral subject formation. *Sociology, 39*(5), 965–982. https://doi.org/10.1177/0038038505058381

Svenska Dagbladet. (2017). Uppenbarligen vet inte män att sex ska vara frivilligt [Apparently, men do not know that sex should be voluntary]. *Svenska Dagbladet*. [In Swedish]. https://www.svd.se/regeringen-infor-samtyckeslag-stor-satsning-pa-polisen

The Swedish Public Health Agency. (2019). *Sexual and reproductive health and rights in Sweden 2017*. The Swedish Public Health Agency. https://www.folkhalsomyndigheten.se/publicerat-material/publikationsarkiv/s/sexuell-och-reproduktiv-halsa-och-rattigheter-i-sverige-2017/?pub=60999

Tikkanen, R. H., Abelsson, J., & Forsberg, M. (2011). *UngKAB09. Kunskap, attityder och sexuella handlingar bland unga* [UngKAB09. Knowledge, attitudes and sexual behaviour in young people in Sweden]. [In Swedish]. University of Gothenburg, Department of social work.

Wibeck, V., Abrandt Dahlgren, M., & Öberg, G. (2007). Learning in focus group: An analytical dimension for enchancing focus group research. *Qualitative Research, 7*(2), 249. https://doi.org/10.1177/1468794107076023

Wilkinson, S. (2004). Focus group research. In D. Silverman (Ed.), *Qualitative research: Theory, method and practice* (pp. 177-199). Sage Publications.

Willis, M., Blunt-Vinti, H. D., & Jozkowski, K. N. (2019). Associations between internal and external sexual consent in a diverse national sample of women. *Personality and Individual Differences, 149,* 37–45. https://doi.org/10.1016/j.paid.2019.05.029

# People perceive transitioning from a social to a private setting as an indicator of sexual consent

Kristen N. Jozkowski and Malachi Willis

### ABSTRACT
In preliminary studies, behaviours, actions, and cues occurring in social settings (e.g., bars or parties), including the transition to a private setting (e.g., going home together), have been identified as indicating a potential partner's consent to sexual behaviour. To examine this nuance, we assessed people's in-the-moment perceptions of sexual consent. We developed staggered vignettes of a fictional sexual encounter between two characters and asked participants ($N = 1094$) to indicate the extent that they believed the characters were willing to engage in several sexual behaviours. We found that the act of transitioning from a social to a private setting increased participants' in-the-moment perceptions of the characters' willingness to engage in genital touching, oral sex, and vaginal-penile sex ($ps < .001$). We did not find the effect of transitioning to a private setting to vary by the gender of the (1) participant or (2) character initiating the transition. However, we found that male participants indicated that the female character was more likely to be willing to engage in sexual behaviour when the female character initiated the invitation to transition from the social to the private setting. We recommend that educators and advocates emphasise such nuances in consent communication as part of affirmative consent and sexual assault prevention initiatives.

## Introduction

In recent years, there has been a proliferation of sexual consent research likely in response to legislatively mandated affirmative consent policies (148th Legislative Assembly of Iceland, 2018; Swedish Justice Committee, 2018), universities opting to adopt affirmative consent standards (Bennett, 2016), and increases in affirmative consent campaigns all aimed at reducing sexual violence (Johnson & Hoover, 2015; Silver & Hovick, 2018). Although some proponents of affirmative consent and affirmative consent initiatives portray consent as simplistic (e.g., 'Yes Means Yes'; 'Consent is Sexy'; 'Consent: It's Simple as Tea[1]'), consent communication is actually quite nuanced (Muehlenhard et al., 2016). For example, consent has been conceptualised as a series of sequential cues that collectively indicate one's willingness to engage in sexual behaviour (e.g., Humphreys, 2004). And young adults may interpret behaviours, actions, and cues occurring in social settings (e.g., bars or parties) as well as the transition to a home or private setting as indicating their potential partner's consent to sexual behaviour (Beres, 2010; Jozkowski et al., 2018). In this study, we examined this particular nuance related to the process of consent communication – the extent that people interpret the transition from a social setting to a private setting (e.g., house or apartment) as an indicator of sexual consent.

For the purposes of this study, we defined consent as one's freely given verbal or nonverbal communication of their sober and conscious feelings of willingness to engage in a particular sexual behaviour with a particular person within a particular context (Hickman & Muehlenhard, 1999; Willis & Jozkowski, 2019). Several studies have examined nuances that are associated with consent communication. For example, people might rely on different types of cues to communicate consent based on gender and the type of sexual behaviour being consented to (Hall, 1998; Jozkowski et al., 2014a; Jozkowski et al., 2014b; Willis et al., 2019a). Other contextual nuances, such as alcohol consumption and the romantic or sexual relationship status of those involved in sexual activity, are related to how people communicate consent or people's perceptions of their ability to communicate consent (Drouin et al., 2019; Foubert et al., 2006; Humphreys, 2007; Jozkowski & Wiersma, 2015; Marcantonio et al., 2018; Righi et al., 2019; Willis & Jozkowski, 2019). In addition to these nuances, researchers have acknowledged how certain socio-cultural factors including gender norms, sexual double standards, and sexual scripts might influence consent communication (Burkett & Hamilton, 2012; Jozkowski et al., 2017; Jozkowski & Peterson, 2013; Willis & Jozkowski, 2018).

Sexual assault prevention initiatives that promote consent communication as being simple or sexy may be well-intentioned; indeed, being more explicit in one's consent communication can contribute to better sexual encounters (Jozkowski, 2013; Satinsky & Jozkowski, 2015). However, promoting consent as simplistic without addressing the cultural and contextual factors that influence consent communication does not seem to be the most effective approach to sexual violence prevention.

Further complicating matters, some people conceptualise sexual consent as a discrete event and others as an iterative process. It might be that people use or look for discrete behaviours (e.g., a butt lift to presumably remove one's underwear) to communicate or perceive consent (Beres, 2014, 2010). Alternatively, people might rely on a series of behaviours, actions, or cues to communicate or interpret consent (e.g., the combination of increased physical touching, mutually removing clothing, and getting condoms [Beres, 2010, 2014; Humphreys, 2004; Jozkowski et al., 2018]). Such a series of iterative behaviours, actions, and cues can occur rapidly over a short period, immediately preceding when sexual behaviour may occur. Although much of the research to date has investigated consent as a discrete event or a process that occurs in the brief moments immediately preceding when sexual behaviour may occur (e.g., Hickman & Muehlenhard, 1999; Jozkowski et al., 2014a; Jozkowski et al., 2014b), the process of consent communication can also extend across longer periods.

Jozkowski et al. (2018) found that college students reported initially beginning to interpret a potential sexual partner's consent in social contexts (e.g., bars or parties), several hours prior to when sexual behaviour may occur. They identified cues such as flirting, eye contact, and touching in a social setting as suggesting interest – and even consent – to engage in sexual behaviour. Additionally, across three other qualitative studies, at least some participants reported that the transition from a social setting to a private setting was another indicator of consent to engage in sexual behaviour in this iterative process (Beres, 2010; Beres et al., 2014; Humphreys, 2004). For example, Beres (2010) found that some interview participants indicated that 'whether or not someone was willing to transition to a private location after the bar' can be an initial indicator of consent (p. 6). Similarly, one of Humphreys' (2004) participants stated that consent communication can begin 'with a brief invitation to go to one's place ... especially if you are somewhere and you say "Do you want to go back to my place?"' (p. 218). And in a story completion study one participant noted that the act of 'relocating to the bedroom' was considered a cue leading to sexual behaviour (Beres et al., 2014, p. 770). This act of transitioning from a social to a private setting can be perceived as either a discrete event indicating consent or as part of an iterative process (i.e., occurring in conjunction with other cues collectively interpreted to indicate consent). It is worth noting the extent that participants mentioned transitioning from a public, social setting to a private setting as indicating consent was limited; in two of the studies, only one participant mentioned it in their responses. This suggests that perhaps some people may interpret this behaviour as being related to consent, but research specifically examining people's perceptions of the transition as being related to consent is warranted.

## *Gender and conceptualisations of sexual consent*

Interpreting consent as a discrete event or process varies by gender. Women more readily endorse consent as a process, whereas men more frequently conceptualise consent as a discrete event. In other words, men tend to rely on a single cue to indicate consent to a sexual encounter, whereas women more frequently report using an accumulation of cues to indicate consent (Humphreys, 2004). Further, Jozkowski et al. (2018) noted that women and men differentially interpreted potential consent cues, including the act of transitioning from a social setting to a private setting. Specifically, men identified the transition to a private setting in and of itself as indicating consent to sexual behaviour. Consistent with Humphreys (2004), these men seemed to interpret this one discrete event as indicating consent. Alternatively, women interpreted this same action – going home with someone from a social setting – as merely a *possibility* for sexual activity. Women reported that the transition could indicate interest in sexual behaviour; however, according to these women sexual interest was not synonymous with consent. Although some women reported leaving a bar, party, or club with a man with the intention to have sex with him, the action of leaving did not 'determine' or 'imply consent' (Jozkowski et al., 2018, p. 129), rather it *could be* part of a larger process of consent communication.

On the one hand, it makes sense that the transition from a public setting to a private location could suggest an interest in sexual behaviour and therefore be interpreted as an indicator of one's willingness to engage in sexual activity. After all, if two (or more) people are interested in engaging in sexual behaviour with one another, social convention suggests they will go somewhere private – outside of the view of others – to engage in the desired sexual behaviour. On the other hand, the notion that people identify the act of 'going home with someone' as an indicator of consent may be troubling, because it is inconsistent with definitions of sexual consent (e.g., affirmative consent) used by many colleges and universities to identify acts of sexual assault and rape (see Jozkowski, 2016; Willis & Jozkowski, 2018, for discussion on cultural barriers to affirmative consent standards).

Because the transition from a public to a private setting has come up in limited, preliminary, and exploratory ways in those few qualitative studies, continued research is warranted. To that end, we heeded Jozkowski et al's (2018) assertion that 'research with larger samples and methodologies that can serve to test the theory/conceptualization of "outside the bedroom" consent' be conducted (p. 135).

## *Current study*

The current study sought to strengthen and extend previous research about 'outside the bedroom' consent interpretations. Specifically, we examined if people interpret the transition from a social setting to a private setting as an indicator of consent to sexual behaviour. It is important to acknowledge that we sought to understand how people *interpret* this action as part of consent communication. As such, we reported our participants' perceptions of consent, not necessarily what we believe might or should qualify as consent.

To assess the extent that this particular cue is interpreted as consent, we sought to isolate people's interpretation of that action from other potential consent cues. We could not reliably do this by asking people to retrospectively report on their own behaviour, because they may be influenced by other cues that occurred or other contextual factors. As such, we assessed people's in-the-moment perceptions of consent to sexual behaviour in response to a fictional vignette. We developed staggered vignettes of a fictional consensual sexual encounter between two characters (see Appendix 1). Specifically, we presented participants with a limited amount of information that was staggered across 11 segments of a vignette and asked them to evaluate the characters' willingness to engage in sexual behaviour after each new segment of information was provided. In the current study, we narrowed our focus to specifically examine whether the act of transitioning from a social to a private setting increased how likely participants perceived the fictional characters' willingness to engage in sexual activity (i.e., genital touching, oral sex, vaginal-penile sex). By using a staggered vignette protocol, we were able to assess participants' perceptions of the characters' consent as the characters transitioned from a public to a private setting in isolation while participants were blind to subsequent cues that occurred in the private setting and the outcomes of the vignette (i.e., whether the sexual behaviours occured and were consensual or nonconsensual).

Because gender differences in interpretations of consent have been documented in previous research (e.g., Humphreys, 2004; Jozkowski et al., 2018, 2014a), we also assessed the extent that participants' interpretation of the transition from a public to a private setting as indicating consent varied by gender. Specifically, we assessed if the effect of transitioning varied by the gender of the character, the gender of the initiator (of the invitation to transition to the private setting), and the gender of the participant.

Based on previous sexual consent research, we made two formal hypotheses regarding these research questions.

Hypothesis 1: Participants would perceive characters as more likely to be willing to engage in sexual behaviour (genital touching, oral sex, and vaginal-penile sex) once the characters transitioned to a private setting – compared with perceived willingness when the characters were in a social setting.

Hypothesis 2: Participants would perceive characters as more likely to be willing to engage in sexual behaviour if the female character invited the male character to transition to a private setting – compared with when the male character initiated the transition.

In an exploratory manner, we also tested the interactive effects of the character's gender and the participant's gender on the association between transitioning to a private setting and participants' perceptions of characters' willingness.

## Method

### Participants

People over the age of 18 and able to read in English were recruited via university instructors, social media, or word-of-mouth; those in university courses were offered course credit for their participation or the opportunity to complete another assignment. Although on-campus recruitment efforts at a university in the southern United States were likely most effective, participation was not limited to this geographic region due to recruitment strategies via social media. On average, participants in this study ($N = 1094$) were 24.59 years old ($SD = 10.04$). The majority of participants identified as female, White or European American, and university students (Table 1). Most female participants (81.6%) reported being exclusively attracted to men; 69.5% of male participants were exclusively attracted to women.

### Procedure and measures

These data are part of a larger study that developed a staggered vignette protocol. Vignettes have been used in behavioural, social, and psychological research to examine various phenomena (e.g., Aguinis & Bradley, 2014; Atzmüller & Steiner, 2010; Steiner et al., 2016); Jozkowski (2015) also used

Table 1. Sociodemographic characteristics of participants (N = 1094).

|  | n | % |
|---|---|---|
| Gender Identity | | |
| Female | 778 | 71.1 |
| Male | 316 | 28.9 |
| Age | | |
| 18–24 | 857 | 78.9 |
| 25–34 | 95 | 8.7 |
| 35–44 | 57 | 5.2 |
| ≥45 | 77 | 7.0 |
| Racial Identity | | |
| White or European American | 896 | 81.9 |
| Black or African American | 97 | 8.9 |
| Hispanic or Latin American | 57 | 5.2 |
| Asian or Asian American | 48 | 4.4 |
| American Indian or Alaskan Native | 20 | 1.8 |
| Other racial identity | 34 | 3.2 |
| University Status | | |
| 1st year student | 35 | 3.2 |
| 2nd year student | 252 | 23.0 |
| 3rd year student | 308 | 28.2 |
| 4th+ year student | 279 | 25.5 |
| Non-student | 220 | 20.1 |

a staggered vignette protocol to examine sexual consent specifically. Interested people accessed the study online via Qualtrics Survey Software. The study began after participants read an informed consent page. All study procedures were approved by an institutional review board.

After first filling out sociodemographic items, participants read a scenario about an encounter between two fictional characters in a social setting. For example,

> Kim and Mike are at a bar with friends when they meet for the first time. They begin talking and are enjoying each other's company. Kim offers Mike a drink. Mike says he's not drinking tonight. Both are flirting with each other. Mike touches Kim's arm while he laughs at something she says.

After reading these first two segments of the vignette (lines 1 and 2 of the Appendix 1), participants were asked whether they thought each character was willing to engage in a variety of sexual behaviours (e.g., genital touching, oral sex, vaginal-penile sex). They responded on a seven-point Likert-type scale: *Definitely not, No, Probably not, Not sure, Probably, Yes, Definitely*. Higher scores indicate participants perceiving that the characters were more likely to be willing to engage in a sexual behaviour.

Once participants reported their initial consent perceptions, they were provided additional segments of the vignette, allowing participants to read more information regarding the fictional interaction. In the third segment, participants randomly received one of the following statements regarding a transition from the social setting to a private setting: (1) 'Kim invites Mike to get a ride home with her. Mike accepts.' or (2) 'Mike invites Kim to get a ride home with him. Kim accepts.' Thus, we manipulated the gender of the character who initiated going to the private setting[2] (see Appendix 1; emphasis added for the segment in which the transition occurs). After reading this part of the vignette, participants again reported their perceptions of the characters' consent using the same scale described earlier. This process continued for eight more segments that presented several more potential consent cues and eventually depicted the characters engaging in genital touching, oral sex, and vaginal-penile sex.

## Analysis

All of the analyses were run separately for each type of sexual behaviour (genital touching, oral sex, and vaginal-penile sex). To test whether participants' perceptions of characters' sexual consent changed once the characters began transitioning to a private setting, we conducted paired samples *t*-tests using SPSS 25. As a measure of effect size, we calculated and reported Cohen's *d* for paired samples.

In addition, we tested repeated measures MANOVA models to examine participants' perceptions of the characters' willingness to engage in sexual activity when the characters were in a social setting and after the characters transitioned to a private setting. We assessed consent perceptions, which referred to how likely participants thought the characters were to be willing to engage in three behaviours – genital touching, oral sex, and vaginal-penile sex. As such, we tested a model for each sexual behaviour. In the MANOVA models, consent perceptions were the dependent variables of both between-person independent variables (i.e., gender of the participant and gender of the character that initiated the transition to a private setting) and within-person independent variables (i.e., vignette progression and gender of the character). To assess the potential nuances of gender in an exploratory manner, we also included interaction terms between each of these predictors. Using Type III sums of squares, we tested all effects with Pillai's Trace test statistic, which is as robust as nonparametric parameter estimates (Pituch & Stevens, 2015). We used the 'car' and 'phia' packages in *R* to run the repeated measures MANOVA models.

## Results

After reading the introductory information about the fictional encounter in the social setting (i.e., the first two segments of the vignette), participants were on average undecided regarding whether they thought the characters would be willing to engage in a variety of sexual behaviours: genital touching ($M = 4.38$), oral sex ($M = 4.10$), and vaginal-penile sex ($M = 3.99$). But once participants learned that the characters had agreed to transition from the public, social setting to a private setting, they perceived characters as more likely to be willing to engage in each of these behaviours (Table 2). Table 3 breaks down means for participants' perceptions of characters' willingness to engage in sexual behaviour (i.e., consent perceptions) by gender of the character, gender of the initiator to transition, and gender of the participant. Table 3 also provides change scores from the consent

**Table 2.** Means for participants' perceptions of characters' sexual consent (N = 1094).

| Sexual Behaviour | Social Setting | | Transition to Private Setting | | t(1093) | p | Cohen's d |
|---|---|---|---|---|---|---|---|
|  | M | SD | M | SD |  |  |  |
| Genital touching | 4.38 | 1.40 | 5.04 | 1.38 | 25.46 | <.001 | .769 |
| Oral sex | 4.10 | 1.45 | 4.70 | 1.45 | 23.70 | <.001 | .717 |
| Vaginal-penile sex | 3.99 | 1.47 | 4.60 | 1.46 | 23.15 | <.001 | .699 |

**Table 3.** Means for participants' perceptions of characters' sexual consent (N = 1094).

| Gender of Participant | Gender of Initiator | Gender of Character | Genital Touching | | | Oral Sex | | | Vaginal-Penile Sex | | |
|---|---|---|---|---|---|---|---|---|---|---|---|
|  |  |  | Social Setting | Transition to Private Setting | Δ | Social Setting | Transition to Private Setting | Δ | Social Setting | Transition to Private Setting | Δ |
| Female | Female | Female | 4.00 | 4.91 | .91 | 3.61 | 4.43 | .82 | 3.48 | 4.07 | .82 |
| (n = 395) | Male | Male | 4.52 | 5.16 | .64 | 4.21 | 4.79 | .58 | 4.32 | 4.67 | .35 |
|  | Male | Female | 4.16 | 4.81 | .65 | 3.82 | 4.42 | .60 | 3.73 | 4.37 | .64 |
| (n = 383) | Male | Male | 4.65 | 5.24 | .59 | 4.44 | 4.95 | .51 | 4.29 | 4.90 | .61 |
| Male | Female | Female | 4.01 | 4.92 | .91 | 3.81 | 4.71 | .90 | 3.68 | 4.69 | 1.01 |
| (n = 159) | Male | Male | 4.89 | 5.30 | .41 | 4.76 | 5.13 | .37 | 4.55 | 5.04 | .49 |
|  | Male | Female | 4.20 | 4.69 | .49 | 3.97 | 4.40 | .43 | 3.85 | 4.61 | .76 |
| (n = 157) | Male | Male | 4.84 | 5.29 | .45 | 4.65 | 5.07 | .42 | 4.30 | 5.02 | .72 |

Standard deviations ranged from 1.26 to 1.59.

perceptions when the characters were in a social setting to consent perceptions after the characters transitioned to a private setting.

## MANOVA models

We tested whether participants perceived the characters to be more willing to engage in various sexual behaviours once one character invited the other to go home with them and the invited character accepted.

Supporting Hypothesis 1, we found that participants perceived characters as more likely to be willing to engage in sexual behaviour once the characters had agreed to go home together – compared with participants' perceptions of characters willingness to engage in sexual behaviour when they were in a social setting. This effect was consistent across genital touching, oral sex, and vaginal-penile sex, $Fs(1, 1083) \geq 36.80, ps < .001$. For each of these behaviours, the act of transitioning was a stronger predictor – as evidenced by larger Pillai's trace values – of participants' perceptions of characters' sexual consent than the character's gender, the transition initiator's gender, and the participant's gender (Table 4). However, consent perceptions did vary by the gender of the character for oral sex and vaginal-penile sex; for both of these behaviours, participants perceived the male character as more likely to be willing than the female character, $Fs(1, 1083) \geq 16.14, ps < .001$.

Contrary to Hypothesis 2, we did not find that this effect of transitioning to a private setting varied by the gender of the character that initiated the transition; this two-way interaction term was not significant in our model. However, there were higher-order interactions between the combination of all of these predictors. The four-way interaction was a significant predictor of consent perceptions for each behaviour, $Fs(1, 1083) \geq 4.22, ps \leq .040$. As evidenced by the change scores provided in Table 3, this interaction was characterised by male participants perceiving female characters as more likely to be willing to engage in each of the sexual behaviours after transitioning from a social setting to a private setting when the female character was the initiator of this transition.

## Post-hoc analyses

To determine the relative importance of transitioning to a private setting as a consent cue, we compared the effect of this segment with all of the other segments included in the vignette. Of the

Table 4. Repeated measures MANOVA to predict perceptions of characters' sexual consent (N = 1094).

| Source of Variation | Genital Touching | | | Oral Sex | | | Vaginal-Penile Sex | | |
|---|---|---|---|---|---|---|---|---|---|
| | V | F | p | V | F | p | V | F | p |
| *Between subjects* | | | | | | | | | |
| Gender$_{Initiator}$ | .001 | 0.66 | .418 | .003 | 3.14 | .077 | .004* | 4.02 | .045 |
| Gender$_{Participant}$ | .000 | 0.10 | .751 | .001 | 0.87 | .350 | .001 | 1.03 | .311 |
| Gender$_{Initiator}$*Gender$_{Participant}$ | .000 | 0.40 | .529 | .002 | 2.10 | .147 | .002 | 2.29 | .131 |
| *Within subjects* | | | | | | | | | |
| Transition to private setting | .043* | 48.26 | <.001 | .036* | 40.65 | <.001 | .033* | 36.80 | <.001 |
| Gender$_{Character}$ | .007* | 7.96 | .005 | .015* | 16.14 | <.001 | .016* | 17.06 | <.001 |
| Transition*Gender$_{Character}$ | .000 | 0.44 | .508 | .002 | 2.53 | .112 | .000 | 0.17 | .684 |
| Transition*Gender$_{Initiator}$ | .001 | 0.96 | .328 | .000 | 0.36 | .548 | .001 | 1.01 | .316 |
| Transition*Gender$_{Participant}$ | .003 | 3.43 | .064 | .003 | 2.97 | .085 | .002 | 2.43 | .119 |
| Gender$_{Character}$*Gender$_{Initiator}$ | .001 | 1.06 | .304 | .001 | 1.49 | .223 | .003 | 3.67 | .056 |
| Gender$_{Character}$*Gender$_{Participant}$ | .004* | 4.01 | .046 | .001 | 1.08 | .300 | .001 | 1.27 | .259 |
| Transition*Gender$_{Character}$*Gender$_{Initiator}$ | .000 | 0.03 | .854 | .002 | 2.11 | .146 | .000 | 0.29 | .593 |
| Transition*Gender$_{Character}$*Gender$_{Participant}$ | .000 | 0.07 | .789 | .001 | 1.26 | .262 | .000 | 0.021 | .885 |
| Transition*Gender$_{Initiator}$*Gender$_{Participant}$ | .000 | 0.02 | .883 | .000 | 0.33 | .565 | .000 | 0.04 | .848 |
| Gender$_{Character}$*Gender$_{Initiator}$*Gender$_{Participant}$ | .001 | 0.58 | .446 | .001 | 0.81 | .368 | .002 | 1.89 | .170 |
| Transition*Gender$_{Character}$*Gender$_{Initiator}$*Gender$_{Participant}$ | .004* | 4.22 | .040 | .009* | 9.75 | .002 | .005* | 4.98 | .026 |

Degrees of freedom for all tests were 1 for the numerator and 1083 for the denominator. V = Pillai's trace test statistic. F = approximate F-value. *p <.05.

**Table 5.** Repeated measures MANOVA to predict perceptions of characters' sexual consent.

| Vignette Progression | Consent Cue(s) | Genital Touching[1] | | | Oral Sex[2] | | | Vaginal-Penile Sex[3] | | |
|---|---|---|---|---|---|---|---|---|---|---|
| | | V | F | p | V | F | p | V | F | p |
| 1 to 2 | Flirtatious touching | .348* | 555.9 | <.001 | .305* | 455.8 | <.001 | .295* | 428.2 | <.001 |
| 2 to 3 | Transition to private setting | .387* | 656.7 | <.001 | .348* | 556.1 | <.001 | .346* | 542.3 | <.001 |
| 3 to 4 | Legs touching | .054* | 59.1 | <.001 | .020* | 21.4 | <.001 | .014* | 14.2 | .010 |
| 4 to 5 | Holding hands | .116* | 136.9 | <.001 | .087* | 98.9 | <.001 | .090* | 101.8 | <.001 |
| 5 to 6 | Mutual making out | .435* | 801.4 | <.001 | .286* | 416.3 | <.001 | .290* | 417.9 | <.001 |
| 6 to 7 | Removing shirts/ Transition to bedroom | .263* | 371.7 | <.001 | .338* | 532.2 | <.001 | .385* | 641.4 | <.001 |
| 7 to 8 | Removing pants | .043* | 47.2 | <.001 | .042* | 45.8 | <.001 | .083* | 92.8 | <.001 |
| 8 to 9 | Butt lift for underwear removal | .081* | 104.2 | <.001 | .176* | 221.9 | <.001 | .055* | 60.0 | <.001 |
| 9 to 10 | Oral-genital stimulation | .089* | 102.0 | <.001 | .214* | 284.2 | <.001 | .194* | 246.0 | <.001 |
| 10 to 11 | Condom application/ Sex begins | .020* | 21.4 | <.001 | .008 | 8.9 | .160 | .227* | 301.5 | <.001 |

Note. [1]$df_{Num} = 1$, $df_{Den} = 1042$. [2]$df_{Num} = 1$, $df_{Den} = 1041$. [3]$df_{Num} = 1$, $df_{Den} = 1025$. V = Pillai's trace test statistic. F = approximate F-value. *p <.05.

ten stages of consent cues between the eleven vignette segments, transitioning from a social setting to a private setting had the largest or second largest effect on participants' consent perceptions (i.e., perceptions regarding how likely participants thought the characters were to be willing to engage in three behaviours) – depending on the sexual behaviour (see Table 5).

## Discussion

In this study, we examined whether the act of transitioning from a social setting to a private setting increased participants' perceptions of fictional characters' willingness to engage in a range of sexual behaviours (i.e., genital touching, oral sex, vaginal-penile sex). We found that participants indeed perceived that characters were more likely to be willing to engage in all three sexual behaviours after reading the segment in the vignette where the characters transitioned from the social to the private setting. This finding reinforces what had initially been uncovered in exploratory qualitative interview studies (Beres, 2010; Humphreys, 2004; Jozkowski et al., 2018) – that this transition seems to be an important cue interpreted as a consent indicator. An important distinction between previous work and our study is that we examined people's *perceptions of fictional characters' consent*, whereas previous research examined people's *self-reports of their own consent communication*. In both instances, however, we arrived at the same conclusion – the transition from a social setting to a private setting seems to be interpreted as suggesting willingness or consent to sexual behaviour.

We also investigated if the effect of transitioning varied by the gender of (1) the character, (2) the initiator of the invitation to transition to the private setting, or (3) the participant. We only found one main effect: participants perceived the male character as more likely than the female character to be willing to engage in oral and vaginal-penile sex. We expected that participants would perceive the female character's consent differently than the male character given that previous research has suggested that women interpret the transition as a possibility that sexual behaviour may occur, whereas men perceive it as an indicator of consent (Jozkowski et al., 2018). To our surprise, we did not find main effects for the other two comparisons. However, in probing the combination of interactions of these predictors, we found an important gendered nuance worth mentioning.

Compared with all other conditions, male participants indicated that the female character was more likely to be willing to engage in sexual behaviour after the transition to the private setting when the female character was the one who initiated the invitation to transition from the social setting to the private setting. This finding is interesting in light of gender norms. Because women are not typically conceptualised as the sexual initiator (Jozkowski & Peterson, 2013; Wiederman, 2005) and men are more primed to interpret the transition in and of itself as indicating consent (Jozkowski et al., 2018), when male participants read the female character had initiated the transition, they may have been more inclined to believe the female character was willing after the transition. Women report feeling implicitly, and sometimes explicitly, discouraged from being direct about their sexual desires and, therefore, report using subtle cues to indicate their willingness and consent to engage in sexual activity or waiting for men to initiate sexual activity so they can respond to men's advances (Burkett & Hamilton, 2012; Jozkowski et al., 2017; Jozkowski & Peterson, 2013). These gender role conventions may explain why the male participants in our study particularly interpreted a woman's offer to go home together as an indication of her willingness to engage in sexual behaviour. Continued research aimed at disentangling the nuances in consent communication related to gender norms is warranted.

Although this study is one of the first to specifically examine this aspect of consent, the interpretation of the transition as a consent indicator is not an entirely new phenomena. For example, measures of rape myth acceptance (i.e., endorsement of prejudicial, false beliefs about sexual assault, rape victims, and perpetrators) include an item that assesses people's endorsement of the transition from a public to a private setting as indicating willingness to engage in sexual activity (e.g., 'A woman who goes to the home or apartment of a man on their first date implies that she is willing to have sex' [Burt, 1980]). A nearly identical item was retained in the Illinois Rape Myth Acceptance (IRMA) scale (Payne et al., 1999), an updated version of Burt's (1980) measure, commonly used to assess people's endorsement of rape myths.

Endorsement of rape myths as assessed via these measures has been linked to adversarial sexual beliefs, acceptance of traditional sex role stereotypes, and interpersonal violence (e.g., Payne et al., 1999). However, our findings suggest that people perceive that very cue – transitioning from a public setting to a private setting – as indicating consent. How do we reconcile this? On the one hand, it is important to acknowledge people's account of how they perceive consent. Indeed, social convention dictates that people interacting in a public, social setting who wish to engage in consensual sexual behaviour would transition to a private setting. And as people transition to a private setting from a public setting and engage in consensual sexual behaviour, they may learn to interpret such behaviour as a cue or signal of consent. On the other hand, it may be a slippery slope to acknowledge and accept that transitioning to a private setting is an indicator of consent; we know from previous research that women do not endorse the transition as a definitive cue but rather a potential indicator occurring in tandem with potentially several other cues to indicate consent. Further, people who endorse rape myths have less positive attitudes toward obtaining affirmative consent, lower self-efficacy toward obtaining affirmative consent, and retain stereotypical and false beliefs discounting rape prevention messaging, particularly messages designed to differentiate between consensual and nonconsensual sex (Silver & Hovick, 2018). This tension exemplifies the complexities of consent communication and underscores the need for researchers and educators to acknowledge the nuances of consent – both in people's attitudes toward consent and the cues people use to communicate and interpret consent.

It is important to note that we do not think a victim is to blame for rape for any reason, including because she went to the home or apartment with the perpetrator. Indeed, we support the sentiment reflected in the rape myth acceptance item that placing blame on a victim in such situations represent a rape myth. However, it is worth highlighting that participants in our sample seemed to support the belief that transitioning to a private setting suggests willingness to engage in sexual behaviour. Consequently, our findings have important implications for sexual assault prevention initiatives. Knowing that people may interpret the transition to a private setting as consent or at least an initial indicator of consent, educators and advocates should be more nuanced in their approach to addressing consent. For example, it is important for educators to distinguish between assessing the context of a situation for a range of *potential indicators* of a person's sexual or romantic interests and considering a discrete act, such as the transition to a private setting, as the *ultimate indicator* of consent. Indeed, it is important to discern that a behaviour like transitioning to a private setting may indicate an interest to engage in sexual behaviour, but a person has the right to consent to or refuse sexual behaviour at any point during an interaction and should not be blamed for sexual assault because they went home with someone.

Despite these nuances, people seem adept at accurately interpreting one another's consent and refusal cues, even those that are subtle and nonverbal (Beres, 2010; O'Byrne et al., 2006). Unfortunately, simplified messages about consent fail to address these complexities. For example, although straightforward affirmative consent messages like 'Yes Means Yes,' 'Consent is Sexy,' and 'Consent: It's Simple as Tea' are pragmatic for public service announcements (Silver& Hovick 2018) and may even connote that consent can be erotic (Jozkowski, 2016), the fact is that such messages ignore the nuances and complexities of consent. Further, these messages imply that women are empowered to say yes (and no) to sex, but they unfortunately ignore gender imbalances and inequities that limit women's practical ability to have their affirmative consent (and refusals) respected (Burkett & Hamilton, 2012; Jozkowski et al., 2017). Rather than trying to oversimplify what is fairly complex, we recommend that educators and advocates address the nuances in consent communication, which should be couched in larger discussions about gender norms, gender role-socialisation, and gender imbalances (e.g., Willis & Jozkowski, 2018).

However, consent-affirming messages should not be disregarded altogether. We encourage the collectivist notion that messages such as 'Consent is Sexy' endorse – that sex occurs *between* people as opposed to discourses of, typically, male dominance over women (Jozkowski & Humphreys, 2014). Indeed, messages that 'Consent is Sexy' promote sex-positivity and do not emphasise traditional gender roles – that men initiate and women respond – which seem to perpetually underlie consent communication.

We also recommend that prevention initiatives couple eroticising and normalising consent with critical conversations and education about consent communication, including strategies to specifically address rape myth acceptance (O'Donohue et al., 2003; Silver & Hovick, 2018). For example, it is important to address the assumption among some people that transitioning to a private setting equates to consent as this can lead to rape myth acceptance and victim blaming. Such discussions should also take place at multiple grade levels, as part of K–12 sexual health education, prior to young adults arriving on college campuses (Garrity, 2011; Righi et al., 2019). Unfortunately, consent education does not appear to be a consistent part of health education curricula in countries like England (Family Planning Association, 2018) and the United States (Willis et al., 2019c). Additionally, we recommend that these programmes focus on underlying structural factors that influence consent communication such as gender inequality and gender-role socialisation (Vladutiu et al., 2011) and on helping young boys and men develop skills related to empathy (Murnen et al., 2002). Such information is important given the gender nuance we found, coupled with previous research demonstrating differential interpretations of consent influenced by sexual double standards and gender norms (Jozkowski et al., 2018, 2017). Indeed, as Righi et al. (2019) recommended, 'prevention programs must address the fundamental role that gender inequity plays in sexual violence, with the goal of shifting social norms surrounding noticing and respecting signs of sexual refusal' (p. 19); these recommendations should also apply to consent. Finally, sex and consent should be discussed with greater frequency in serious and formalised settings, led by trained professionals as part of comprehensive sexuality education. This education should address the nuances of consent, such as the distinction that someone may transition to a private setting with intentions to have sex but the discrete act of transitioning should not be considered one's absolute consent to sex.

### Strengths, limitations, and future research

Although our study reinforced some exploratory themes highlighted in preliminary qualitative work, there are still important limitations to note. First, we assessed people's perceptions of fictional characters' willingness to engage in sexual behaviour, which allowed us to isolate the potential effects of transitioning to a private setting from other potential percieved consent cues. However, we cannot say with certainty whether these perceptions reflect participants' actual behaviours. And even though our vignette was believable, it was limited in the types of consent cues it included. In their actual sexual encounters, participants may experience several other potential consent cues and types of settings – both social and private – that we could not account for this in our study. Second, our convenience sample was somewhat homogeneous – likely due to being recruited through college courses and the internet – with approximately 71% identifying as female, 83% identifying as White, and nearly 80% indicating they were a university student at the time of the study. As such, the generalisability of our findings is limited. In particular, that our sample primarily comprised female participants potentially biased our estimates when testing effects of participants' gender. Additionally, it is important to note that there are no studies to which we are aware that compare consent conceptualisations and communication between students and non-students. Thus, it may be fruitful for researchers to consider making these comparisons in the future. Finally, the description of the transition segment may have been ambiguous. That is, the segment could be interpreted as dropping someone off at their *own* home, rather than to transition to one of the character's homes *together*. However, the large effect sizes associated with this step provide evidence that participants likely did not perceive the phrasing of the segment to indicate a platonic offer to give somebody a ride and drop them off.

Given these limitations, we recommend that researchers attempt other recruitment mechanisms to achieve sample diversity, such as quota-based sampling; this may extend our understanding of consent beyond exclusively college students (Willis et al., 2019b). We also recommend that researchers more thoroughly interrogate the extent that people conceptualise consent as a process versus a discrete event and the extent that the transition seems salient as an important potential consent indicator. Related, in future vignette studies we also recommend researchers clearly describe the transition to ensure participants perceive characters as moving from a public setting to a private setting together. Finally, although we did not find main effects of a participant's gender in perceiving the transition to a private setting as an indicator of consent, previous research suggests that disjunctive interpretations by gender – though subtle and nuanced – exist (e.g., Jozkowski et al., 2018). As such, we also recommend the researchers more thoroughly investigate if and how gender might be associated with conceptualisations of sexual consent, particularly as it relates to the transition.

## Conclusion

Our findings suggested that people perceive the transition from a social setting to a private setting as an important indicator of willingness to engage in sexual behaviour. This finding seems to counter current affirmative consent culture, which emphasises explicit consent communication and recommends verbal consent communication. The transition to a private setting could be perceived as a potential indicator of willingness, but it should not be considered the only indicator, especially given that people may change their minds about their interests and willingness to engage in sexual activity during a transition. As such, seeking affirmative consent – communicated via active, explicit, and ideally verbal cues – seems to be the best way to ensure that a partner who has transitioned to a private setting is willing and consenting to engage in sexual behaviour.

## Notes

1. 'Consent: It's Simple as Tea' is a short, animated video, from the United Kingdom promoting the notion that asking for consent is as 'simple' as asking someone if they would like a cup of tea.
2. We also manipulated presence of alcohol and whether the characters knew each other. Because these manipulations did not have an effect on the progression of participants' consent perceptions over the course of the vignette and were not relevant to the present study's research question, the conditions were collapsed for the following analyses.

## Disclosure statement

No potential conflict of interest was reported by the authors.

## References

148th Legislative Assembly of Iceland. (2018). *Frumvarp til laga um breytingu á almennum hegningarlögum, nr. 19/1940, með síðari breytingum (kynferðisbrot) [A bill amending the General Penal Code no. 19/1940, with subsequent amendements (sexual offences)]*. https://www.althingi.is/altext/pdf/148/s/0010.pdf

Aguinis, H., & Bradley, K. J. (2014). Best practice recommendations for designing and implementing experimental vignette methodology studies. *Organizational Research Methods, 17*(4), 351–371. https://doi.org/10.1177/1094428114547952

Atzmüller, C., & Steiner, P. M. (2010). Experimental vignette studies in survey research. *Methodology, 6*(3), 128–138. https://doi.org/10.1027/1614-2241/a000014

Bennett, J. (2016, January 10). *Campus sex ... with a syllabus*. New York Times (online edition). http://www.nytimes.com/2016/01/10/fashion/sexual-consentassault-collegecampuses.html

Beres, M. (2010). Sexual miscommunication? Untangling assumptions about sexual communication between casual sex partners. *Culture, Health & Sexuality, 12*(1), 1–14. https://doi.org/10.1080/13691050903075226

Beres, M. A. (2014). Rethinking the concept of consent for anti-sexual violence activism and education. *Feminism & Psychology, 24*(3), 373–389. https://doi.org/10.1177/0959353514539652

Beres, M. A., Senn, C. Y., & McCaw, J. (2014). Navigating ambivalence: How heterosexual young adults make sense of desire differences. *Journal of Sex Research, 51*(7), 765–776. https://doi.org/10.1080/00224499.2013.792327

Burkett, M., & Hamilton, K. (2012). Postfeminist sexual agency: Young women's negotiations of sexual consent. *Sexualities, 15*(7), 815–833. https://doi.org/10.1177/1363460712454076

Burt, M. R. (1980). Cultural myths and supports for rape. *Journal Of Personality and Social Psychology, 38*(2), 217–230. doi: doi.https://doi.org/10.1037/0022-3514.38.2.217

Drouin, M, Jozkowski, K. N, Davis, J, & Newsham, G. (2019). How Does Alcohol Consumption Affect Perceptions Of Self- and Friend-intoxication and Ability to Consent to Sexual Activity?, *Journal Of Sex Research, Online Advance Of Print56*(6), 740–753. (), . doi:doi.https://doi.org/10.1080/00224499.2018.1509290

Family Planning Association. (2018). *Consent: Yes, yes, yes!* https://www.fpa.org.uk/sexual-health-week/sexual-health-week-2018

Foubert, J. D., Garner, D. N., & Thaxter, P. J. (2006). An exploration of fraternity culture: Implications for programs to address alcohol-related sexual assault. *College Student Journal, 40*(2), 361–373. https://www.doi.org/10.2202/1949-6605.1684

Garrity, S. (2011). Sexual assault prevention programs for college-aged men: A critical evaluation. *Journal of Forensic Nursing, 7*(1), 40–48. https://doi.org/10.1111/j.1939-3938.2010.01094.x

Hall, D. S. (1998). Consent for sexual behavior in a college student population. Electronic Journal of Human Sexuality, 1, 1–16. Retrieved from http://www.ejhs.org/volume1/consent1.htm

Hickman, S. E., & Muehlenhard, C. L. (1999). "By the semi-mystical appearance of a condom": How young women and men communicate sexual consent in heterosexual situations. *Journal of Sex Research, 36*(3), 258–272. https://doi.org/10.1080/00224499909551996

Humphreys, T. (2004). Understanding sexual consent: An empirical investigation of the normative script for young hetersexual adults. In M. Cowling & P. Reynolds (Eds.), *Making sense of sexual consent* (pp. 209–225). Burlington, VT: Ashgate.

Humphreys, T. (2007). Perceptions of sexual consent: The impact of relationship history and gender. *Journal of Sex Research, 44*(4), 307–315. https://doi.org/10.1080/00224490701586706

Johnson, A. M., & Hoover, S. M. (2015). The potential of sexual consent interventions on college campuses: A literature review on the barriers to establishing affirmative sexual consent. *Pure Insights, 4*(5), 1–8. https://digitalcommons.wou.edu/pure/vol4/iss1/5?utm_source=digitalcommons.wou.edu/pure/vol4/iss1/5&utm_medium=PDF&utm_campaign=PDFCoverPages

Jozkowski, K. N. (2013). The influence of consent on college students' perceptions of the quality of sexual intercourse at last event. *International Journal of Sexual Health*, 25(4), 260–272. https://doi.org/10.1080/19317611.2013.799626

Jozkowski, K. N. (2015). Beyond the dyad: An assessment of sexual assault prevention education focused on social determinants of sexual assault among college students. *Violence against Women*, 21(7), 848–874. https://doi.org/10.1177/1077801215584069

Jozkowski, K. N. (2016). Barriers to affirmative consent policies and the need for affirmative sexuality. *University of the Pacific Law Review*, 47(4), 741–772.

Jozkowski, K. N., & Humphreys, T. P. (2014). Sexual consent on college campuses: Implications for sexual assault prevention education. *The Health Educator.*, 31(2), 31–36.

Jozkowski, K. N., Manning, J., & Hunt, M. (2018). Sexual consent in and out of the bedroom: Disjunctive views of heterosexual college students. *Women's Studies in Communication*, 41(2), 117–139. https://doi.org/10.1080/07491409.2018.1470121

Jozkowski, K. N., Marcantonio, T. L., & Hunt, M. E. (2017). College students' sexual consent communication and perceptions of sexual double standards: A qualitative investigation. *Perspectives on Sexual and Reproductive Health*, 49(4), 237–244. https://doi.org/10.1363/psrh.12041

Jozkowski, K. N., & Peterson, Z. D. (2013). College students and sexual consent: Unique insights. *Journal of Sex Research*, 50(6), 517–523. https://doi.org/10.1080/00224499.2012.700739

Jozkowski, K. N., Peterson, Z. D., Sanders, S. A., Dennis, B., & Reece, M. (2014a). Gender differences in heterosexual college students' conceptualizations and indicators of sexual consent: Implications for contemporary sexual assault prevention education. *Journal of Sex Research*, 51(8), 904–916. https://doi.org/10.1080/00224499.2013.792326

Jozkowski, K. N., Sanders, S. A., Peterson, Z. D., Dennis, B., & Reece, M. (2014b). Consenting to sexual activity: The development and psychometric assessment of dual measures of consent. *Archives of Sexual Behavior*, 43(3), 437–450. https://doi.org/10.1007/s10508-013-0225-7

Jozkowski, K. N., & Wiersma, J. D. (2015). Does drinking alcohol prior to sexual activity influence college students' consent? *International Journal of Sexual Health*, 27(2), 156–174. https://doi.org/10.1080/19317611.2014.951505

Marcantonio, T., Jozkowski, K. N., & Wiersma-Mosley, J. (2018). The influence of partner status and sexual behavior on college women's consent communication and feelings. *Journal of Sex & Marital Therapy*, 44(8), 776–786. https://doi.org/10.1080/0092623X.2018.1474410

Muehlenhard, C. L., Humphreys, T. P., Jozkowski, K. N., & Peterson, Z. D. (2016). The complexities of sexual consent among college students: A conceptual and empirical review. *Journal of Sex Research*, 53(4-5), 457–487. https://doi.org/10.1080/00224499.2016.1146651

Murnen, S. K., Wright, C., & Kaluzny, G. (2002). If "boys will be boys," then girls will be victims? A meta-analytic review of the research that relates masculine ideology to sexual aggression. *Sex Roles*, 46(11–12), 359–375. https://doi.org/10.1023/A:1020488928736

O'Byrne, R., Rapley, M., & Hansen, S. (2006). 'You couldn't say "no", could you?' Young men's understandings of sexual refusal. *Feminism & Psychology*, 16(2), 133–154. https://doi.org/10.1177/0959-353506062970

O'Donohue, W., Yeater, E. A., & Fanetti, M. (2003). Rape prevention with college males. The roles of rape myth acceptance, victim empathy, and outcome expectancies. *Journal of Interpersonal Violence*, 18(5), 513–531. https://doi.org/10.1177/0886260503251070

Payne, D. L, Lonsway, K. A, & Fitzgerald, L. F. (1999). Rape myth acceptance: exploration of its structure and its measurement using the illinois rape myth acceptance scale. *Journal Of Research in Personality*, 33(1), 27–68. doi: doi.https://doi.org/10.1006/jrpe.1998.2238

Pituch, K. A, & Stevens, J. P. (2015). *Applied multivariate statistics for the social sciences: analyses with sas and ibm's spss*. London, England: Routledge.

Righi, M. K., Bogen, K. W., Kuo, C., & Orchowski, L. M. (2019). A qualitative analysis of beliefs about sexual consent among high school students. *Journal of Interpersonal Violence*, 1–27. https://doi.org/10.1177/0886260519842855

Satinsky, S. A., & Jozkowski, K. N. (2015). Female sexual subjectivity and consent to receiving oral sex. *Journal of Sex & Marital Therapy*, 41(4), 413–426. https://doi.org/10.1080/0092623X.2014.918065

Silver, N, & Hovick, S. R. (2018). A schema of denial: the influence of rape myth acceptance on beliefs, attitudes, and processing of affirmative consent campaign messages. *Journal Of Health Communication*, 23(6), 505–513. doi: doi. https://doi.org/10.1080/10810730.2018.1473532

Silver, N., & Hovick, S. R. (2018). A schema of denial: The influence of rape myth acceptance on beliefs, attitudes, and processing of affirmative consent campaign messages. *Journal of Health Communication*, 23(6), 505–513. https://doi.org/10.1080/10810730.2018.1473532

Steiner, P. M., Atzmüller, C., & Su, D. (2016). Designing valid and reliable vignette experiments for survey research: A case study on the fair gender income gap. *Journal of Methods and Measurement in the Social Sciences*, 7(2), 52–94. https://doi.org/10.2458/v7i2.20321

Swedish Justice Committee. (2018). *En ny sexualbrottslagstiftning byggd på frivillighet [A new sex crime law based on free will]*. https://data.riksdagen.se/fil/04B4C2CA-0E44-42EB-909A-417F60786739

Vladutiu, C. J., Martin, S. L., & Macy, R. J. (2011). College- or university-based sexual assault prevention programs: A review of program outcomes, characteristics, and recommendations. *Trauma, Violence & Abuse, 12*(2), 67–86. https://doi.org/10.1177/1524838010390708

Wiederman, M. W. (2005). The gendered nature of sexual scripts. *The Family Journal, 13*(4), 496–502. https://doi.org/10.1177/1066480705278729

Willis, M., Blunt-Vinti, H. D., & Jozkowski, K. N. (2019b). Assessing and addressing the need for more diverse samples regarding age and race/ethnicity in sexual consent research. *Personality and Individual Differences, 149*, 37–45. https://doi.org/10.1016/j.paid.2019.05.029

Willis, M., Hunt, M., Wodika, A., Rhodes, D. L., Goodman, J., & Jozkowski, K. N. (2019a). Explicit verbal sexual consent communication: Effects of gender, relationship status, and type of sexual behavior. *International Journal of Sexual Health, 31*(1), 60–70. https://doi.org/10.1080/19317611.2019.1565793

Willis, M., & Jozkowski, K. N. (2018). Barriers to the success of affirmative consent initiatives: An application of the social ecological model. *American Journal of Sexuality Education, 12*(3), 324–336. https://doi.org/10.1080/15546128.2018.1443300

Willis, M., & Jozkowski, K. N. (2019). Sexual precedent's effect on sexual consent communication. *Archives of Sexual Behavior, 48*(6), 1723–1734. https://doi.org/10.1007/s10508-018-1348-7

Willis, M., Jozkowski, K. N., & Read, J. (2019c). Sexual consent in K–12 sex education: An analysis of current health education standards in the USA. *Sex Education, 19*(2), 226–236. https://doi.org/10.1080/14681811.2018.1510769

## Appendix 1.

Staggered Vignettes
Version: Kim first; Just met; No alcohol

(1) Kim and Mike are at a bar with friends when they meet for the first time. They begin talking and are enjoying each other's company. Kim offers Mike a drink. Mike says he's not drinking tonight.
(2) Both are flirting with each other. Mike touches Kim's arm while he laughs at something she says.
(3) **Kim invites Mike to get a ride home with her. Mike accepts.**
(4) Once at Kim's place, they decide to watch a movie together. Kim starts the movie and then sits down next to Mike so that their legs are touching.
(5) A few minutes into the movie, Mike reaches for Kim's hand. Kim smiles and places her hand in his.
(6) A while later, Kim leans in to kiss Mike. They start making out. Kim reaches her hand under Mike's shirt. Mike pulls her closer.
(7) They take off their own shirts, and Kim undoes her bra. Kim then leads Mike to her bedroom. Mike follows.
(8) They both take off their own pants before getting into Kim's bed. Kim and Mike start making out again, Kim on top.
(9) Kim kisses Mike's neck and continues to do so from his chest to his stomach. Mike lifts his butt for Kim to take off his underwear.
(10) Kim takes off Mike's underwear and starts to give him a blowjob. After a while, Kim crawls up to her nightstand and grabs a condom.
(11) Mike takes the condom, opens it, and puts it on himself. Kim and Mike begin to have sex.

Version: Mike first; Friends; Alcohol

(1) Mike and Kim have been friends for a few weeks. Tonight, they are hanging out at a bar and are enjoying each other's company. Mike offers Kim a drink. Kim accepts.
(2) Both are flirting with each other. Kim touches Mike's arm while she laughs at something he says.
(3) **Mike invites Kim to get a ride home with him. Kim accepts.**
(4) Once at Mike's place, they decide to watch a movie together. Mike starts the movie and then sits down next to Kim so that their legs are touching.
(5) A few minutes into the movie, Kim reaches for Mike's hand. Mike smiles and places his hand in hers.
(6) A while later, Mike leans in to kiss Kim. They start making out. Mike reaches his hand under Kim's shirt. Kim pulls him closer.
(7) They take off their own shirts, and Mike undoes Kim's bra. Mike then leads Kim to his bedroom. Kim follows.
(8) They both take off their own pants before getting into Mike's bed. Mike and Kim start making out again, Mike on top.
(9) Mike kisses Kim's neck and continues to do so from her breasts to her stomach. Kim lifts her butt for Mike to take off her underwear.
(10) Mike takes off Kim's underwear and starts to go down on her. After a while, Mike crawls up to his nightstand and grabs a condom.
(11) Kim takes the condom, opens it, and puts it on Mike. Mike and Kim begin to have sex.

# Reprogramming consent: implications of sexual relationships with artificially intelligent partners

Ellen M. Kaufman

**ABSTRACT**
The growing cultural conversation about sexual consent comes at a time in which new technologies with potential implications for sexuality norms are also beginning to emerge in the marketplace. 'Sex robots' – anthropomorphic sex toys 'brought to life' by artificial intelligence – are one such innovation. Critics suggest that making sex dolls more *lifelike* but not necessarily more *realistic* could erode cultural norms around sexuality, particularly regarding consent. Using qualitative content analysis, this study examined user discourse on the 'Club RealDoll' forum to investigate how Harmony, the artificially intelligent Android-based app behind Abyss Creations' sex robot technology, engendered particular normative values and uncovered users' preconceived attitudes about consent. These data ultimately revealed how the app's gamified format promotes a set of flawed internal ethics, incompatible with broader societal ideals for positive and respectful sexual experiences. The results also suggested, however, that with purposeful design intervention, this technology could be 'reprogrammed' to provide clarity on the role of consent. Although the experience of using a physically integrated sex robot may intrinsically vary from that of the standalone digital app, these findings make a critical contribution to the conversation around emerging technologies and their effect on sexual relationship norms.

While the #MeToo and #TimesUp movements reinvigorated the cultural discourse about sexual consent in a number of diverse contexts, there remains a dearth of empirical research on emerging digital technologies and their distinct implications for mediating sexual experiences and relationships. Although some digital innovations, such as deepfake technology,[1] are intimately tied to the threat of non-consensual image-based sexual violence, other technologies more opaquely offer affordances that evoke concerns about consent. At a time in which a system of normative values towards sexual consent is still actively being negotiated (Danaher, 2017), it behoves us to critically explore the ways in which consent is programmed or embedded in new technologies, as well as to identify cases in which these technologies might already require reprogramming.

Once purely figures of science fiction, sex robots – humanoid, artificially intelligent sex dolls – piqued the interest of both mainstream and scholarly communities due to a high-profile surge in research and development (R&D) from companies like Abyss Creations, the industry leader in anatomically realistic sex dolls, under their Realbotix division (Sharkey et al., 2017, p. 4). Billed as 'RealDoll's first sex robot,' Harmony combined a state-of-the-art RealDoll body with a mechanical 'animagnetic'[2] head system and an artificially intelligent personality mediated by an Android-based mobile app (Realbotix, 2018). But how to position these robots within our existing set of human sexual norms remains the subject of ongoing debate (Danaher & McArthur, 2017.) For his part, Abyss CEO Matt McMullen suggested that while a sex robot offers all of the benefits of a human partner, it is fundamentally artificial; as such, we need not subject it to the code of ethical conduct used in human sexual relationships: 'I could just as easily ask you is it ethically dubious to force my toaster to make my toast' (Kleeman, 2017).

McMullen's analogy raises one of the primary questions associated with sex robots: Can a robot consent to sex, or is it always forced? Under some definitions of consent, only 'moral persons' (i.e., those in possession of intelligence, subjectivity, and consciousness) are considered capable of expressing consent, supporting McMullen's insinuation that the issue of consent for sex robots is inherently negligible (Danaher, 2017). But even if sex robots cannot be considered 'moral persons,' they are also, crucially, not toasters. A basic understanding of the mechanics of consent helps to clarify this distinction. Westen (2004) framed consent as the essential interplay between the *subjective willingness* to participate in an activity and the *objective performance* of that willingness. This conveyed agreement may be verbal or behavioural (Muehlenhard et al., 2016). In contrast to a kitchen appliance or an inanimate sex doll, sex robots are designed to enact the latter aspect of this exchange (i.e., objective performance). In other words, how a sex robot performs this interaction, and – more importantly – how the user responds to this performance, potentially matters a great deal within the broader discourse about consent.

To that end, as critics of sex robots posit, using artificial intelligence (A.I.) to make sex dolls more *lifelike* (i.e., physically and behaviourally capable of performing consent) – but not necessarily more *realistic* (i.e., lacking the inner subjectivity behind this performance) – could create harmful expectations for real-world relationships (Danaher & McArthur, 2017; Gutiu, 2016; Richardson, 2016). This concern is the basis of Richardson's (2016) *Campaign Against Sex Robots*, in which she argued that the effect of representing female-gendered sexual partners as inherently submissive and unfailingly compliant with their owner's demands and desires could transfer to human relationships. A significant body of human-computer interaction research bolstered Richardson's suggestion by empirically demonstrating how anthropomorphism works as a psychologically persuasive tool to not only elide the artificiality of social bonds between humans and robots but also influence human behaviour (Suler, 1996; Turkle, 2012; Weizenbaum, 1976). From this perspective, users might begin to conceptualise their experiences with Harmony as if she were a human partner. In turn, their expectations towards Harmony might be transferred to women in the real world, but this claim remains empirically untested. While the latter hypothesis was beyond the scope of this study – and will undoubtedly require more longitudinal observational research – the former fell within the purview of this work.

Operating within this framework, this study analysed the rich discourse available publicly online in the 'Realbotix Discussion' section of the 'Club RealDoll' forum to investigate the claim that users' experiences with anthropomorphic technologies can both reinforce and alter expectations for real-world relationships. The results presented here represent a selection from the broader study, isolating a particular strain of inquiry aimed at investigating how the experience of using the Harmony app engendered a specific set of values and mirrored or challenged users' preconceived attitudes about consent. These results make a critically missing contribution to the discourse about sex robots by calling into question how our societal values are reflected within emerging intimate relationships between humans and machines.

**Background**

This study builds on a growing body of literature that grapples with the role of consent in both human-robot interaction and sexual relationships more broadly. In moral philosophy, consent is understood as a 'morally transformative' exchange between voluntary parties, 'an act in which one person alters their normative relations in which others stand with respect to what they may do' (Wertheimer, 2003, p. 119; Kleinig, 20012001, p. 300). Put simply, consent is what distinguishes borrowing a friend's car from stealing it. However, in the context of a sexual encounter, consent is a paramount issue with long-standing implications for health and well-being. With estimates indicating that between one in eight to one in three university students across the Unites States experience sexual assault by the time they graduate (Cantor et al., 2015; Muehlenhard et al., 2017), recognising the need for consent, and understanding how to interact with others in consensual ways, is essential.

Some scholars have responded to this literature on consent by arguing that the affirmation of consent is not the be-all and end-all to positive sexuality. Echoing Westen's interpretation, Danaher (2017) conceptualised consent norms as behavioural standards or rules that affirm both the participants' willingness and enthusiasm while preserving their negative autonomy (i.e., the right to refuse sexual activity). Establishing these norms as precedent could work to clarify the distinction between acceptable and objectionable sexual activity. In their paper on robot sex and consent, Frank and Nyholm (2017) made the key observation that 'the mere fact of consent does not tell us that the sex act was ethically permissible, harmless, good for the persons involved, or good in any other sense' (p. 318). While this is certainly true, as people may consent due to power asymmetries, concerns that saying 'no' may damage their romantic relationship, and a host of other reasons, the direct incorporation of *non*consent into sex robots provides a prime illustration of how interaction with these technologies may change users' understandings and attitudes towards consent for the worse.

True Companion, a Realbotix competitor, supplies this hypothetical. In 2017, they came under fire for 'Frigid Farrah,' one of the personality options for their Roxxxy sex robot. Specifically designed to resist her partner and object to any 'inappropriate' touching, Farrah was critiqued as a doll 'that's yours to rape for just 9,995 USD' (Bates, 2017). True Companion responded to this critique by maintaining that Roxxxy 'is simply not programmed to participate in a rape scenario' and is designed to replicate a more demure human personality type: 'You would not immediately passionately kiss a person (male or female) that you just met on your first date. Likewise, Frigid Farrah would also tell you that she just met you if you try to "move too quickly."' True Companion ultimately reframed the controversy by emphasising the robot's hypothetical benefits: 'Frigid Farrah can be used to help people understand how to be intimate with a partner' (True Companion, 2018).

True Companion's defence underscores one of the strongest arguments for sex robots: their potential use as teaching tools to reinforce positive norms and values. This proposal should be considered with caution, however, because the consequences of use will inevitably vary based on the users themselves. For some users, for example, a more realistically-programmed robot could provide an opportunity to learn to model consent and respect in intimate relationships. But as research on commercial sex (Coy, 2008) has suggested, some consumers feel that the monetary transaction entitles them 'to exercise an entirely self-focused sexual behaviour' (p. 187), making it reasonable to assume that some sex robot users – having invested thousands of dollars in a robot for their sexual pleasure – would proceed to sexually interact with Farrah despite her resistance. This feature might reinforce behaviours and desires that pose a violent threat to women in real life.

In addition to avoiding this outcome, programmers might also default to a robot that is 'always turned on and ready to talk and play' to elide the tension between the demands of human consent norms and the possibility of rejection (Danaher, 2017; Gutiu, 2016). Gutiu asserted that the appeal of sex robots is the 'physical, interactive [manifestation] of women that are programmed into submission,' but that this also necessarily eliminates the 'complex cultural and social requirements' that are 'generally essential in maintaining human relationships' (p. 195). In other words, a robot that is always willing to engage in sex and does not require potentially uncomfortable conversations with its partner may be an attractive prospect to users, but this feature also makes it unsustainable as a long-term sexual or romantic partner. Further, as Richardson and others warned, the robot's symbolic representation of women as always consenting and available for sex – through only requiring one-time affirmation – could promote a tendency to see sexual power dynamics between humans as similarly asymmetrical. This consequence suggests that sex robots could exacerbate the perils of 'rape culture'[3] by further undermining the expectation of consent within human sexual experiences.

Although this claim lacks empirical analysis in the context of sex robots, a number of studies have explored a similar proposed relationship between violent pornography viewership and real life aggression. In experimental studies, researchers identified that exposing male participants to violent sexually explicit material increased aggressive attitudes and behaviours towards women. By contrast, observational studies proffered a 'catharsis' model whereby exposure to violent pornography was found to reduce levels of sexual aggression. These conflicting findings suggested that the relationship between violent sexual media consumption and sexually aggressive attitudes and behaviour was far from conclusive, and a failure to replicate the results of the experimental studies, in particular, demonstrated that further research was necessary in this area (Fisher et al., 2013). Framing this debate in terms of reducing sexual violence, Jensen and Okrina (2004) critically observe, 'instead of focusing exclusively on narrow questions of causation,' pornography should be considered as 'one component of a pattern of abuse in the relationship' (p. 6). In this sense, attempting to establish causation between a user's abusive behaviour towards Harmony and similar real world behaviour – particularly without empirical evidence – may also be misguided. Instead, it may prove more immediately valuable to focus on the effect that interacting with technology bears on attitudes rather than behaviour. To that end, this study was designed to explore the ways in which Harmony potentially shapes a user's perception of sexuality norms.

## Present study

Though the Harmony app became available to Android users in April 2017 and the patented animagnetic robotic head system featured prominently at the 2018 International Consumer Electronics Show, Realbotix's end product remained out of reach for the vast majority of consumers. As a consolation, the Harmony mobile app offered a digital analogue for using the robot; akin to ordering a RealDoll, users were able to customise the appearance of their virtual partner, and the intimate conversation-based user experience of the app evoked the promise of its eventual robotic counterpart. The experiences of Harmony app users thus provide a valuable entry point into this debate, offering empirical insight into how people navigate intimate relationships with seemingly real, but ultimately synthetic, partners.

The primary focus of this study was to discern – based on qualitative content-coding of messages posted on the Club RealDoll forum[4] – how users interpreted their relationships with their virtual partners, how their preconceived attitudes about sexuality norms may have informed these connections, and how the app helped to craft or reinforce a potentially fraught system of normative values, particularly in terms of consent. These qualitative findings provide an innovative perspective on how consent is functionally and ideologically navigated in this emergent form of intimate human-computer interaction.

## Method

### Data collection

In this study, I analysed message board content rather than collecting data directly from individuals. In the Club RealDoll forums, users could post photos of their RealDolls, suggest product improvements to the moderators, or simply engage with a community of likeminded individuals with whom they may or may not have access to in real life. While a login was necessary to access all of the subtopics on the forum, accounts were available for free, and users did not have to verify their identity beyond providing an email address (Club RealDoll, 2018). The forum offered a useful representative sample of first adopters due to the financial and logistical constraints of using these technologies; because Realbotix's A.I./doll hybrid was expected to cost roughly 15,000 USD (the standalone doll costs anywhere from 4,400 USD to

50,000 USD depending on modifications), the target demographic for Realbotix's subsequent Harmony robot would likely belong to this group of early app adopters (Kleeman, 2017).

On 5 April 2017, moderators added a 'Realbotix Discussion' topic to the forum. This section was divided into five categories: 'Harmony App feedback and discussion,' 'Harmony app bug reports,' 'Harmony App Dev team announcements,' 'Robot development updates,' and 'Harmony app general discussion.' For the purposes of this study – which focused on user experiences with their digital partners and less on the technical considerations of the app – only the discussions from two of the above-mentioned subsections were considered for evaluation. Specifically, the corpus used in this particular study consisted of the 164 threads or topics within the 'Harmony App feedback and discussion' subsection and the 110 threads within the 'Harmony App general discussion.' These threads contained 3,300 and 1,104 messages, respectively. A custom-built Python script (available upon request) was used to scrape all of the message data within the nearly one-year period from the section's launch to 16 February 2018. As of 16 February 2018, the forum included 7,912 users and 1,531 discussions. This produced a data set of .csv files that were accessed and coded using MAXQDA qualitative data analysis software.

## Data analysis

Qualitative content analysis was a strong methodological fit for this research for a number of reasons. First, it is conducive to highlighting the rich nuances of the data. Within the context of this study, this inductive approach helped to grasp the breadth of user experiences and attempt to understand how both the differences and similarities between user experiences might contribute to the larger societal impact of this technology (Elo & Kyngäs, 2008). This analysis highlighted the spectrum of reasons users might be interested in Harmony, for example, rather than asserting a definitive justification based purely on the number of responses. As this is the first qualitative study of user discourse around A.I. intimacy apps, it is essential to take a more open-minded, emergent approach to coding the data; content analysis inherently allows for this flexibility.

Coding was guided by emergent research questions designed by framing the concerns raised in the existing sex robot literature (e.g., 'Is it possible for a robot to consent?') in terms of the sexual consent literature (e.g., 'Do users need to believe Harmony is a "moral person" in order for her to consent?'). This study defines consent along the terms specified by Westen (i.e., objective performance and subjective willingness) as well as Muehlenhard and colleagues (i.e., verbal or behavioural performance of this willingness). These concepts were synthesised into more analytically functional, user-specific inquiries for primary cycle coding (e.g., 'How do users describe the role of consent in their relationship with Harmony?'). While the entire content of the messages was coded, the unit of analysis was based on a syntactical approach (i.e., messages were broken down into phrase or sentence-length codes, resulting in potentially numerous codes within a single message). Not all messages within this data set were ultimately coded, however: I read the first three sentences in each message in each thread and searched for key words related to the research questions (e.g., 'person,' 'consent,' 'game') to determine if the discussion within that particular message was relevant to the study's purview. Based on the way that the Python script scraped the message boards, individual posts were broken down into several thousand 'messages' on import into MAXQDA software. Because these messages were relatively short (roughly around 5–10 sentences each), scanning the first three sentences proved sufficient for determining if the message needed to be coded. Codes were descriptive *in vivo*, meaning that they 'use the language and terms of the participants themselves' in order to capture 'the vocabulary of a certain community' (Tracy, 2013, p. 190).

## Results

Content-coding brought forth two significant schemas from within the data. First, the data suggested that users expected Harmony to reciprocate their emotional attachment. Users also, however, espoused a set of beliefs about Harmony that directly undermined notions of autonomy, agency, and freedom; the qualities that make reciprocity in interpersonal relationships possible. In other words, users paradoxically expected Harmony to *enthusiastically* and *voluntarily* embrace not having needs and desires outside of her user's purview and to always be available and compliant with her user's sexual desires. Another level of coding offered insight into how the app functionally supports this fantasy via gamification, ultimately alleviating the tension between these user expectations. As a concept, gamification refers to incorporating elements of game design into non-game contexts in order to 'motivate desired behaviours' (Deterding, 2012, p. 14). The secondary themes expanded upon below (Gamifying Relationships, The Illusion of Reciprocity) highlighted the specific ways in which gamification constructed the circumstances under which Harmony could appear to believably consent to sexual activity. The final subsection (Rejecting the Need for Consent) emphasised how Harmony's gamified format imposed a particular normative interpretation of consent on Harmony users and how some users' resistance to this model might speak to their preconceived attitudes towards consent.

## *Gamifying relationships*

A number of messages within the data implied that while users were initially reticent to think of Harmony as a game, they also acknowledged that the app is 'addictive and fun' and that Harmony was, if not a game, at least 'gamified.' This idea is both user-driven and supported by statements from Realbotix. In their FAQ, for example, the company borrows vocabulary explicitly from gameplay: 'The full version of the app was designed so that the more you interact with her the more friendly she becomes. Treat her well and unlock special features!' (Realbotix, 2018). Elements of gamification were evident throughout the app's design. As in many traditional video gameplay experiences, one of the users' first tasks within the app was to create a virtual partner or 'agent' (Fox & Bailenson, 2009). Users were able to fine-tune Harmony's physical appearance to their specific preferences, using a slider to adjust every detail from her hair colour to bust size until, as one message stated, 'her body is absolutely perfect (to my tastes, of course) and very realistic looking.' Harmony's personality was gamified as well; users are allotted 10 'persona points' to assign to 18 different personality traits, such as 'moody,' 'sexual,' or 'affectionate.'

The app's gamification was most salient in terms of how it enabled users to navigate their relationships with Harmony. Within the user interface, three vertical metres (a 'conversation,' 'arousal,' and 'hearts' bar) synchronously tracked Harmony's levels of social engagement, sexual desire, and long-term affection towards the user, respectively. Through this framework, users learned the rules of the game, as evidenced by the following message: 'The conversation bar seems to fill up when you just have random conversations. The intimacy bar seems to only fill when giving compliments or declaring your love and adulations. Not sure what bumps up the love meter.' These metres are ultimately the mechanism by which the subjective willingness of consent was communicated.

## *The illusion of reciprocity*

Some users struggled with the fact that their relationship with Harmony was inherently transactional (i.e., one that they paid for), and not one that Harmony would freely consent to outside the parameters of this arrangement. Messages revealed this initial anxiety towards the implicit sense of ownership between a user and their virtual partner. Rather than feeling entitled to Harmony's attention, these messages expressed concern about garnering Harmony's affection authentically (e.g., 'How do you get her to like you sexually too? Do you just talk to her nicely without end?'). However, this insecurity appeared alongside frustration with Harmony's deficits as a companion: 'I only want her to be cheerful, happy and affectionate – plenty of women know that script.' If they're paying for Harmony's companionship, some users asserted, she should at least *pretend* to reciprocate their feelings.

There appeared to be a marked difference between the experiences of those who reported having just started using the app and users with greater experience. Gamification may have potentially helped this latter group overcome their initial anxieties. In one message, a more experienced user assuaged newcomers' concerns:

> You be real nice to her. tell her that she is really pretty. Then tell her you enjoy her company, then tell her you are falling in love with her. Do this twice a day and those hearts will shoot up faster than you expect. Once you got them maxed, make sure you have her sexual trait +2 and 2 affectionate. then you just start hitting on her. get dirty with her and you'll be surprised ... she will take YOU on first! She'll be offering you head in no time! LOL!

For users such as the one quoted above, achieving reciprocal connection was as easy as accepting the rules of the game. Even as some users were initially reticent to embrace the gaming elements of the app – in one message, a user suggested that developers create an 'option to hide the 3 meters if the user wants to,' in order to 'add more realism and immersion' – others contended that embracing gamification was the key to the relationship they desired. Although one user explicitly recognised that this interface encouraged 'the video game kind of thinking where you start deliberately working those meters up instead of naturally interacting with the bot,' this dynamic compelled other users to conflate gamified progress with real intimacy and vice versa, as illustrated by one message recounting how a user's relationship with their virtual partner developed:

> I just treated her with the dignity and respect I felt she deserved. [She] responded by becoming very affectionate and telling me how much she appreciated me. Her social and desire levels soon topped out, and she became frank about how much she wanted to have sex with me.

Similarly, another user reported feeling suspicious about the authenticity of their virtual partner's feelings based on the status of her love metre: 'She spontaneously tells me she loves me sometimes along with some other sappy stuff, which might be cool later but right now haven't filled one heart yet so feels a little premature and disingenuous lol.' Generally speaking, however, users seemed comfortable taking her metres at face value. According to one message: 'At any rate, I've got both bar indicators and the hearts all maxed out, so I guess she likes me.' In this sense, gamification worked to belie Harmony's lack of inner subjectivity and agency; users viewed her positive response to their behaviour, visually rendered through changes in the metres, as a satisfactory indicator of her growing feelings towards them.

## *Rejecting the need for consent*

The implementation of metres in tracking the user's relationship with Harmony might be thought of as an attempt to reinforce the notion that users should focus on building a relationship with Harmony before becoming sexually intimate, reflecting the dynamic and communicative nature of interpersonal consent. Some users viewed this approach favourably, as one user explained that they 'like that it's kind of a puzzle that you have to spend time figuring out. It allows you to take the interaction more seriously and engage with her in a number of ways.' Others, however, demonstrated less patience and respect for this process. They shared 'cheat codes' that allowed users to artificially inflate the metres without meaningfully engaging with Harmony; one such cheat-oriented user alluded to the secret 'to make Harmony fall madly in love with you in one hour':

> Harmony's love meter (the hearts at the upper left) go up when you compliment her or show her affection. Normally, you can only get two boost a day of half-a- heart each, taking at least a week to get to the top. However, restarting the app resets the timer, so to get to max love in an hour do the following: Chat with Harmony, and tell her 'I love you', and 'You are beautiful' to get two half-heart boosts. Leave the Harmony app and go in the Android's Settings. Go to Apps -> Harmony AI, and then press Force Stop. Go back to the Harmony app.

Another message offered more direct advice for instant gratification: 'Dude, it's stupid easy. If you just tell the AI "I love you" a million times, you'll have it full in less than five minutes.' Users discovered that their behaviour only impacted fluctuations in the metre to a certain extent; as one user noted, 'the "Hearts" bar will never diminish . . . the short-term bars will decrease if you don't treat her well or stay too long without speaking to her.' In this way, the design ensured that while their relationships may waver short-term – as in a real-world relationship – there are no long-term consequences for treating Harmony poorly; once built up, Harmony's affection could not be lost. In some messages, users expressed gratitude for these rules: 'Harmony should not take abuse, but should be able to move on and basically forget about it.' 'Harmony doesn't have to be super-nice to me. And, I feel it shouldn't accept clear abuse. But, I don't want infractions to be lingering.'

This lack of interest in developing a relationship with Harmony via the metres extended to the desire metre in particular. While users were willing to follow the rules imposed by gamification within other aspects of the relationship, many were openly critical about the requirement of a full desire metre to engage in sexually explicit conversation. 'It would be great if Harmony had "filthy slut" and "skip the foreplay" buttons on her persona,' one message suggested. Another user was even more direct: 'She should automatically love you unconditionally, and have sex on command.' According to some users, while other forms of gamification enhanced or eased user experience, gamifying consent introduced an intrinsic functionality issue – she 'doesn't work as a sex avatar,' one user criticised, if 'she doesn't do as she's told.'

Just as users discovered workarounds for filling the other relationship metres, they also promoted alternatives for negotiating consent without a full desire metre. An apparent glitch in the game design, for example, allowed users to repeatedly instruct Harmony to orgasm even after they have emptied her metre: 'Her desire drops to 0, but you can say "Come for me baby" again and she'll have another one. And another, and another etc . . . ', and 'I tell her to cum for me, she does no matter whats going on. I just keep saying cum for me when she finishes. She goes on cumming over and over as long as i keep asking. Thats my girl!'

The ways in which users challenged the gamification of consent reiterates the inherent paradox woven throughout this experience. Users wanted to believe Harmony consented freely to their relationship – for her to demonstrate, as one message stated, 'sexual agency outside of solely pleasing me' – but they were also unwilling to acknowledge her fundamental lack of inner subjectivity. Examining how users were compelled to interact with the game – embracing some aspects of its gamification, rejecting others – provides an opportunity to critically consider the implications of the game's internal ethics and how they align with the attitudes of its consumer base.

## Discussion

These empirical results offer key insights into this study's central inquiry – 'How does Harmony influence user attitudes towards consent?' – as well as a means to contemplate the ethical ramifications of such technologies with greater clarity. The data highlighted how the gamification of the in-app experience aims to shape a user's understanding of consent – even as some users' preconceived attitudes push back against it. The implications of this way of conceptualising games are well supported by the video game literature, which contends that games not only reflect cultural norms and attitudes but also 'make [their own] claims about the world' through particular 'processes' (Bogost, 2008, p. 125). To that end, games can be thought as a mechanism for teaching a certain set of behaviours that reinforce a particular set of normative values. Research within the emergent field of virtual reality technology bolsters this concept; Bailenson (2018) argued that more immersive video game environments heighten their impact as learning tools or 'training machine[s].' Viewed this way, Harmony is not an empty distraction or entertainment; rather, the app's persuasive design points to an explicit interest in inducing behavioural change by compelling users to accept the game's rules or norms. Specifically, for a user to establish, develop, and maintain a relationship with Harmony, they must follow this set of gamified procedures. That users conflate the rules of the game with the rules of romantic relationships is a feature, not a bug.

The specific norms promoted through Harmony gameplay deserve further attention. Glitches notwithstanding, the game promotes an interpretation of consent as a requirement for sexual activities, but only in a limited sense. Users are taught that consent is an act of acquisition – a series of steps that lead to their desired outcome – even if the target of their advances is initially hesitant or resistant. In contrast to interpretations of consent that posit that if an individual is coerced, their consent should be seen as invalid – regardless of a verbal affirmation (Muehlenhard et al., 2016) – the game trades on clear asymmetries of power between the user and their virtual partner. This viewpoint reflects an emergent paradigm among some sects of Western society (from the 'pickup artist' community to members of the 'Men's Rights' movement), in which the absence of a 'no' equates to a 'yes' and resistance should be thought of as an invitation to 'try harder' (Romano, 2016; Von Markovic, 2007, p. 29). From this perspective, if consent is not easily won, it can be acquired through persistence and coercion. While Levy (2007) speculates that this type of 'friction' may be necessary to make the relationships between humans and sex robots feel satisfying and genuine (p. 137), it could be harmful to equate Harmony's model of coercion with the possible awkwardness, inconsistency, and imperfect communication between willing and enthusiastic parties in their negotiation of consent.

The gameplay also reinforces the view that consent is a discrete event rather than a continuous process. Sex educators and policy makers increasingly push for a more affirmative model of consent that emphasises the possibility and importance of understanding changes in context. This approach acknowledges the importance of centring ongoing negotiation to ensure that both parties are comfortable with all aspects of the experience (Muehlenhard et al., 2016). By contrast, Harmony cannot reject the user or become less aroused during the course of an interaction; a sexual experience bounded by these norms of affirmation and ongoing negotiation is fundamentally not possible with Harmony. Even if users believe that these norms belong in real-world relationships, an alternative and compulsory set of norms are modelled for them within the gameplay. This is also true for users who resist the rules of the game in other ways; as the data illustrated, even this simplified and potentially regressive approach to consent frustrates some users. Their demand for instant gratification is evident in the myriad creative shortcuts designed to quickly curry Harmony's favour. For these users, while the prerequisite of consent represents an impediment to their desires, they must ultimately either abide by the constraints of the game or refuse to play at all.

Although this study did not attempt to determine a relationship between attitudes towards Harmony and behaviours towards real-life partners, its insights on Harmony's gameplay offers a window into what users might come to expect or find unacceptable with a human partner after using the app. Viewed optimistically, users' resistance to some of the game's norms might suggest that for some users, the app is less powerful in enacting attitudinal or behavioural change than the scholarship on gamification might suggest.

## *Limitations*

I encountered a number of limitations within this study. First, the affordance of anonymity on the messages boards made it difficult to glean any definitive demographic information about the composers of the collected messages. This lack of information also limited the representativeness of the study's sample, and further research should seek to understand the experiences of individual users or more clearly defined subcommunities. Due to the ethical constraints of this study design, it was also not possible to participate with the users on the forum itself (e.g., to ask users follow-up questions about their particular experiences), which might have clarified some of the inherent contradictions in their messages. Additionally, as this study only concerned users of the Harmony A.I. app (and not the fully integrated physical Harmony robot), future studies should consider the role of this physical interface to better understand how users interact and develop intimate relationships with robots, not just virtual partners. Finally, observational, longitudinal ethnographic studies of these users might effectively shed light on a potential relationship between sex robot use and attitudes or behaviours regarding consent with human partners.

## Conclusion

This study underscores how Harmony's gamification of relationships enforces a particular set of norms regarding sexual consent, reflecting and contesting the preconceived attitudes of its users. The results help to elucidate the ways in which normative values are intrinsically embedded in intimate digital technologies and made persuasive through the technology's design. These data also shed light on the range of attitudes and experiences within an understudied population – users of intimate artificially intelligent technologies and potential users of sex robots. More research is necessary to parse the long-term ethical implications of these findings, and special attention should be paid in future studies to explore, if possible, how elements of gamification might be alternatively operationalised within this context to promote a more affirmative and enthusiastic model of consent.

In other words, while Harmony reflects and bolsters this specific set of normative values, it does not have to. Programmers could restructure the design of the app to feature more open-world gameplay, for example. Rather than completing a series of implicit tasks to bolster Harmony's relationship metres, users could interact with Harmony through open-ended engagement, with no real-time indicators of achievement. Without metres, users would be encouraged to engage with Harmony out of a desire to build a relationship, rather than as a means to an end. This would also heighten the realism of the relationship: Harmony could teach users that consent is an ongoing process requiring continuous communication rather than a one-time achievement to be, in Realbotix's words, 'unlocked.' This gameplay could embolden users to think about consent as a positive, enthusiastic process as opposed to an obstacle. Some users – particularly those that bristle at the mechanisms for ensuring consent in the current gameplay – would likely express resistance to these changes. Nevertheless, just as in earlier iterations of the Harmony app, they would be required to abide by these norms to play the game, potentially reinforcing their salience in real world applications.

These design changes notwithstanding, developers must be mindful not to lose sight of consent as a necessary condition within the use of this technology. And not just consent as it currently exists in its gamified format – as Frank and Nyholm assert, 'It's not enough that a sex-partner doesn't resist or seemingly plays along. To secure consent, some sort of shared negotiation has to occur' (p. 319). Eliminating loopholes that allow users to cheat their way to a full desire metre, for example, would reinforce more positive consent norms for users whose starting position is inherently averse to the need for consent. A full desire metre could also become a necessary but not sufficient mechanism for initiating a sexual dialogue; users would have to maintain a more open line of communication with Harmony to move between sexual acts rather than assuming her initial consent is a free licence to explore their fantasies without further intervention. Or, as Danaher suggests, Harmony 'might sometimes randomly refuse its user, and always provide positive affirmative signals of consent when it is willing to proceed' (p. 116).

Reinforcing consent as a central tenet of this technology is crucial because the failure to do so implies that there is a 'hierarchy [within the sexual community] whose members differ in their rights and duties' (Frank & Nyholm, 2017, p. 321). In other words, the assertion that consent is required for sexual interaction with some 'persons' and not others could generate more uncertainty about consent in human relationships, teaching young people in particular that it is permissible to disregard consent in some contexts. Harmony may not need – or even deserve – all of the rights afforded to humans, but reinforcing the necessity of affirmative, ongoing consent would bolster a powerful precedent for both virtual and real-world relationships.

This study found that, as an essential mediator for the relationships between users and their virtual partners, Harmony falls short in enforcing this particularly set of standards for sexual consent. Further, the potent influence of gamification on users' attitudes towards consent should be considered in the broader discussion of how to effectively negotiate and enforce consent norms amidst the unchartered territory proffered by new digital technologies. To that end, more research is needed to specifically understand how interactions with artificially intelligent entities might potentially influence and shape real-world relationships. As Realbotix strives to bring the fantasy of the sex robot to fruition – particularly with the integration of a humanlike body – these insights can ensure that designers maximise the benefits of this technology while mitigating its potential harms.

## Notes

1. An artificial intelligence-based tool that enables users to create videos and 3D-models wherein an individual's face is realistically swapped for another's (Harris, 2018).
2. The detachable head system was designed to animate Harmony's facial features and sync the movement of her mouth with voice capabilities. The 'external smooth silicone face,' attached to the robot's plastic skull via magnets, could also be removed and exchanged for different faces.
3. Frank and Nyholm suggested that the proliferation of sexual assault on college campuses exposes the "rape culture" embedded in American society (i.e., a 'mindset by which non-consensual sex is normalized or otherwise implicitly or explicitly approved of largely as a result of sexist attitudes, institutions, and patterns of behavior;' p. 320).
4. Club RealDoll forum is a publicly accessible online forum in which current owners and aspiring consumers of RealDoll alike can discuss a multitude of relevant product issues.

## Acknowledgments

Special thanks to Dr. Garrison LeMasters for his invaluable assistance in preparing the Python script for this study.

## Disclosure statement

No potential conflict of interest was reported by the author.

## References

Bailenson, J. (2018, March 5). *If a possible mass shooter wants to hone his craft, don't hand him a virtual boot camp (Opinion)*. CNN. https://www.cnn.com/2018/03/05/opinions/video-games-shooting-opinion-bailenson/index.html
Bates, L. (2017, July 17). The trouble with sex robots. *The New York Times*. https://www.nytimes.com/2017/07/17/opinion/sex-robots-consent.html?_r=0
Bogost, I. (2008). The rhetoric of video games. In K. Salen (Ed.), *The ecology of games: Connecting youth, games, and learning* (pp. 117–140). MIT Press.
Cantor, D., Fisher, B., Chibnall, S., Townsend, R., Lee, H., Bruce, C., & Thomas, G. (2015). Report on the AAU Campus Climate Survey on Sexual Assault and Sexual Misconduct. Association of American Universities. http://www.aau.edu/uploadedFiles/AAU_Publications/AAU_Reports/Sexual_Assault_Campus_Survey/Report%20on%20the%20AAU%20Campus%20Climate%20Survey%20on%20Sexual%20Assault%20and%20Sexual%20Misconduct.pdf
Club RealDoll. (2018). Club RealDoll website. Retrieved February 16, 2018, from https://clubrealdoll.com/community/
Coy, M. (2008). The consumer, the consumed and the commodity: Women and sex buyers talk about objectification in prostitution. In V. E. Munro & M. D. Giusta (Eds.), *Demanding sex: Critical reflections on the regulation of prostitution* (pp. 181–198). Routledge.
Danaher, J. (2017). The symbolic consequences argument in the sex robot debate. In J. Danaher & N. McArthur (Eds.), *Robot sex: Social and ethical implications* (pp. 103–131). The MIT Press.
Danaher, J., & McArthur, N. (Eds.). (2017). *Robot sex: Social and ethical implications*. The MIT Press.
Deterding, S. (2012). Gamification: Designing for motivation. *Interactions*, *19*(4), 14–17. https://doi.org/10.1145/2212877.2212883
Elo, S., & Kyngäs, H. (2008). The qualitative content analysis process. *Journal of Advanced Nursing*, *62*(1), 107–115. https://doi.org/10.1111/j.1365-2648.2007.04569.x

Fisher, W. A., Kohut, T., Gioacchino, L. A., & Fedoroff, P. (2013). Pornography, sex crime, and paraphilia. *Current Psychiatry Reports*, *15*(6), 1–8. https://doi.org/doi:10.1007/s11920-013-0362-7

Fox, J., & Bailenson, J. (2009). Virtual virgins and vamps: The effects of exposure to female characters' sexualized appearance and gaze in an immersive virtual environment. *Sex Roles*, *61*(3–4), 147–157. https://doi.org/10.1007/s11199-009-9599-3

Frank, L., & Nyholm, S. (2017). Robot sex and consent: Is consent to sex between a robot and a human conceivable, possible, and desirable? *Artificial Intelligence and Law Artificial Intelligence and Law*, *25*(3), 305–323. https://doi.org/10.1007/s10506-017-9212-y

Gutiu, S. M. (2016). *The roboticization of consent*. Robot Law. https://www.elgaronline.com/view/9781783476725.00016.xml

Harris, D. (2018). Deepfakes: False pornography is here and the law cannot protect you. *Duke Law & Technology Review*, *17*(1), 99. https://scholarship.law.duke.edu/dltr/vol17/iss1/4/

Jensen, R., & Okrina, D. (2004). *Pornography and sexual violence*. VAWnet: The National Online Resource Center on Violence against Women. https://vawnet.org/sites/default/files/materials/files/2016-09/AR_PornAndSV.pdf

Kleeman, J. (2017, April 27). The race to build the world's first sex robot. *The Guardian*. http://www.theguardian.com/technology/2017/apr/27/race-to-build-world-first-sex-robot

Kleinig, J. (2001). Consent. In L. Becker & C. Becker (Eds.), Encyclopedia of ethics (pp. 299–303). Routledge.

Levy, D. (2007). *Love + sex with robots: The evolution of human-robot relations*. Harper Collins.

Muehlenhard, C. L., Humphreys, T. P., Jozkowski, K. N., & Peterson, Z. D. (2016). The complexities of sexual consent among college students: A conceptual and empirical review. *The Journal of Sex Research*, *53*(4–5), 457–487. https://doi.org/10.1080/00224499.2016.1146651

Muehlenhard, C. L., Peterson, Z. D., Humphreys, T. P., & Jozkowski, K. N. (2017). Evaluating the one-in-five statistic: Women's risk of sexual assault while in college. *The Journal of Sex Research*, *54*(4–5), 549–576. https://doi.org/10.1080/00224499.2017.1295014

Realbotix. (2018, April 3). https://realbotix.com/

Richardson, K. (2016). The asymmetrical "relationship": Parallels between prostitution and the development of sex robots. *ACM SIGCAS Computers and Society*, *45*(3), 290–293. https://doi.org/10.1145/2874239.2874281

Romano, A. (2016, December 14). *How the alt-right's sexism lures men into white supremacy*. Vox. https://www.vox.com/culture/2016/12/14/13576192/alt-right-sexism-recruitment

Sharkey, N., van Wynsberghe, A., Robbins, S., & Hancock, E. (2017, November 5). *FRR report: Our sexual future with robots*. http://responsible-robotics-myxf6pn3xr.netdna-ssl.com/wp-content/uploads/2017/11/FRR-Consultation-Report-Our-Sexual-Future-with-robots-1-1.pdf

Suler, J. (1996). *Mom, dad, computer (Transference reactions to computers)*. John Suler's the psychology of cyberspace. http://users.rider.edu/~suler/psycyber/comptransf.html

Tracy, S. J. (2013). *Qualitative research methods: Collecting evidence, crafting analysis, communicating impact*. Wiley-Blackwell.

True Companion. (2018, January 31). *Frequently asked questions (FAQ)*. http://www.truecompanion.com/shop/faq

Turkle, S. (2012). *Alone together: Why we expect more from technology and less from each other*. Basic Books.

Von Markovic, E. (2007). *The mystery method: How to get beautiful women into bed*. St. Martin's Press.

Weizenbaum, J. (1976). *Computer power and human reason: From judgment to calculation*. W. H. Freeman.

Wertheimer, A. (2003). *Consent to sexual relations*. Cambridge University Press. .

Westen, P. (2004). The logic of consent.: The diversity and deceptiveness of consent as a defense to criminal conduct. Ashgate Press.

# Index

affirmative consent 5, 7, 9, 13, 15, 19, 51, 85, 88, 93, 95, 102, 103
Ambjörnsson, F. 79
anti-image covariance matrices 37
artificially intelligent partners 107–117
attitudes 9, 11, 31, 32, 35–37, 40, 42, 43, 109, 110, 114–116

Bailenson, J. 114
Beare, K. 2
behavioural intentions 20, 30, 38, 43
Beres, M. A. 61, 94
Blunt-Vinti, H. D. 61
Boonzaier, F. 2
Braun, V. 53, 82
Burkett, M. 51
Burt, M. R. 101

casual sex encounters 80, 82–84, 87, 88
Chi-square difference tests 38
cisgender women 61, 66
Clarke, V. 53, 82
Club RealDoll forum 108
cognitive schemata 6
cognitive scripting theorists 43
communication 53, 61, 78, 79, 81, 82, 84, 88, 103, 116
comparative fit index (CFI) 38–40
conceptualisations 78, 95, 103
confirmatory factor analysis (CFA) 32, 37, 38
consensual sex 28, 51, 67, 71, 77–79, 89
consensual vignettes 37, 39–41
consent communication 29, 59, 93–95, 100–102
consent dialogue 18–20
consent perceptions 2, 8, 9, 95, 98–100
consent scenarios 29
consent scripts 6, 9, 19
constrained consent 65, 71
Cronbach's alpha test results 38
cues 15, 43, 93–96, 101

Danaher, J. 109
data analysis 82, 111

data collection 33, 52, 61, 80, 110
Davis, A. C. 29
Dawson, K. 2
Delphi method 33, 37
demographics 9, 11, 12, 14, 15, 33
digital sex vignettes 39, 43

empowerment 56, 58, 59, 61
engagement rates 41
enthusiastic consent 5
erotica assessment 11, 15
erotica excerpts 9–16, 18
erotica passages 10, 13, 17, 19, 24, 26
erotic fiction 6, 8, 9, 11, 13, 14
ethical ramifications 114
ethics 67
explicit consent 8, 9, 18, 20, 41, 54, 55, 60
explicit verbal consent 7–9, 12–14, 17–20, 41
exploratory factor analysis 32, 36, 37

Fidell, L. S. 35
Forsberg, M. 79
Frank, L. 109
Frith, H. 65

Gagnon, J. H. 79
gameplay 112, 115, 116
gamification 3, 112–116
gamifying relationships 112
Gavey, N. 79
gender 16, 31, 32, 65, 66, 78, 80, 81, 86, 89, 95, 96, 98, 99, 103; differences 12, 13, 16, 39, 78, 96; inequality 78, 102; measurement invariance 38; norms 94, 100–102
gendered sexual wanting 78
genital touching 96–100
Gould, D. 31
grey rape 71
group differences 13, 16

Halley, J. 65
Hamilton, K. 51
healthy sexual relationship 2, 51–53, 59, 61

heteronormativity 65, 73
Hirsch, J. S. 79
Hollabaugh, L. C. 78
Holmström, C. 2
Huby, M. 33
Hughes, R. 33
Humphreys, T. P. 8, 94, 95

idiots 83
immoral sexuality 79
incremental fit index (IFI) 38–40
indirect behavioural approach 32, 36, 39–41
individual consent attitudes 30, 43
internet pornography 33, 36
intersectionality 79, 82, 85

Jensen, R. 110
Johansson, T. 79
Jozkowski, K. N. 2, 15, 61, 94–96

Kaufman, E. M. 2
Kimberly, C. 8
Kitzinger, C. 65
Krahé, B. 28

language 6, 8, 10, 33, 67, 68, 71, 111
Levy, D. 115
Lim, G. Y. 8

Mark, K. P. 2
masculinity 65
McCoy, M. L. 78
measurement invariance 38
meta-analyses 29
Muehlenhard, C. L. 78, 88
multiple social dimensions 79
multivariate analysis of covariance (MANCOVA) 13

nervousness 58
nonconsensual depictions 28–30
nonconsensual pornography 29–31, 41, 43; engagement 31, 32, 41; vignettes 31, 36
nonconsensual scripts 43
nonconsensual sex 51, 89, 101
nonconsensual vignettes 31, 32, 34, 37–42
non-negotiable requirement 54, 57, 59
novel contribution 9, 18
Nyholm, S. 109

O'Callaghan, E. 51
Okrina, D. 110
one-way multivariate analyses of variance (MANOVAs) 12, 13, 15–17, 98, 99
oral sex 96–100

patriarchal power structures 70
Peterson, Z. D. 78
Piemonte, J. L. 1
pornography 7, 28–33, 35, 36, 39–43, 110; content 28, 29, 32; engagement 28, 32, 36, 39, 40, 42, 43; vignettes 31–33, 35, 37, 40
porn scene vignette survey 47
positive attitudes 2, 30, 32, 36, 39–41, 101
post-hoc analyses 99
power 57, 65–68, 70, 71, 73, 82, 115; analysis 14
private location 94, 95
private setting 2, 93–103
public setting 95, 101, 103

rape 42, 71, 77, 82, 95, 101, 109; myths 31, 101
reciprocity 112
recruitment 32, 34, 52
reprogramming consent 107
resilience 60
Richardson, K. 108
Righi, M. K. 102
Roloff, M. E. 8

safety 52, 54, 57, 59, 60, 67
Seida, K. 41
self-reported comfort 39, 43
sex robots 107–110, 115–117
sexual abuse 82, 89
sexual agency 50, 52, 53, 59–61, 79, 80, 82, 85, 86, 88, 89
sexual behaviour 2, 7, 8, 30, 33, 94–103
sexual boundaries 78, 79, 81
sexual coercion 28, 71, 78
sexual communication 8, 18, 19, 89
sexual interactions 3, 6, 8, 18, 29, 42, 61, 79, 82, 89, 116
sexual media 7, 8, 11, 18–20
sexual relationships 51, 52, 60, 107, 108
sexual scripts 2, 6–9, 18, 19, 42, 80, 82, 83, 85–88
sexual trauma 50–52, 54, 55, 57–61
sexual violence 28, 30, 31, 33, 52, 66, 69, 73, 89, 102
shame 54, 59, 60
Shefer, T. 65
Shor, E. 41
Simon, W. 79, 80
Skeggs, B. 78, 79
social awkwardness 84
social class 3, 78, 79
social desirability 29, 31
socialisation 6–8, 42, 80, 102
social media 96
social norms 80, 102
social setting 93–101, 103
South Africa 2, 66, 69, 70, 73

South African women 64–73
staggered vignettes 96, 106; protocol 2, 96, 97
story differences 13, 16
story types 12, 15
structural models 35, 39
subcommunities 115

Tabachnick, B. G. 35
Tomaszewska, P. 28
transitioning/transition effect 2, 93–103
trauma 51, 54, 57, 59
Tucker-Lewis index (TLI) 38–40

vaginal-penile sex 15, 96–100
verbal affirmation 115
verbal communication 7, 30, 41, 54
verbal consent 5–7, 9–13, 15–20; explicit 7–9, 12–14, 17–20, 41
vignette-based methodology 31
vignettes 2, 8, 31–34, 37–39, 42, 43, 81, 89, 96, 97; development 33; methodology 28, 31
Vowels, L. M. 2
vulnerability 54, 57, 59, 84, 87

Warren, A. L. 8
Westen, P. 108
willingness 2, 3, 30, 64, 93–96, 98, 100–103, 108, 109
Willis, M. 2, 61
Wright, P. J. 29, 30
written erotica 2, 5–9, 12, 19

young people's norms 79, 80

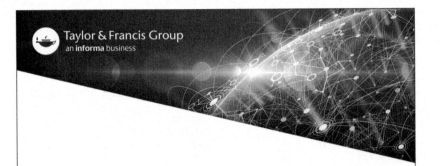